Past and Present Publications

Concepts of cleanliness

This book is published as part of the joint publishing agreement established in 1977 between the Fondation de la Maison des Sciences de l'Homme and the Press Syndicate of the University of Cambridge. Titles published under this arrangement may appear in any European language or, in the case of volumes of collected essays, in several languages.

New books will appear either as individual titles or in one of the series which the Maison des Sciences de l'Homme and the Cambridge University Press have jointly agreed to publish. All books published jointly by the Maison des Sciences de l'Homme and the Cambridge University Press will be distributed by the Press throughout the world.

Cet ouvrage est publié dans le cadre de l'accord de co-édition passé en 1977 entre la Fondation de la Maison des Sciences de l'Homme et le Press Syndicate of the University of Cambridge. Toutes les langues européennes sont admises pour les titres couverts par cet accord, et les ouvrages collectifs peuvent paraître en plusieurs langues.

Les ouvrages paraissent soit isolément, soit dans l'une des séries que la Maison des Sciences de l'Homme et Cambridge University Press ont convenu de publier ensemble. La distribution dans le monde entier des titres ainsi publiés conjointement par les deux établissements est assurée par Cambridge University Press.

This book is also published in association with and as part of Past and Present Publications, which comprise books similar in character to the articles in the journal *Past and Present*. Whether the volumes in the series are collections of essays – some previously published, others new studies – or monographs, they encompass a wide variety of scholarly and original works primarily concerned with social, economic and cultural changes and their causes and consequences. They will appeal to both specialists and non-specialists and will endeavour to communicate the results of historical and allied research in readable and lively form. This new series continues and

For a list of titles in Past and Present Publications, see end of book.

Concepts of cleanliness

Changing attitudes in France since the Middle Ages

GEORGES VIGARELLO

translated by JEAN BIRRELL

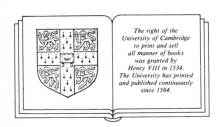

*The right of the
University of Cambridge
to print and sell
all manner of books
was granted by
Henry VIII in 1534.
The University has printed
and published continuously
since 1584.*

CAMBRIDGE UNIVERSITY PRESS
Cambridge
New York   New Rochelle   Melbourne   Sydney

EDITIONS DE LA MAISON DES SCIENCES DE L'HOMME
Paris

Published by the Press Syndicate of the University of Cambridge
The Pitt Building, Trumpington Street, Cambridge CB2 1RP
32 East 57th Street, New York, NY 10022, USA
10 Stamford Road, Oakleigh, Melbourne 3166, Australia

Originally published in French as *Le Propre et le sale: l'hygiene du corps depuis le
Moyen Age* by Editions du Seuil, Paris, 1985 and © Editions du Seuil, 1985

First published in English by Maison des Sciences de l'Homme and Cambridge
University Press 1988 as *Concepts of cleanliness: changing attitudes in France since
the Middle Ages*

English translation © Maison des Sciences de l'Homme and Cambridge
University Press 1988

Printed in Great Britain
at the University Press, Cambridge

British Library cataloguing in publication data

Vigarello, Georges.
Concepts of cleanliness: changing attitudes
in France since the Middle Ages. – (Past
and Present publications).
1. France. Man. Personal hygiene, 1500–1985
I. Title   II. Le Propre et la sale. *English*
III. Series
613.4′0944

Library of Congress cataloguing in publication data

Vigarello, Georges.
[Propre et la sale. English]
Concepts of cleanliness: changing attitudes in France since the
Middle Ages / Georges Vigarello; translated by Jean Birrell.
    p. cm.
Translation of: Le propre et le sale.
Bibliography.
Includes index.
ISBN 0 521 34248 1
1. Bathing customs – France – History.   2. Hygiene – Social aspects –
France – History.   I. Birrell, Jean.   II. Title
GT2846.F7V5413 1988
391′. 64′0944 – dc19   88-4125 CIP

ISBN 0 521 34248 1
ISBN 2 7351 0234 3 (France only)

For L.

Contents

Introduction

In the course of recounting the familiar exploits of Don Carlos, mysteriously abducted by masked ruffians, *Le Roman comique* (1651) describes its hero making his toilet. The prisoner is noble and the surroundings are sumptuous. Scarron describes both actions and objects: the attentiveness of the servants, naturally, and the magnificence of certain objects, such as the chandelier of chased silver-gilt, but also the indicators of cleanliness. These, however, defy our understanding; they are at the same time close to, and totally remote from, our own. They may bear some resemblance to certain practices of today, but they are, in fact, far removed from them. Scarron's interest focusses on indications which have today become subsidiary, whilst he pays little attention to others which have become, in contrast, essential. There are things missing and things left vague; it is as if our own most routine actions have yet to be invented, though some, nevertheless, have their equivalents here. In particular, the single act of washing which he mentions is very brief: 'I forgot to tell you that I think he washed his mouth, as I know he took great care of his teeth.'[1] Attention to cleanliness is more explicitly concentrated on linen and clothes. 'The masked dwarf stepped forward to serve him, and had him take the most beautiful linen in the world, the whitest and the most sweet-smelling.'[2]

There is no mention of water at any point in these scenes, except for the water which washed his mouth. Attention to cleanliness was a matter of sight and smell. It existed, with its own requirements, routines and frame of reference, but it served appearance above all. A norm was expressed and visible. The difference from today is that it applied primarily not to the skin but to linen, to what was most immediately visible. This example alone shows that it is foolish to deny the existence of practices of cleanliness in a pre-scientific culture.

1 P. Scarron, *Le Roman comique* (1651) in *Romanciers du XVIIe siècle* (Paris, 1973), p. 560.   [2] *Ibid.*

The norms, in this regard, do not start from nothing. They have their basis and their purpose. What we need to examine is how they change and are elaborated, how they are manifested and transformed.

A history of cleanliness should first, therefore, show how new requirements and constraints gradually emerge. It has to retrace a journey in which the scene from *Le Roman comique* constitutes only a stage. Other, less refined, scenes have preceded it, where, for example, changing the shirt did not have the same importance. Linen, in particular, received little attention, and did not serve as a criterion of distinction, in the scenes of royal receptions described two centuries earlier in *Le Roman de Jehan de Paris*.[3]

Cleanliness here reflects the civilising process, in its gradual moulding of bodily sensations, its heightening of their refinement, and its release of their subtlety. It is a history of the refining of behaviour, and of the growth of private space and of self-discipline: the care of oneself for one's own sake, a labour ever more squeezed between the intimate and the social. On a wider plane, it is the history of the progressive pressure of civilisation on the world of direct sensations.[4] It reveals the extension of their range. A cleanliness defined by regular washing of the body supposes, quite simply, a greater sharpness of perception and a stronger self-discipline than a cleanliness which is essentially defined by the changing of linen and its degree of whiteness.

It is essential, before embarking on such a history, to put aside our own frame of reference; cleanliness has to be recognised in behaviour long forgotten. The 'dry' wash of the courtier, for example, who wiped his face with a white cloth rather than wash it, responded to a standard of cleanliness which was altogether rational in the seventeenth century. It was considered and justified, even though it makes little sense today, when feelings and meanings have changed. We have to rediscover this lost sensibility.

It is also necessary to overturn the hierarchy of categories of authority; it was not, for example, hygienists who laid down the criteria of cleanliness in the seventeenth century, but the authors of manuals of etiquette, experts in manners, not scholars. The slow accumulation of constraints was accompanied by the displacement of the knowledge on which they were based.

---

[3] See below, chapter 4.
[4] The work of Norbert Elias, *La Civilisation des moeurs* (Paris, 1973, 1st ed. in German, 1939, trans. English as *The Civilising Process*, Oxford, 1978) is crucial here.

Representing this process as a succession of accretions, or as an accumulation of pressures brought to bear on the body, however, risks giving a false picture. It was not simply a question of the accumulation of constraints. Such a history needs to connect with other histories. Cleanliness is inevitably affected by images of the body, by images, more or less obscure, of the corporeal shell, by even obscurer images of the body's physical composition. It was, for example, because water was seen as capable of penetrating the body, that bathing had a very special significance in the sixteenth and seventeenth centuries; hot water, in particular, was believed to weaken the organs and leave the pores open to unwholesome air. Thus there existed a set of ideas about the body which had their own history and causes. They, too, affected sensibility, and influenced norms, which could not change in isolation from them. They operated on ground already occupied, and never controlled a passive body. Images of the body had to change before constraints could change. So, too, did latent conceptions of the body, such as those which dictated its functioning and its capabilities.

So a history of bodily cleanliness brings into play a wider and more complex history. All the ideas which gave the body its contours, shaped its appearance and suggested its internal mechanisms had primarily a social terrain. The cleanliness of the seventeenth century, attached essentially to linen and external appearance, and expressed in, for example, the display of objects or the fine points of vestimentary symbols, was obviously very different from the cleanliness which, at a later date, was expressed in the protection of the body's organism, or of whole populations. In the same way, a court society which conformed to the aristocratic criteria of appearance and display, differed from a bourgeois society more concerned with the physical and demographic strength of peoples. A concentration on purely external appearance changed to a more complex attention to physical resources, to strength, and to hidden forces. Thus the history of bodily cleanliness is also social history.

Finally, the word 'cleanliness' is employed here in a wide sense, as applying to the whole body or to the whole collection of objects capable of standing for it.

Part I *From water for pleasure to water as threat*

1. *The water that infiltrated*

In 1546, Barcelona, in the grip of the plague, was no longer receiving provisions. Neighbouring towns and villages, fearing contagion, refused all contacts and all trade. Worse, the ships despatched to Majorca in search of supplies by the Council of the Five Hundred were repulsed with cannon fire.[1] Such episodes became common. At the end of the Middle Ages and in the classical period, contact was widely seen as a major risk in times of epidemic. The traditional flight from infected towns became in itself dangerous; it came up against neighbourhoods capable of open violence. Those people who fled from Lyons in 1628 were stoned by the peasantry, and condemned to rove or return to their city.[2] The inhabitants of Digne, compelled in 1629 by a degree of the Parlement of Aix to remain within the town walls, were put under the surveillance of a cordon of armed guards by the neighbouring communities.[3] They threatened to set fire to the town if the cordon was broken. Cities struck by plague became prisons doomed to horror.

Within these communities temporarily shut in on their awful plight, the external constraints accelerated the formulation of internal regulations if only, here too, in the hope of confining the calamity. Mayors, magistrates and provosts of the merchants issued injunctions dealing with social hygiene; social contacts were progressively limited, certain places shut off or condemned. The Salle Légat of the Hôtel-Dieu in Paris, for example, was isolated in 1584 and made ready to receive only victims of the plague.[4] In many towns notaries could not approach stricken houses; wills were dictated at a distance, before witnesses, from upper storeys.[5] The measures also

---

[1] J.-N. Biraben. *Les Hommes et la Peste en France et dans les pays européens et méditerranéens* (Paris, 1976), vol. 2, p. 98.

[2] J. Guiart, 'La peste à Lyon au xviie siècle', *Biologie médicale*, 5 (1929), p. 5.

[3] Biraben, *Les Hommes et la Peste*, vol. 2, p. 167.

[4] M. Brièle, *Document pour servir à l'histoire des hôpitaux de Paris* (Paris, 1883), vol. 2, p. 16.   [5] Guiart, 'La peste à Lyon', p. 10.

dealt with personal hygiene: to suppress social intercourse was to suppress practices which risked opening up the body to infected air, such as violent labour which heated the limbs, warmth which relaxed the skin, and, above all, bathing. Liquid, by its pressure, or even more by its warmth, could open up the pores and heighten the danger. The fight against plague here reveals ideas which are totally remote from our own; water was capable of penetrating the skin, which had implications for practices of cleanliness.

It was this same fear which led people to cease to frequent schools, churches, steam-baths and bath-houses. Contacts, and thus the possibility of infection, had to be limited. In the case of baths, the dynamic of separation related to the very image of the body and its functioning. Doctors, in times of plague from the fifteenth century on, denounced these establishments, where naked bodies rubbed shoulders. 'People already afflicted with contagious diseases'[6] might be the cause of ill-fated mixing. Disease might spread in consequence. 'Steam-baths and bath-houses, I beg you, flee them or you will die.'[7] These regulations were at first tentative. In the plague of 1450, Des Pars called in vain on the Paris magistrates to prohibit steam-baths, but provoked only the wrath of their owners. Their threats were such that he beat a hasty retreat to Tournai.[8] Regular temporary closure during each epidemic nevertheless gradually established itself within the logic of separations. In the sixteenth century, these closures became official and systematic. An ordinance of the provost of Paris, frequently repeated between the plagues of 1510 and 1561, prohibited anyone 'from going to steam-baths, and steam-bath keepers from heating their baths until after next Christmas, on pain of a summary fine'.[9] A similar resolution was passed in more and more towns. It became general; introduced in Rouen in 1510[10] and in Besançon in 1540,[11] it had existed in Dijon since the end of the fifteenth century.[12] In most epidemics, it was during hot weather, more favourable to outbreaks of plague, that the prohibition was promulgated.

---

6 N. de Delamare, *Traité de la police* (Paris, 1722, 1st ed. 1698), vol. 1, p. 628.

7 G. Bunel, *Ouevre excellente et à chacun désirant soi de peste préserver* (Paris, 1836, 1st ed. 1513), p. 17.

8 J. Riolan, *Curieuses Recherches sur les écoles de médecine de Paris et de Montpellier* (Paris, 1651), p. 218.   9 Delamare, *Traité de la police*, vol. 1, p. 628.

10 L. Boucher, *La Peste à Rouen aux xvie et xviie siècles* (Paris, 1897), p. 26.

11 M. Limon, *Les Mesures contre la peste à Besançon au xvie siècle* (Paris, 1906), p. 9.

12 J. Garnier, *Les Etuves dijonnaises* (Dijon, 1867), pp. 28–9.

THE WIDE OPEN SKIN

Why should historical significance be attributed to these prohibitions? Because behind the fear of social contacts lurked a host of other anxieties, amongst them fear of the frailty of the bodily shell. The skin was seen as porous, and countless openings seemed to threaten, since the surfaces were weak and the frontiers uncertain. Behind the simple refusal of proximity lay a very specific image of the body: heat and water created openings, the plague had only to slip through. These images were potent and far-reaching, and their consequences for classical hygiene need to be assessed. It is in this context that the prohibitions we have described assume significance. Baths and steam-baths were dangerous because they opened up the body to the atmosphere. They exercised an almost mechanical action on the pores, temporarily exposing the organs to the elements.

It was no longer touch, or a principle of proximity, which was at issue, but a principle of openness. The body had less resistance to poisons after bathing, because it was more open to them. It was as if the body was permeable; infectious air threatened to flood in from all sides. 'Steam-baths and bath-houses should be forbidden, because when one emerges, the flesh and the whole disposition of the body are softened and the pores open, and as a result, pestiferous vapour can rapidly enter the body and cause sudden death, as has frequently been observed.'[13] Comparing the body to familiar objects only reinforced this image of penetration. The architectural metaphor played a central role, with the body seen as a house invaded and occupied by the plague. You had to know how to shut the doors. But water and heat undid them at will, opened them up and maintained the breach. The plague had only to move in. 'Bath-houses and steam-baths will from now on be deserted, because, the pores and the little air holes in the skin being, as a result of the heat, more easily opened, pestilential air gets in.'[14]

This fear lasted throughout the seventeenth century. The plague, breaking out in one place or another almost annually throughout the period, engendered the same prohibitions: to heat the body 'would be to open the doors to the poisons in the atmosphere and swallow it in

---

[13] A. Paré, *Oeuvres* (Paris, 1585, 1st ed. 1568), p. 56.
[14] N. Houel, *Traité de la peste* (Paris, 1573), p. 16.

great gulps'.[15] Invariably, such an 'encounter of air and poison'[16] with heated flesh suggested an almost inevitable result. It transformed danger into destiny.

The first concerted actions against the plague, especially from the sixteenth century, thus conjured up a frightening picture of a body with a permeable exterior. Its surface could be penetrated by water and by air, a frontier rendered even more uncertain in the face of an evil whose material basis was invisible. Perhaps the pores were even weak in themselves, independently of being heated. They needed permanent protection from attack. This, for example, rendered the shape and nature of clothing in time of plague all-important: smooth fabrics, dense weave and close fit. Infected air should slide over with no possibility of entry. The ideal of being enclosed varied only in its manifestations. 'One should wear clothes of satin, taffeta, camlet, tabby and the like, with hardly any pile, and which are so smooth and dense that it is difficult for unwholesome air or any sort of infection to enter or take hold, especially if one changes frequently.'[17] Clothing in times of plague confirms this image, dominant throughout the sixteenth and seventeenth centuries, of a body which was completely porous, and which necessitated quite specific strategies: the avoidance of wool or cotton, materials which were too permeable, and of furs, whose deep pile offered a haven to unhealthy air. Men and women alike longed to have smooth and hermetically sealed clothes enclosing their weak bodies. And if taffeta and tabby were too grand, the poor could resort to 'sacking and oil-cloth'.[18]

Practices of hygiene and, in particular, practices of cleanliness could not be considered without reference to these assumptions. If water could penetrate the skin, it needed to be handled with care. It could seep in and disturb. In certain cases, as in hydrotherapy, the mechanism might be beneficial. Immersing themselves in the pools of Spa, Pougues or Forges, sixteenth-century bathers confidently expected an amelioration of their diseases. A bath of warm thermal water, like a bath in 'ordinary' water, could, for example, dissolve stone; this was how Montaigne treated his kidney stones.[19] It could

[15]   D. Jouysse, *Bref Discours de la préservation et de la cure de la peste* (Amiens, 1668), p. 3.
[16]   C. de Rebecque, *Le Médecin français charitable* (Lyon, 1683), p. 608.
[17]   F. Citoys, *Avis sur la nature de la peste* (Paris, 1623), p. 20.
[18]   J.-J. Manget, *Traité de la peste et des moyens de s'en préserver* (Lyons, 1722), p. 199.
[19]   M. de Montaigne, *Journal de voyage en Italie* (Paris, 1974, 1st ed. 1774), pp. 377–8.

also restore some substance to systems which were 'too dry'. It was employed by Rivière for 'emaciated and wasted bodies'.[20] It also acted on the colour of jaundice, and soothed certain congestions.[21] In these cases, liquids mingled. And lastly, the penetration of the water might even correct certain sour or vicious humours. This treatment 'refreshed far more than any other medicine'.[22]

But for the most part, baths threatened to disturb an equilibrium. They invaded, damaged, and above all, exposed the body to many more dangers than pestilential air. The very earliest observations on steam-baths and the transmission of plague already referred to more obscure dangers. 'Bath-houses and steam-baths and their after-effects, which heat the body and the humours, which debilitate the constitution and open the pores, cause death and sickness.'[23] Disease, in the sixteenth and seventeenth centuries, was spreading, even proliferating. People had disquieting visions of contagious communication, as with syphilis,[24] or visions of the most miscellaneous penetrations, such as steam-bath pregnancies resulting from the impregnation of female sexual organs by sperm floating in the tepid water. 'A woman can conceive through using baths in which men have spent some time.'[25] The risks multiplied. Once infiltrated, the skin was not only wide open to pestilence, but also to unwholesome air, to cold, and to nameless ills. The weakness was diffused, and all the more global and imprecise since it was through the pores that humours and thus strength escaped. The openings worked both ways. It was as if internal substances threatened to flee; thus the 'bath debilitated'.[26] It provoked 'feebleness'.[27] It 'diminished hugely strength and vigour'.[28] The risks were no longer confined simply to contagion. And this picture had sufficient success to spread beyond the discourse of doctors. It was absorbed into thinking to the extent of becoming a commonplace. It was all-pervasive. It became impossible to contemplate a bath without surrounding it with imperative constraints: rest, staying in bed, protective clothing. The

---

[20] L. Rivière, *Les Pratiques de la médecine* (Lyons, 1682), p. 10.
[21] Rebecque, *Le Médecin français*, p. 419.
[22] Rivière, *Les Pratiques de la médecine*, p. 10.
[23] T. Le Forestier, *Régime contre épidémie et pestilence* (Paris, 1495), p. 102.
[24] Cf. G. Barraud, *L'Humanisme et la Médecine aux XVIe siècle* (Brussels, 1942), p. 83.
[25] R. de Graff, *Histoire anatomique des parties génitales de l'homme et de la femme* (Basle, 1699, 1st ed. 1678).
[26] H. de Monteux, *Conservation de santé et Prolongation de la vie* (Paris, 1572), p. 96.
[27] Paré, *Oeuvres*, p. 1154.   [28] *Ibid.*

practice could not fail to be a source of anxiety. The accumulated precautions and the impossible protections turned it into something both complicated and rare.

When, one May morning in 1610, an emissary from the Louvre found Sully taking a bath in his house at the Arsenal, complications ensued; a series of obstacles prevented Sully, for the sake of his body, from attending on the king, who required his presence. The minister's own entourage, even the emissary himself, adjured him not to brave the outside air. 'Having found you in the bath, and observing that you wished to get out to do as the king ordered, he said to you (because we were nearby): Monsieur, do not quit your bath, since I fear that the king cares so much for your health, and so depends on it, that if he had known that you were in such a situation, he would have come here himself.'[29] Henri IV's envoy proposed to return to the Louvre, he would explain to the sovereign and return with his orders. Not one of the witnesses was surprised to see such a situation disrupt relations between the king and his minister. On the contrary, everyone insisted that Sully should not expose himself. And Henri IV's reply justified the precautions taken. 'Monsieur, the king commands you to complete your bath, and forbids you to go out today, since M. Du Laurens has advised him that this would endanger your health.'[30] So there had been consultation. Advice had been sought and offered. The recourse to Du Laurens, the royal doctor, reveals the nature of the concern. The episode assumed all the aspects of an 'affair'. It immediately involved numerous people, and it was protracted, as the risks lasted several days. 'He orders you to expect him tomorrow in your nightshirt, your leggings, your slippers and your night-cap, so that you come to no harm as a result of your recent bath.'[31] So it was the liquid experienced in this manner which could be harmful. It was the consequences of the bath as such which were at issue.

This commotion over a bathtub was not mere idle tittle-tattle; it emphasises the strength in the seventeenth century of the association between water and the penetration of the body, and it confirms the dominant image of an exterior which was easily permeable. It emphasises also, paradoxically by its very intensity, the rarity of the practice of bathing.

Half a century later, when Louis XIV's doctors decided to bath him,

[29] M. de Sully, *Mémoires* (Paris, 1662), vol. 6, p. 427.   [30] *Ibid.*, p. 428.
[31] *Ibid.*

it was for explicitly medical reasons. The patient had experienced 'starts, raging fits, convulsive movements . . . followed by rashes: red and violet spots on his chest'.[32] The bath took place during his convalescence. It was to 'moisten' a body which had been bled eight times within the last few days. Once again there was no shortage of precautions: a purge and an enema the day before to prevent any possible surfeit which might result from the water infiltrating, rest so as not to exacerbate any over-excitement, and interruption of the treatment at the slightest discomfort to avoid anything untoward. 'I had the bath prepared, the king got in at ten o'clock; for the rest of the day he felt weighed down with a nagging headache such as he had never experienced before, and with the whole demeanour of his body quite changed from what it had been in the preceding days. I did not wish to persist with the bath, having seen enough wrong to have the king get out.'[33] Thus the treatment was quickly interrupted. A year later, Fagon resorted to it again, very cautiously, for a few days. This was the last time. 'The king was never pleased to become accustomed to bathing in his chamber.'[34]

The disquiet was obscure and diffused, as if the mere encounter of water and body was in itself a cause for concern. The penetration might sometimes, by its very force, restore lost equilibrium. But the essential disturbance it involved demanded vigilance. Openings, interchanges and pressure on the humours constituted above all a disorder. Their consequences were ever more various.

The bath, except for medical reasons when absolutely necessary, is not only superfluous, but very prejudicial to men . . . The bath destroys the body, and, filling it, renders it susceptible to the effects of the bad properties of the air . . . slacker bodies are more sickly and have shorter lives than hard ones. Bathing fills the head with vapours. It is the enemy of the nerves and ligaments, which it loosens, in such a way that many a man never suffers from gout except after bathing. It kills the child in the mother's womb, even when it is warm . . .[35]

The catalogue of ills also included 'weakness of the chest',[36] dropsy, and various evil humours resulting from the penetrating vapours.[37]

---

[32] A. d'Aquin, G.-C. Fagon, A. Vallot, *Journal de la santé du roi Louis XIV (1647–1711)* (Paris, 1862), p. 67.
[33] *Ibid.*, p. 73.   [34] *Ibid.*, p. 92.
[35] T. Renaudot, *Recueil général des questions traitées et conférences du bureau d'adresse* (Paris, 1655), vol. 2, p. 533.
[36] N. de Blégny, *Livre commode des adresses de Paris* (1878, 1st ed. 1692), p. 184.
[37] C. de Rebecque, *L'Apothicaire français charitable* (Lyons, 1683), p. 474.

Various attempts were made in the seventeenth century to ward off these dangers, but they served only to render the activity even more complicated. And they confirmed the view of the bodily covering as porous. In 1615 Guyon suggested that the day before bathing the body should be submitted to the heat of a dry steam-bath;[38] the idea was to evacuate the humours so as to render the penetration of the water less pressing. Actions designed to prepare the body for bathing became more numerous and more complex. But whatever was done, penetration and its attendant dangers remained. The most extreme, indeed absurd, suggestion came from Bacon, who in 1623 required the water to have a composition identical to that of the bodily matter. The liquid, after all, had to compensate for the substances which were lost, and do no harm itself by mixing. The constituents of the bath had to be treated till they were similar to those of the body. Interchanges would consequently be less dangerous. 'The first and principal requirement is that baths should be composed of materials whose substances are similar to those of the flesh and the body, and which can sustain and nourish the interior.'[39] Such an expectation was fanciful, obviously, and simply added new variations to the theme of infiltration.

Times of plague strengthened the impression of bodily frontiers which could be penetrated, of bodies open to poison. Such rapid and terrible contagion suggested that an active element could infiltrate both breath and skin. The bodies most at risk must be the most porous. Their systems, succumbing within hours, must obviously be the most penetrable. This seemed to be the real danger. The plague thus established this disquieting vision, which flourished. Fear of bathing outlasted times of plague, and the permeability of the skin became a permanent source of anxiety. It was in Héroard's mind when he confined the infant Louis XIII to his room after having him take two baths in 1611.[40] It was why Guy Patin, though occasionally mentioning bathing in his medical texts, omitted it entirely from his treatise on health.[41] The mechanical effects, with their therapeutic

---

[38] L. Guyon, *Façon de contregarder la beauté* in *Cours de médecine théorique et pratique* (Lyons, 1689, 1st ed. 1615), vol. 2, p. 221.

[39] F. Bacon, *Histoire de la vie et de la mort* (trans. Paris, 1647, 1st ed. London, 1623), p. 392.

[40] J. Héroard, *Journal sur l'enfance et la jeunesse de Louis XIII* (1601–1628) (Paris, 1868), vol. 2, p. 70.

[41] G. Patin, *Lettres* (Paris, 1846, 1st ed. 1683), vol. 1, p. 109, and *Traité de la conservation de la santé* (Paris, 1682).

ambivalence, were dominant. R. Bonnard's engraving, 'Une dame qui va entrer au bain',[42] might wrongly suggest the contrary. The scene appears familiar, even though the setting is sumptuous. Neither doctor nor drugs are to be seen. A maidservant busies herself round a decorated bathtub, covered with lace, surrounded by hangings, and standing on a dais. Two carved taps set into the wall supply the water. A woman clothed in silk takes a flower offered by an elegant gentleman. The extreme refinement of the occasion renders it almost allegoric. The bath will be a gracious activity, and possibly amorous. But the caption reveals its meaning as a rule to be observed: 'A bath taken at the right time acts on me like medicine, and damps down the fire about to consume me'.[43] Despite the sexual ambiguity, cleanliness was not explicitly at issue. It was a matter of the restoration of lost equilibrium, and of knowing when it was right to bathe. Water in itself only upset the balance.

Before examining the role of these ideas more directly, and assessing their importance, we must look further at their effects on thinking. They were influential in very different fields, by the application of an identical logic.

The new attention paid to childhood in the sixteenth century, for example, and the emphasis placed on its frailty, rapidly confirmed such ideas. The theme of infiltration was again all-pervasive from the sixteenth century on. It was because the bodies of new-born babies were thought to be completely porous that a technique of massage developed which employed both the hand and the warmth of water. The bath was intended both to cleanse the skin of the blood and mucous substances of birth, and at the same time to allow the limbs to be moulded to the desired physical form. Midwives used the water to facilitate this sort of massage. Immersion was intended, amongst other things, to correct the shape. 'Remember, too, while the bones of the limbs are softened by the heat of the bath in which they have just been washed, to give each limb, by gentle manipulation, the form and

---

[42] R. Bonnard, 'Une dame qui va entrer au bain', Paris, 1691, estampe BN.
[43] *Ibid.* Audiger indirectly reveals how unimportant bathing was in the seventeenth century. When describing all the activities in which a chambermaid in the service of a woman of quality should excel, he stressed the care of linen, the art of arranging ribbons and lace, and dressing hair; he also cited 'skill in making a bath for the feet and pastes for cleaning the hands'. These skills were not required in the service of a rich man; in this case it was a question of knowing how 'to shave and comb' and 'keep the master's clothes very clean and decent', *La Maison réglée* (1691), pp. 102, 51.

the straightness that is required to produce complete perfection.'[44]
This bath in the first few days had several purposes, amongst which
cleanliness did not yet figure. It involved manipulation precisely
because it permeated the flesh. It helped 'to adjust the limbs to the
proper shape'.[45] For the same reason the skin of the nurse, most
fragile of all, had to be permanently clogged up. 'To strengthen the
skin and equip it to withstand external accidents, which might
damage and harm it as a result of its weakness, it should be spread
with the ash of mussels which can be found all over in rivers and
marshes, or with ash made from calves' horns, or with the ash of lead
well pulverised and mixed with wine.'[46] The most diverse substances
could be used to saturate the skin. Salt, oil and wax, in particular,
would all serve to stop up the pores. The body was even coated as if it
were a glossy and protected object. 'Children, once out of the womb,
should be wrapped in roses crushed with salt to strengthen the
limbs.'[47]

The swaddling clothes which enveloped skin treated in this way,
and imprisoned limbs previously 'annointed with oil of roses or
bilberries . . . to close the pores',[48] had a specifically protective role. It
was for the same reason, too, that baths were strictly limited in
childhood. There was a risk that they would prolong softness in
systems already too moist. The slow drying out of the body which
accompanied growth might be impeded. The clay would remain too
soft. Once the new-born child 'appeared nice and dry, ruddy and rosy
all over',[49] further bathing seemed almost to tempt fate. The legs of
the Dauphin, the future Louis XIII, were never washed before he
reached the age of six. Their first immersion, with the exception of a
very brief one immediately after birth, took place when he was
seven.[50]

[44]   S. de Sainte-Marthe, *La Manière de nourrir les enfants à la mamelle* (Paris, 1698, 1st
       ed. sixteenth century), p. 52.
[45]   S. de Valembert, *Cinq Livres de la manière de nourrir et gouverner les enfants*
       (Poitiers, 1565), p. 46.
[46]   E. Rodion, *Des divers travaux et enfantements des femmes* (trans. Paris, 1583, 1st ed.
       1537), p. 94.
[47]   B. de Glainville, *Le Propriétaire des choses très utiles et profitables au corps humain*
       (fourteenth century) (Paris, 1518), unnumbered pages.
[48]   Paré, *Oeuvres*, p. 947.
[49]   M. Ettmuler, *Pratique de médecine spéciale* (trans. Lyons, 1691, 1st ed. 1685), vol. 2,
       p. 484.
[50]   Héroard, *Journal sur l'enfance*, vol. 1, p. 349: 'Bathed for the first time, put into the
       bath and Madame [his sister] with him'.

On the basis of this same image of fragile pores, anxieties proliferated and fed each other. Hot water attacked a passive body which it permeated and left open. Where children were concerned, there was added a whole range of comparisons with substances which were flexible and malleable; thus it was tempting to mould their docile limbs. The problem was to balance the dangers of bathing against freeing the skin.

All these fears and contrivances produced a logic quite other than the precautions of today. They supposed a frame of reference for bodily functions quite alien to ours. Though they seem to be marginal to hygiene, they could, in fact, affect it. That such influence is possible is hardly open to doubt. When, for example, sixteenth-century books on health refer to certain bodily smells, they also refer to the need to remove them. But they assume friction and perfume, not washing, to achieve this. The skin should be rubbed with scented linen. 'To cure the goat-like stench of armpits, it is useful to press and rub the skin with a compound of roses',[51] that is, to wipe vigorously, applying perfume, but not actually to wash.

Rules for polite behaviour are equally significant in this connection. It was these which, from the sixteenth century, dictated good manners and good taste at court. They constituted an inventory of 'noble' behaviour in its most humdrum aspects, real-life, commonplace situations, private or public, but always envisaged from the point of view of manners. The texts refer repeatedly to the 'cleanliness of the body'. They ignored bathing, but that is not what is most important in this connection. They focussed attention on the parts which were visible – the hands and face. 'Washing the face in the morning in cold water is both clean and healthy.'[52] They sometimes equate correct behaviour and hygiene even more pointedly: 'It is a point of cleanliness and of health to wash the hands and face as soon as one rises.'[53]

Caution with regard to water is also visible in this type of text. Water, from the seventeenth century in particular, became more disquieting as the face became more fragile. Great care was taken in

[51] Monteux, *Conservation de santé*, p. 265.
[52] D. Erasmus, *La Civilité puérile* (Paris, 1977, 1st ed. 1530), p. 66.
[53] Anon., *Bienséance de la conversation* (Pont-à-Mousson, 1617), p. 34.

seventeenth-century books of etiquette to ensure that the face was wiped rather than washed. 'Children should clean their face and their eyes with a white cloth, which cleanses and leaves the complexion and colour in their natural state. Washing with water is bad for the sight, causes toothache and catarrh, makes the face pale, and renders it more susceptible to cold in winter and sun in summer.'[54] The same fears applied here as with bathing, and affected both actions and their context. Actual washing was no longer involved, though cleansing persisted, and even, in a sense, became more precise. One action gave way to another; splashing with water was replaced by wiping. The influence of the image of the body is clear to see; skins which had been infiltrated were susceptible to every ill.

As early as the beginning of the seventeenth century, Jean du Chesne, describing, as a scrupulous hygienist, all the actions which followed getting up, emphasised wiping and rubbing. Water was not involved. Cleanliness was achieved by wiping. The toilet was both 'dry' and active. 'Having opened his bowels, he should as his first act comb his hair and rub his head, always from front to back, right to the neck, with suitable cloths or sponges, for some little time, so that the head is well cleansed of all dirt; while the head is being rubbed, he might well walk about, so that the legs and arms are gradually exercised.'[55] Next comes cleaning the ears and the teeth, with water used only to wash the hands and the mouth. Lastly, the very frequently described act of Louis XIV, washing his hands in the morning in a mixture of water and spirits of wine, poured from a rich ewer into a silver saucer,[56] does not imply washing the face. The mirror held at a distance by a valet emphasises that there was, in any case, 'no toilet-table nearby'.[57]

On a more everyday plane, some seventeenth-century school rules institutionalised wiping. The pupils of both Jacqueline Pascal and the Ursulines washed their hands and mouths when they got up. On the other hand, they only wiped their faces. Their toilet also involved attending to their hair, the older children combing that of the younger ones. Water was hardly used. Only when they were dressed, and various items had been tidied away, did the pupils of the Ursulines

[54]   Anon., *La Civilité nouvelle contenant la vraie et parfaite instruction de la jeunesse* (Basle, 1671), p. 69.
[55]   J. du Chesne, *Le Portrait de santé* (Paris, 1606), p. 361.
[56]   L. de Saint-Simon, *Mémoires* (Paris, ed. Boisille, 1879–1928), vol. 28, p. 336.
[57]   *Ibid.*, p. 340.

splash water on their hands and face. 'When dressed, after having neatly folded away their things, they wash their mouth and their hands.'[58] In the case of Jacqueline Pascal, who described in great detail a veritable orchestration of the process of rising, water was mixed with wine to give it acidity, but was still not used on the face. 'While they made their beds, one of them brought breakfast and what was needed to wash their hands, and wine and water for washing the mouth.'[59] In the eighteenth century, the rules of Jean-Baptiste de La Salle perpetuated these instructions unchanged; the fears were sufficiently strong to persist. 'It is correct to clean the face every morning by using a white cloth to cleanse it. It is less good to wash with water, because it renders the face susceptible to cold in winter and sun in summer.'[60] Rétif carried out these same actions at the choir school of the Centre Hospitalier de Bicêtre, which he attended in 1746. Water still had a precise and limited use. 'Not a moment was lost; prayers in the morning: after getting up, one rinsed one's mouth with water and vinegar; one took breakfast.'[61] These examples of cleansing are all the more interesting in that the rejection of water does not rule out the practice of cleanliness. A norm existed, with specific utensils and methods, but it involved minimal washing.

A rapid reading of successive texts can give an impression of a distinct reduction in the requirements of hygiene dating from the sixteenth century. Water, after all, to some extent disappeared. Closer reading suggests rather a change; the insistence on wiping, on the whiteness of linen, and on the fragility and the colour of the skin are in fact evidence of increased attention. Texts are longer and more specific, as if concern was stronger. In treatises on manners, for example, most themes were more developed with the passage of time. The standards were more rigorous in the manual of Jean-Baptiste de La Salle in 1736 than in that of Erasmus in 1530, even though the latter mentions washing the face. La Salle dwells on the care of the hair, which is to be cut and combed, and should have the grease regularly removed by the use of powder and bran (without washing); he dwells on the care of the mouth, which is to be washed every morning, and

[58] Ursulines, *Règlements des religieuses de la congrégation de Paris* (Paris, 1705, 1st ed. 1650), vol. 1, p. 131.
[59] J. Pascal, 'Règlement pour les enfants' (Paris, 1657), in *Lettres et Mémoires* (Paris, 1845), p. 232.
[60] J.-B. de La Salle, *Les Règles de la bienséance chrétienne* (Rheims, 1736), p. 11.
[61] N. Rétif de La Bretonne, *Monsieur Nicolas* (Paris, 1924, 1st ed. 1794), vol. 1, p. 138.

the teeth briskly rubbed; he describes in detail the care of the nails, which are to 'be cut every week'.[62] The same concerns are present in Erasmus, but are described more allusively, and less distinctly. In Erasmus, rapid images and advice follow in quick succession, and he is briefer. The use of the comb, for example, is in comparison described more elliptically. 'It is remiss not to comb your hair, but though you must be proper, you should not titivate yourself like a girl.'[63] On the same subject, La Salle covers methods of care and frequency of actions, and he specifies and discusses the procedures. His explanations become additions and reinforcement. It is the same with the face. The use of water is reduced, but in favour of a care and an attention to detail which maintains and even strengthens the norm. Wiping, as described here, can even constitute a new demand. Acts of cleanliness were not abolished, but altered. They were affected by the image of the body. To understand this, all reference to the criteria of today has to be put aside and the existence of a cleanliness which assumed other methods than washing accepted.

The problem is, however, more complex. Two specific practices, public and private bathing, which had once existed, both disappeared almost completely between the sixteenth and seventeenth centuries, at the very period when the particular horror of the plague was being formulated. It is as if the image of the body had had a determining effect. These practices merit particular attention; they were the principal victims of the rejection of water. And it is their widespread disappearance which can give the impression of a lowering of standards of hygiene.

[62]   La Salle, *Les Règles de la bienséance*, p. 34.
[63]   Erasmus, *La Civilité puérile*, pp. 66–7.

2. *The disappearance of certain practices*

The rejection, even condemnation, of bathing in the sixteenth century is all the more striking because the practice had acquired its own institutions, customs and times, and its appointed places and trappings. A common historiographical theme, bathing was already mentioned by several seventeenth-century historians. Jean Riolan, for example, referred to it almost mythically in 1651. 'Bath-houses and steam-baths were so common in Paris that, amongst the marvels of this town, an Italian called Brixianus praised it for its baths and steam-baths 150 years ago.'[1] These establishments evoked practices which, at the very time when Riolan was writing, were being 'abolished and lost'.[2] This disappearance needs to be carefully examined before it can be understood.

STEAM-BATHS AND BATH-HOUSES

A crier patrolled the streets of thirteenth-century Paris to summon people to the heated steam-baths and bath-houses. These establishments, already numbering twenty-six in 1292,[3] and with their own guild, were a familiar feature of the town. They were commonplace enough for it not to be shocking to offer a session in a steam-bath as a tip to artisans, domestic servants or day-labourers. 'To Jehan Petit, for him and his fellow valets of the bedchamber, which the queen gave him on New Year's Day to visit the steam-baths: 108s.'[4] What they would find was a steam-bath, with in addition, according to price, a bath in a tub, wine, a meal, or a bed.[5] Naked bodies sweated and were sponged down side by side in the steam from water heated by wood

---

[1] Riolan, *Curieuses Recherches*, p. 218.   [2] *Ibid.*, p. 219.
[3] Guillaume de Villeneuve, *Les Crieries de Paris* (thirteenth century), quoted by M. Barbarau, *Le Costoiement ou Instructions du père à son fils* (Paris, 1760); E. Boileau, *Le Livre des métiers* (thirteenth century), (Paris, 1879), pp. 628–9.
[4] 'Compte des menus plaisirs de la reine' (art. 376), quoted by V. Gay, *Glossaire archéologique* (Paris, 1887), vol. 1, p. 683.
[5] C. de Beaurepaire, *Nouveaux Mélanges historiques* (Paris, 1904), p. 94.

fires. Baths were taken in a room, often separate, crammed with heavy round iron-bound bathtubs. A steam-bath did not necessarily involve immersion, though a bath could be had. There were, for example, six bathtubs at Saint-Vivien in 1380, with three beds and sets of bedding. It was primarily a place for bodies to sweat and bathe.[6] In contrast, the surroundings in the fifteenth-century minia-ture of Valerius Maximus are plusher, with sumptuous table-covers, wall-hangings and a tiled floor.[7] It was a complex activity, with other services complementing the pleasures of water, and it was socially diversified, being both popular and refined. Steam-baths, in sum, were much frequented, even familiar, places.

Yet this institution disappeared in the course of several decades of the sixteenth century, and was not replaced. Of the four steam-baths in Dijon, the last was destroyed in the mid-sixteenth century.[8] Those in Beauvais, Angers and Sens were gone by the end of the century.[9] The *Livre commode des adresses* listed only a tiny number of public baths in Paris in 1692, including one for women in the Rue Saint-André-des-Arts.[10] Most were medicinal in purpose. Out of thirteen establishments in Strasbourg, only four seem to have survived.[11] Martin, whose journal for 1637 recreates the life of a Strasbourg shopkeeper, mentions occasional visits to the steam-baths 'for an inflammation of the teeth and another on the eyes'.[12] The cupping-glasses he had applied to 'the upper part of his shoulders'[13] had as their sole purpose a compensation of humours. The practice was clearly therapeutic. The enforced sweating was intended to purify the humours.

A few establishments survived in the seventeenth century, in particular in Paris, which acted both as hotels and as places where a bath could be taken. They were used only by the aristocracy, and infrequently. Visits with cleanliness in mind were never common: before marriage, for example, or before an amorous encounter or a

[6] *Ibid.*
[7] Valerius Maximus, 'Faits et Dits mémorables' (fifteenth century) Paris, BN, ms. fr., 289; fol.414.   [8] Garnier, *Les Etuves dijonnaises*, p. 30.
[9] P. Goubert, *Beauvais et les Beauvaisis de 1600 à 1730* (Paris, 1960), p. 232; F. Lebrun, *La Mort en Anjou au XVIIIe siècle* (Paris, 1971), p. 266.
[10] Blégny, *Livre commode des adresses*, p. 183.
[11] A. Seyboth, *Strasbourg historique et pittoresque de ses origines à 1870* (Strasbourg, 1894). Seyboth gives a detailed list of businesses, street by street, with dates, which makes the count possible.
[12] D. Martin, *Le Parlement nouveau* (Strasbourg, 1637), quoted by C. Nerlingen, *Strasbourg* (1900), p. 125.   [13] *Ibid.*

journey, or on return. One courtier went there ceremonially the day he was introduced to his future wife.[14] Another spent some time there to erase the fatigue of a journey.[15] Madame de Sévigné did not find it 'unreasonable' for someone 'the night before setting off, to sleep at the bath-house . . . so long as [the baths were] not at [her] house'.[16] The purpose of such places was ambiguous; they were above all hotels providing absolute discretion. M. de Laval, for example, hid in one after a turbulent marriage, and to escape from his pursuers.[17] Others used them for secret love affairs. They were luxurious establishments, often situated well away from prying eyes, perhaps tucked away at the end of a cul-de-sac, like the Hotel Zamet, Rue de la Cerisaie, frequented by Henri IV himself.[18] Madame de Sévigné's distrust sprang from such ultra-discreet practices. Bathing was only a secondary purpose of such places. They were restricted, in any case, to a very limited clientele. Steam-baths had effectively disappeared.

Iconography similarly bears witness to this disappearance. The public steam-baths, with their bed linen and wall-hangings, their wooden bathtubs and their serving maids carrying pails on yokes across their shoulders, still illustrated in the illuminated manuscripts of the *Decameron* in 1430,[19] or in the series of men and women bathing by Dürer from the end of the fifteenth century,[20] disappeared in their turn from engravings and paintings.

'GETTING OUT THE BATHTUBS'

The other practice which largely died out was private. It was an activity of the nobility in particular, or at least of the refined. It was the *seigneurs* who, in the mid-fifteenth century *Cent Nouvelles nouvelles*, had baths prepared for them,[21] as if water was a sign of wealth. A demonstration of status, it became the occasion for display; a bath enhanced celebrations and receptions. The accounts of Philip

---

[14]   Mme de La Guette, *Mémoires* (Paris, 1982, 1st ed. 1681), p. 89.
[15]   G. de Chavagnac *Mémoires* (Paris, 1699), vol. 1, p. 207.
[16]   Mme de Sévigné, *Lettres* (Paris, 1972), vol. 1, p. 28 (letter dated 26 June 1655).
[17]   G. Tallemant des Réaux, *Historiettes* (Paris, 1960), vol. 2, p. 344 (ms. 1659).
[18]   Sauval, *Les Antiquités de Paris* (Paris, 1724), vol. 2, p. 146.
[19]   G. Boccaccio, *Le Décaméron* (fourteenth century) (Paris, 1978), p. 39, translated into English as *The Decameron* (London, 1972, reprinted 1986).
[20]   C. Ephrussi, *Les Bains de femmes de Dürer* (Nuremburg, no date, but around 1930).
[21]   Anon., *Cent Nouvelles nouvelles* (1450), in *Conteurs français du XVIe siècle* (Paris, 1979), p. 33.

the Good, which record the duke's activities as well as his expenditure, enable us to trace 'the baths taken in his house'.[22] Food was always provided, meat in particular. They were the occasion for invitations and festivities, for animated gatherings of people and things. 'On 30 December 1462, the Duke regaled himself at the baths in his residence, in the company of Mgr de Rovestaing, Mgr Jacques de Bourbon, the son of the Comte de Russye and many other great lords, knights and squires.'[23] The practice, clearly, was prestigious. In a sense it even enhanced nobility, the bath adding an extra dimension of pleasure and refinement. 'The Duke invited to dine with him the ambassadors of the wealthy Duke of Bavaria and the Count of Wurtemberg, and had a total of five meat dishes prepared to regale himself at the baths.'[24] Such a scene might even be enjoyed by royalty. The reception offered on 10 September 1476 by J. Dauvet, first president of Parlement, to Queen Charlotte of Savoy and 'many other women of her company' resembled in every detail those described in the accounts of the Duke of Burgundy. 'They were received and regaled most nobly and lavishly, and four beautiful and richly adorned baths had been prepared.'[25] Water enhanced the festivities, and demonstrated the generosity of the host.

It was a practice, lastly, of great noble women, mentioned in a fourteenth-century *Contenance des fames*, even though the author finds it excessively precious.

> Mult la tiendrait à dédain
> Si elle ne prenait souvent le bain[26]

The third of the *Cent Nouvelles nouvelles* uses the occasion of one such female bath. A rare enough event, evidently, since the whole neighbourhood knew when the great lady 'had her bathtubs got out'.[27] It was when he learnt of this happening that the castle miller sought a pretext for surprising the lady in her bath. This equivocal scene apart, the neighbourhood gossip shows that such baths remained

22 L.-P. Gachard, 'Les comptes de Philippe le Bon, duc de Bourgogne', *Collections des voyages des souverains des Pays-Bas* (Brussels, 1876), voi. 1, p. 89.
23 *Ibid.*, p. 87.   24 *Ibid.*, p. 91.
25 J. de Troyes, *Histoire de Louis unzième* (1483), published by J. Michaud and J. Poujelat in *Nouvelle Collection des mémoires pour servir à l'histoire de France* (Paris, 1837), vol. 4, p. 280.
26 A. Jubinal, *La Contenance des fames* (fourteenth century) in *Nouveau Recueil des contes dits* (Paris, 1842), vol. 2, p. 175.
27 Anon., *Cent Nouvelles nouvelles*, p. 33.

very special. They were probably infrequent. The accounts of Philip the Good, for example, suggest on average a bath every four or five months.[28]

These private practices also more or less disappeared in the sixteenth and seventeenth centuries. Steam-baths no longer followed royal courts, as had, for example, that of Isabelle of Bavaria, frequently transported from castle to castle.[29] Instead, displays of water animated gardens and their fountains. It was these, not baths, that Perrault included amongst the superiority of the 'moderns', dwelling at length on the lawns and pools of Versailles.[30] Fears of the body being infiltrated thus appear to have had very concrete consequences.

The bathrooms and the marble bath which Louis XIV installed at Versailles, in an act designed vaguely to recall ancient Rome, were replaced, a few years later, by accommodation for the Comte de Toulouse, the legitimised bastard. After various vicissitudes, the bath itself became a garden pool.[31] It was incorporated into a different water circuit, designed only to please the eye, a scene of nature tamed. Water, whose machinery gave, at great cost, cadence to park design, was employed primarily for cascades and fountains in the seventeenth century. It was meant to beguile the eyes. Its dancing was a mark of plenty and of power. It was a sign of supreme domination over a capricious element.[32] This lavishness, however, did not extend to the practice of bathing. But it was not lack of water which rendered the marble bath redundant so much as the preference accorded to dramatic aquatic contrivances.

Very few inventories drawn up after death mention bathtubs. Pierre Goubert found only one in the Beauvaisis at the time of Louis XIV.[33] No Parisian doctor owned one in the mid-seventeenth century, despite the existence of hydrotherapy.[34] Those in the Château de Vaux, the Hôtel Lambert and the Hôtel Conti were

---

[28] Gachard, 'Les comptes de Philippe le Bon', vol. 1, pp. 87–99.
[29] A. Vallet de Virville, 'Comptes royaus' (1403–1423), *Chronique du roi Charles VII roi de France* (Paris, 1858), vol. 3, p. 277.
[30] C. Perrault, *La Querelle des anciens et des modernes en ce qui regarde les arts et les sciences* (Paris, 1688), vol. 1, p. 247.
[31] C. P. de Luynes, *Mémoires, 1735–1738* (Paris, 1860), vol. 10, pp. 180–8.
[32] Cf. B. Teyssèdre, *L'Art au siècle de Louis XIV* (Paris, 1967), p. 145: 'Le maître des eaux'.   [33] Goubert, *Beauvais et les Beauvaisis*, p. 232.
[34] F. Lehoux, *Le Cadre de vie des médecins parisiens aux XVIᵉ et XVIIᵉ siècles* (Paris, 1976).

simply imitations of the royal example, and clearly do not compensate for its equivocal role.[35] They were regarded, in any case, as curiosities.[36] And the few architects who referred to baths and steam baths in the seventeenth century, did so in imitation of the classical plan of Vetruvius.[37] The reference remained formal. The introduction of this item should not mislead. 'Steam-baths and baths are not necessary in France as in the provinces where they are used to them . . . All the same, if for some reason a seigneur wishes to have them in his house, they should be situated . . .'[38] Fear constrained the use of water. The image of the permeable body, in a context of inadequately mastered risks, made bathing difficult to contemplate. These ideas were accompanied by a real discontinuity in practice. 'In these countries, baths are only prepared to restore lost health.'[39] Montaigne, who himself bathed on his travels, and who dreamed of the infiltrated water taking strange routes the better to dispel bodily indispositions, stressed the disappearance of bathing as early as the sixteenth century, a custom 'lost, which was widely observed in times past by almost all nations'.[40] Only a few therapeutic establishments survived. A type of bathing which had once possessed its own traditions, even its own institutions, its locations and social references, had disappeared. It is as if the plague, with its far-reaching effects on the imagination, had put a stop to a physical activity, as if conceptions of the body had, by degrees, resulted in the suppression of practices directly concerned with bodily hygiene.

It would be wrong, however, to confuse this with practices of cleanliness, and interpret the disappearance of the bath as a step backwards for hygiene, as one historiographical tradition has for long attempted to assert.[41] What disappeared along with steam-baths had no necessary connection with washing. Steam-baths do not necessarily testify to standards of cleanliness which can then be shown to have been abandoned. It was not a matter of an essential element of cleanliness which had dramatically receded. The favour which the queen granted to Jehan Petit and his fellows in 1410 was as much a

[35] H. Havard, *Dictionnaire d'ameublement* (Paris), vol. 4, p. 845.
[36] *Ibid.*
[37] M.-V. Vitruve, *Livre d'architecture, ou art de bâtir* (trans. Paris, 1547).
[38] L. Savot, *L'Architecture française* (Paris, 1624), p. 102.
[39] Rebecque, *L'Apothicaire française*, p. 473.
[40] M. de Montaigne, *Essais* (1595), (Paris, 1950), p. 810.
[41] A. Franklin, *La Vie privée d'autrefois* (Paris, 1908); and, amongst others, R. Pernoud, *Lumière du Moyen Âge* (Paris, 1981, 1st ed. 1944).

matter of pleasure as of washing.[42] The image of water has not always had the associations it has today. A particular journey, over a long period of time, was necessary for it to achieve the 'transparency' of contemporary hygiene. There are other ways of experiencing water than ours. The bath offered by J. Dauvet to Queen Charlotte, with all its ostentatious display, showed the festive dimension prevailing over cleanliness.[43] Bathing dominated by notions of play, for example, had many other cultural roots than bathing seen as indispensible to health. Other factors, and probably other vulnerabilities, were involved.

This being so, it at once becomes easier to understand the disappearance of these practices. The plague, certainly, played a part, as some contemporaries realised. 'Twenty-five years ago, nothing was more fashionable in Brabant than public baths; today, there are none, the new plague has taught us to avoid them',[44] said Erasmus in 1526. But for its role to have had so great an effect, it was probably necessary for other factors, which we must now consider, to converge.

[42]   See note 4, p. 21.   [43]   See note 25, p. 24.
[44]   D. Erasmus, *Les Hôtelleries* (trans. Paris, 1872, 1st ed. 1526), p. 18.

3. *The old pleasures of water*

We must return to the subject of medieval steam-baths in order to gain a better understanding of those practices which the sixteenth century saw gradually disappear. Their purpose was primarily pleasure, even impropriety; the water was, above all, for enjoyment. In other words, washing was not the real point of the bath.

MINGLED BODIES

Wealth, addressing Lover in the *Roman de la Rose*, describes, in a few verses, a thirteenth-century version of Rabelais' Thélème. Heads are wreathed with flowers, nature is fertile, and interiors protected. Encounters multiply, dedicated to desire. The *Ostel de la folle largesse* is, in fact, a steam-bath. Is this surprising?

> Là vont vallez et demoiselles
> conjointes par vieles makereles
> cerchent prez et jardins et gauz
> plus renvoisiez que papegauz
> puis revont entre aus estuves
> et se baignent ensemble en cuves . . .[1]

Here, the steam-bath promises mingling and pleasure – communal baths, a room, beds and feasting. The scene occurs frequently in the *Roman de la Rose*:

> Ce n'est par ce que bon leur semble
> que baigner se doivent ensemble.[2]

It is also a theme of Gothic imagery. There is a steam-bath on the portal of the cathedral at Auxerre. The Prodigal Son is massaged and rubbed by several women, whilst a serving-maid pours water into the

---

[1] G. de Lorris and J. de Meung, *Roman de la Rose* (thirteenth century) (Paris, 1966). vol. 2, p. 57, v. 10065. [2] *Ibid.*, vol. 2, p. 186, v. 14348.

tub. The sirens and serpents surrounding the scene serve only to emphasise its attractions.[3] Elsewhere, for example in the Hôtel de Ville at Damme, people bathe in one same tub, while fellow guests and servants circulate about.[4] Such mixing of sexes and age groups, nude, reveals a lost sociability. It astonished Brantôme when he visited Switzerland in the sixteenth century. 'Men and women mix indiscriminately together in baths and steam-baths without any impropriety occurring.'[5] It was also the practice in thermal baths in the Middle Ages, where naked bodies of both sexes shared the same water. The Fountains of Youth in fifteenth-century Flemish paintings were partly inspired by steam-baths; men and women, transformed into young and slender bodies, swim naked round the spring of life, the better to draw from it strength and youthfulness. Consciously resurrecting pagan themes, as in Bosch's 'Garden of Delight',[6] which combines Dionysiac eroticism with a lost paradise, they illustrate a promiscuity which was already beginning to be archaic, or, at any rate, less tolerated. Sensibility here abetted budding prohibition. In the fifteenth century, bath-house regulations no longer, in theory, permitted these earlier promiscuities.

The history of steam-baths connects at this point with the history of the gradual establishment of physical distance. It reflects the emergence of thresholds; once these were established, certain types of mixing became more difficult, certain contacts no longer permissible. The internalisation of the norms spread by seigneurial courts imperceptibly changed perceptions of decency and modesty. Sensibilities could no longer accommodate such mixed nudity in confined spaces. The separation of the sexes was introduced in many steam-baths at the end of the fourteenth century. A rule of alternance prevailed at Digne, Dijon and Rouen,[7] for example, with certain days reserved for women, others for men, and yet others for Jews and actors (which shows, in the last case at least, that 'decency' was not seen in the same light for lesser social and cultural categories).

[3] C. Enlart, *Manuel d'archéologie française* (Paris, 1902), pp. 88–9.
[4] L. Maeterlinck, *Le Genre satirique dans la peinture flamande* (Brussels, 1907), p. 175.
[5] P. de Bourdeilles (called Brantôme), *Les Femmes galantes*, in *Oeuvres* (Paris, 1864), vol. 9, p. 290 (ms. 1585).
[6] J. Bosch, 'Le Jardin des délices', (1500), Madrid, Prado Museum.
[7] Garnier, *Les Etuves dijonnaises*, p. 26; de Beaurepaire, *Nouveaux Mélanges historiques*, p. 22; J. Arnoud, *Etude historique sur les bains thermaux de Digne* (Paris, 1886).

Separate locations became the rule in Paris and Strasbourg,[8] among other towns, with different places for each sex.

The phenomenon was gradual and confused. The same prohibition was promulgated as much as a century later in some towns than others. And it was never, in practice, universal. A fifteenth-century miniature of Valerius Maximus[9] epitomises such promiscuity – men and women together in one same tub, touching and caressing, even beds where couples lie intertwined. In 1515 Pogge mocked the 'separation' in the baths of Baden, 'honeycombed with little windows which allow male and female bathers to take refreshments and chit-chat together', whilst the surrounding gallery made it easy for them to meet.[10] In 1441, the municipal officers of Avignon prohibited married men from visiting steam-baths,[11] as they were formally recognised as places of prostitution. The steam-baths of Fontaine-le-Comte were demolished in 1412 as a result of the disorderly behaviour of the 'girls' who lived there.[12] The allusion of Eustache Deschamps is quite explicit:

> Bruxelles adieu où les bains sont jolis
> Les étuves, les fillettes plaisantes.[13]

The magistrates of Péronne attributed an unequivocal purpose to their city's steam-baths. 'All prostitutes are ordered to keep to the place built for them at the steam-baths, and not to be so bold or impudent as to sleep or reside outside the said place except in the daytime, to eat and drink decently, without noise, scandal or disorder.'[14] Both confinement and exclusion were involved here.

Gatherings of a particular type were often held in steam-baths. Philippe de Bourgogne once hired the bath-house at Valenciennes, with prostitutes, in honour of the English ambassador who was paying him a visit.[15] In many towns the expression 'going for a steam-bath' had a special meaning. Clients were welcomed by alluring and

---

[8] Boileau, *Le Livre des métiers*, pp. 155–6 (note); F. Piton, *Strasbourg illustré* (Strasbourg, 1885), p. 151.
[9] Valerius Maximus, 'Faits et Dits mémorables'.
[10] G.-F. Pogge, *Les Bains de Bade* (fifteenth century) (Paris, 1847).
[11] P. Pansier, 'Règlement de prostitution à Avignon', *Janus* (Paris, 1902), p. 144; J. Rossiaud, 'Crises et consolidations' (1330–1530), in J. Le Goff, *La Ville médiévale* (Paris, 1980).
[12] R. de Belleval, *Lettres sur le Ponthieu* (Paris, 1868), p. 154.
[13] E. Deschamps, 'Rondel 552', *Oeuvres* (Paris, 1876–1903), vol. 4, p. 6, vv. 4–10.
[14] Cabanès, *La Vie aux bains* (Paris, 1904), p. 194.
[15] R. Kendall, *L'Angleterre pendant la guerre des Deux-Roses* (Paris, 1984, 1st ed. London, 1979) p. 283.

attentive hostesses, 'living in sin and dissolute in love', often poor girls from the country, 'free with their bodies'.[16]

TRANSGRESSION

The history of steam-baths relates to yet another history, that of games and festivities, of pleasure and play. In this case it is also the history of lawlessness and wrong-doing, which appeared inseparable from them.

In the course of his travels in the old Low Countries at the very beginning of the sixteenth century, that is, just when such places were disappearing, Dürer kept a record of all his expenses, down to the last penny. He consistently recorded in conjunction what he spent on the tavern, the baths and on gambling. They were all alike to him. 'Aix-la-Chapelle, spent at the baths with friends: 5 deniers. I spent 5 silver pfennigs at the inn and at the baths with friends. I lost 7 deniers gaming.'[17] This was leisure activity on the fringes of respectability. The baths were inextricably linked with festive sociability, with all its distractions, dissipation and even excesses. This is very clearly demonstrated by law-suits in connection with such establishments.

When, on 29 August 1466, Jehannotte Saignant, mistress of steam-baths, was placed on a hurdle before being put in a sack and drowned in the waters of the Ouche by the Dijon public executioner, her crimes were various without always being particularly grave. There had been trouble over her business, in the first place – she had assisted the burglary by one of her clients of the house of M. de Molène, secretary to the Duc de Bourgogne. The assault had been directed against his wife and was never clearly established. Then there had been illicit prostitution: Jehannotte's steam-bath was provided with 'bawdy young serving-maids, very pleasing and highly alluring'[18] in the service of the house. Lastly, there had been poisoning: the mistress of steam-baths had employed a 'special' herb to prepare food and wine for a female client to whom she 'wished ill'. The result was 'tragic' for the bather. 'It seemed as if she had gone mad . . . ever since, for a long time, she had been constantly on the point of death, and, in the end, without ever recovering her health, she died.'[19]

---

[16] J.-P. Legay, *La Rue au Moyen Age* (Rennes, 1984), p. 150.
[17] A. Dürer, *Le Journal de voyage dans les anciens Pays-Bas* (1520–1) (trans. Brussels, 1970), p. 71.
[18] Garnier, *Les Etuves dijonnaises*, p. 41.   [19] *Ibid.*, p. 79.

The trial had been long and difficult, and the evidence rarely clear. Only the prostitution seemed certain. If Jehannotte Saignant paid for her crimes, she was also paying for the reputation surrounding steam-baths and their disreputable trade.

When, for example, in 1479, Des Pars counted up violent incidents in the steam-baths of Ghent, and reached 1,400 crimes and woundings in the space of ten months, he was both defining and constructing reality.[20] It was not so much the figure itself which was important as its calculation. The very fact of undertaking the exercise revealed an attitude towards the steam-bath and its way of life. By localising a certain violence, such a calculation singled it out and attempted, by implication, to explain it. It was the violence of licence and non-conformity, the very violence which disciplined habits and the civilising process were trying to control. It was as if a certain spontaneity and impulsiveness, hitherto more or less integrated or even seen as normal, was now seen only as intemperance. More than anywhere, there were found here the 'uncontrolled' behaviour, the hasty deeds, the 'excessively' impulsive actions, all the 'contentious words', in fact, which led to 'knives being drawn',[21] described in fifteenth-century trials arising out of incidents in steam-baths.

Dedicated to pleasure, steam-baths were a focus of urban disorder. What was also held against Jehannotte Saignant was the atmosphere of unrest, even dissipation, which surrounded her business. 'So much shouting, bawling and jumping about was heard that it was amazing that the neighbours put up with it, the law ignored it, and the ground supported it.'[22] The motives of the bathers – meetings, entertainment and feasting – fostered complicity with wrong-doing. It was as if the liberty of the instincts which steam-baths appeared to authorise, permitted the rejection of many other prohibitions. The social mixing conjured up pictures of latent disorderliness and potential violence. The priority accorded to desire encouraged lawlessness, real or imaginary. The steam-baths were gradually and increasingly seen as sources of instability. As towns became more structured in the fifteenth century, with centre and suburbs differentiated, certain quarters replanned, and control beginning to be established over their immediate surroundings, steam-baths were a source of unease by virtue of their example of constant, promiscuous, even delinquent,

[20] Maeterlinck, *Le Genre satirique*, p. 180.
[21] G. Espinas, *La Vie urbaine à Douai au Moyen Âge* (Paris, 1913), vol. 4, p. 682.
[22] Garnier, *Les Etuves dijonnaises*, pp. 27–8.

sociability. They authorised, in sum, a licence which was ill-assimilated, which disturbed more than it calmed, which corrupted more than it protected. Places of dissipation, they were perceived as sources of trouble, and increasingly ill-tolerated. This mode of perception and the reality on which it was based was inevitably detrimental to the continued existence of steam-baths. They were already forbidden in the city of London and its suburbs at the beginning of the fifteenth century. The ordinance issued by Henry V in 1411 referred to the 'grievances, abominations, damages, disturbances, murders, homicides, larcenies, and other common nuisances' caused by the 'men and women of bad and evil life . . . in the stews . . . in the City and suburbs'.[23] Many closures had similar penal causes – brawls, suspicious deaths or various 'agitations'. Pierre Melin lost his steam-baths at Aix because he had his manservant commit a murder there in 1478.[24] The last steam-baths in Dijon were suppressed in 1556 by the town Chamber; Etienne Boulé was sentenced to destroy his furnaces. The people themselves seem to have had a role in this decision. The ordinance took account of the 'clamours, complaints, and protests about wicked and scandalous doings there, and the fact that many serving women were debauched and drawn into wrong-doing'.[25] And the prohibition in 1566 by the Estates General of Orléans of all brothels throughout the kingdom accelerated the disappearance of steam-baths, many of which were hit by this law. The *Ostel de la folle largesse* became, in the sixteenth century, an institution which towns gradually rejected. The unrest they sparked off could not be tolerated. The liveliness and bustle of their clientele were seen only as disorderliness and disturbance.

Thus a visit to the steam-baths turned into a confrontation with the law. It fed into a chronicle of lawlessness. Such places were not comparable with the hygienic establishments which, much later, encouraged order and enforced norms. They belonged first and foremost to the world of pleasure, with its conviviality and its excesses, summed up by a fifteenth-century German saying from the steam-baths: 'With water on the outside and wine within, let us make merry'.[26] It was therefore not a direct opposition to natural impulses, as would have been implied by an extension of the sphere of hygiene,

[23] H. T. Riley, *Memorials of London and London Life in the thirteenth, fourteenth and fifteenth centuries* (London, 1868), p. 647.
[24] G. Arnaud d'Agnel, *Les Comptes du roi René* (1453–80) (Paris, 1908), vol. 3, p. 473.
[25] Garnier, *Les Etuves dijonnaises*, p. 41.   [26] Ephrussi, *Les Bains*, p. 13.

but, on the contrary, a complicity with the world of unbridled instincts. Water was an extra dimension of pleasure. It added a sense of licence. The bathers made it an element in their play. In the long conflict in which culture opposed desire, steam-baths did not serve 'order'. They had no part in the rules for civilised behaviour or the precepts of hygiene. This is not to say that no washing took place. But it remained of little significance, the essential being the pleasurable practices in which it was only a subsidiary element.

The rejection was linked to a gradual strengthening of social and urban standards. The church was only giving expression to this when, at this period, it designated 'the trade of steam-bath owner infamous, on a par with that of brothel-keeper'.[27] Since the fifteenth century, preachers had poured forth their fierce denunciations. It is the confusion of steam-baths with other establishments, rather than their moralising, which is of interest in their sermons. This is how they defined 'dangerous' places: 'Citizens, do not give your sons the freedom or the money to visit brothels, steam-baths or taverns'.[28] But the utterances of the preachers alone do not explain the disappearance of steam-baths. What was involved, it seems, was social functioning itself.

The factors contributing to this disappearance had, therefore, at least a double logic: progressive intolerance by the human environment of places seen as turbulent, violent and corrupting, and fears of the weakness of the body, based on ideas about dangerous openings and fluxes. The impact of the plague was much greater because it affected a practice already unstable and under threat.

THE 'MULTITUDE OF GOD'S GOODS'

Baths taken in private were never a source of disorder as were steam-baths. It was a practice of a privileged minority. Brawls and knives were never, clearly, as prominent there, or the link with urban delinquency as strong. These were baths taken in the seclusion of noble houses and mansions, in which connection it is hard to imagine a disorderly dimension. The practice posed neither the legal nor the social problem of the steam-bath. Its disappearance owed even more

27   O. Maillard, *Confessions* (fifteenth century), quoted by A. Samouillan, *Olivier Maillard, sa prédication et son temps* (Paris, 1891), p. 500.
28   O. Maillard, *Sermons* (fifteenth century) (Paris), sermon 28; c.f. also A. Méray, *La Vie au temps des libres prêcheurs* (Paris, 1878).

to ideas about water and images of the body. Fear of the organs being penetrated must have weighed more heavily. No other explanation is adequate. Like the practices discussed above, it had its origins primarily in festive behaviour. It was rooted in the same principle of licence and pleasure. Its context was similarly one of enjoyment rather than hygiene. In the same way, therefore, dedicated to pleasure rather than principle, the activity remained to some extent vulnerable. Such a status could contain the seeds of its decline.

In this instance, comparisons are possible. We can compare over time scenes apparently similar, with the same context and the same surroundings, and identify both what has disappeared and what has replaced it. The point-by-point comparison of these private scenes, separated only by the passage of time, suggests once again that this ancient employment of water was not primarily a matter of hygiene. Two examples will introduce the comparison and emphasise the differences.

The first of the *Cent Nouvelles nouvelles*, written in 1450 for Philip the Good, tells how the Receiver of Haynau, attracted by the beauty of his neighbour, a lady from Valenciennes, attempted to seduce her. His strategy took the form of a series of invitations and feasts, to which her husband was at first invited alone. The Receiver's plan was to make him a close friend. 'And as far as possible, dinners, suppers and banquets with baths and steam-baths, and other pastimes, at his house and elsewhere, never took place without his presence.'[29] The seduction of the young woman would occur in due course. Secret meetings, subtle persuasion – the Receiver was adroit and pressing. His suit was heard and understood. The young woman consented. Further discreet assignations had to be arranged. An ordinary enough tale, it is true, but the setting for these meetings conveys the ambience of the bath. When a journey by her husband enabled the worthy to receive her alone at his house, 'he at once had the bathtubs got out, the steam-baths heated, tarts and hippocras brought, and a multitude of God's goods'.[30] The entertainment was prolonged. 'After they had gone down to the chamber, they got into the bath, before which the splendid supper was laid out and served'.[31] Baths were the scene of social enjoyment, gatherings where guests both ate and amused themselves. It was also, in this case, the scene of amorous exchanges, an erotic preliminary. Water enhanced the pleasures of

---

[29] Anon., *Cent Nouvelles nouvelles*, p. 21.   [30] *Ibid.*, p. 22.   [31] *Ibid.*

the senses. For this fifteenth-century worthy, the practice was an element in the art of hospitality, of entertaining, and, even, of sensuality. These festive occasions, public or private, confirm that water was exploited first and foremost for pleasure. It meant warmth and contacts, more or less sensual.

Comparable scenes appearing in the tales, stories and even memoirs of the seventeenth century, are, at several key points, completely different. They show what has changed. When, in the course of his libertine adventures, the abbé Choisy, disguised as a woman, proposed to share a bed with a certain female dependant, most points of reference are reversed. Water was totally absent; cleanliness was present. 'I had in my house an old attendant of my mother's, to whom I paid a pension of 100 écus; I summoned her. "Mademoiselle", I said, "this girl is proposed as my chambermaid, but I want to know beforehand if she is really clean. Examine her from head to toe". She promptly stripped the young girl down to her skin . . .'[32] The cleanliness demanded by Choisy, certainly, also implied the absence of a secret disease. The word had both a social and a medical sense. The abbé's suspicion was all the greater because of the gulf which separated the aristocrat and the apprentice linen maid. It was not, in this case, without a certain cynicism. There remains, however, a more specific concern; a witness testified to the cleanliness of a body which had been stripped naked. The acts which followed were also significant. 'I completed my toilet and was soon in bed; I had a strong desire to kiss the little darling.'[33] Cleanliness and the toilet involved neither a bath nor even washing. Water had no role, despite the fact that cleanliness was an issue, and trouble taken to achieve it.

Each incident, from noble rake to libertine abbé, possessed what the other lacked. At key points, the two situations were completely opposite. In the fifteenth century, the Receiver of Haynau bathed to give greater intensity to his festivities and pleasures. The seventeenth-century adventurer, future academician and great lord though he was, could not conceive of bathing, though he lingered over protracted sessions during which he and his lady friends did their hair, dressed, and pondered at length the positioning of a hand-

[32] Abbé de Choisy, *Mémoires de l'abbé de Choisy habillé en femme* (mss. end seventeenth century) (Paris, 1966), p. 312.   [33] *Ibid.*, p. 313.

kerchief or a jewel. The use of water disappeared, whilst standards of cleanliness and pains taken increased.

Thus, we must not think of the bath with its modern connotations, but think instead of a cleanliness which existed in the absence of washing; we must accept a bodily cleanliness which would not be recognised by that name today; we must study a series of objects whose cleanliness long served for that of the body, to the exclusion of washing it – places, linen, clothes, various accessories, etc. We must discover the body there, where it no longer resides.

Part 2　*The linen that washed*

4. *What was covered and what was seen*

Platter, a poor scholar in the mid-fifteenth century, described his efforts to rid himself of the vermin with which he was infested. He spoke of their return as that of an inescapable companion. The protective measures to which he resorted were elementary, but sufficiently significant to throw light, in a number of ways, on a key stage in ancient cleanliness.

> You cannot imagine how the scholars, young and old, as well as some of the common people, crawled with vermin . . . Often, particularly in summer, I used to go and wash my shirt on the banks of the Oder; then I hung it on a branch, and whilst it dried, I cleaned my clothes. I dug a hole, threw in a pile of vermin, filled it in and planted a cross on top.[1]

These actions are revealing. Platter knew nothing of washing the body; it was exclusively a matter of washing his linen. On this point, too, the record is precious. Platter, it seems, possessed only one shirt. He washed it himself in the river, more or less regularly, in an attempt to destroy the parasites which infested it.

Personal cleanliness was symbolised by clean linen. Attention was concentrated on the coverings which concealed the skin. Platter's actions were, of course, those of a poor scholar, but poverty alone does not explain them. His actions evoke archaic indicators of cleanliness. Their 'poverty' was a social poverty. Vermin and a limited use of linen were the common lot before Platter's birth. And the equation of changing clothes and cleanliness, excluding any washing of the body, was a long-lasting phenomenon.

VERMIN

Measures against vermin also introduce an earlier world than that of Platter. In fourteenth-century Montaillou, delousing went on all the time, a mark of affection and respect; in bed or in front of the fire,

[1] T. Platter, *La Vie de Thomas Platter* (trans. Geneva, 1862, 1st ed. 1499), p. 24.

mistresses diligently deloused their lovers, serving-maids their masters, daughters their mothers, and mothers-in-law their future sons-in-law. Certain women with particularly nimble fingers even made a profession of it; in summer people sat in the sun and gossiped on the 'flat roofs of low houses'[2] whilst enjoying the services of professional delousers. Vermin were still a daily fact of life at the end of the Middle Ages for a large part of the population. Their presence is constantly referred to. The chief method envisaged by the *Ménagier de Paris* in the fifteenth century for getting rid of them or killing them was to pack bed covers, linen and clothes so tightly inside chests 'that the fleas would be deprived of light and air and gripped tight, and would thus quickly perish and die'.[3] Descriptions of these insects or simply references to them were common in the fifteenth century, testimony to how widely they were found. 'The flea bites those who wish to sleep, and spares no-one, neither king nor pope . . . The flea is not easy to catch because it jumps nimbly, and when it is about to rain it bites fiercely.'[4] Even fifteenth-century compilations of rules of etiquette, aimed, amongst others, at noble children, accepted vermin as a natural phenomenon. At least they should not be allowed to be too obvious. But they were visible; they were there, within reach, a constant and familiar presence. 'It is unbecoming and not very nice to scratch your head at table, or pick lice and fleas or other vermin from your neck or your back and kill them in front of people.'[5] Early in the sixteenth century, an envoy of the Duke of Ferrara, lodging in the Château of Fontainebleau, then newly-built, spoke ironically about 'fleas, lice, bugs and certain flies which never let him rest' and expressed his surprise 'that God had seen fit to create such useless creatures'.[6] For protection, you could, like Platter, change your clothes, or you could, at the very least, keep them clean. This is what was recommended by books of etiquette from the Middle Ages on. The advice was brief and generalised. No precise or detailed guidance was offered. What mattered most was that clothes should be

[2] E. Le Roy Ladurie, *Montaillou, village occitan de 1294 à 1324* (Paris, 1975), p. 204. (Trans. into English as *Montaillou: Cathars and Catholics in a French village, 1294–1324* (London, 1978).)

[3] *Le Ménagier de Paris* (fourteenth century) (Paris, 1846), vol. 1, p. 172.

[4] de Glainville, *Le Propriétaire des choses très utiles.*

[5] J. Sulpizio, *Des bonnes moeurs et honestes convenances que doit garder un jeune homme* (fifteenth century) (Lyons, 1555), p. 7.

[6] Quoted by L. Guyon, *Diverses Leçons* (Lyons, 1604), p. 826.

respectable and decent. Their surface was all that, in practice, people saw.

It is, however, the texts which explain the presence of vermin, or try to describe their emergence and proliferation, which illustrate most clearly the extreme tenuousness of the connection which was thought to exist between them and bodily cleanliness. Hygienists, for example, attributed the proliferation of this parasitical fauna simply to an excess of bodily humours. Lice and fleas were the result of uncontrolled exhalations. They were born of corrupt substances. Thus a reduction of the humours would assist in their control. A long tradition, surviving into the seventeenth century, elaborated causes which had rarely any explicit relation to bodily cleanliness. Animalcules and itching were secreted from 'inside', a spontaneous generation resulting from an invisible mingling of substances. 'The causes of [infant] scurvy are two-fold, because it is brought about by the relics of the months of purging of women, or by the poor quality of the nurse's milk, which easily goes bad inside the stomach of the child, and cannot be transformed into good chyle.'[7] The fight against scurvy in children thus had as its first target the nurse's milk; 'treatment' consisted of changing the nurse or changing her diet.

These teeming creatures could only be born of bodies. They came out from the skin like certain maggots seemed to emerge from decomposing flesh. The image was easily transposed. Their presence indicated an internal disorder or a corruption of obscure substances; death already present, perhaps, secretly at work, or its mark or hold on living flesh. No connection was made with the care of the skin. Cleanliness was not mentioned, as if it had neither importance nor relevance. In this context, it simply did not exist; it had no role in health. The focus of interest lay elsewhere. Spreading scabs, watery discharges and proliferating parasites did not suggest any direct connection with cleanliness. They were essentially the expression of a bodily condition. Getting rid of these pests, therefore, meant treating internal mechanisms. Such reasoning continued unchanged for centuries; that of Mauriceau, surgeon-obstetrician to Parisian bourgeois women in the seventeenth century, was the same as that of Guy de Chauliac, surgeon to the Avignon popes in the fourteenth century.

---

[7] J. Guillemeau, *De la nourriture et du gouvernement des enfants* (Paris, 1609), pp. 166–7.

For the latter, too, lice and mites were born of 'corrupt humours',[8] and the more children overflowed with humours, the more likely they were to fall victim.

This theory of organic disorders clearly shows that the link between vermin and cleanliness was far from being as obvious as it was later to become. A whole pathological context was involved. It is as if eyes could not see something soon to be clearly visible; as if a relationship soon to be obvious was then hidden. 'These filthy spots, these scabs and ulcers which disfigure the bodies and particularly the faces and heads of little children, called milky crust or scald-head . . . whose accidental differences are all that authors describe, come, in my opinion, from a lymph that fishes in a more or less viscous acid.'[9] For protection against these teeming invasions and afflictions of the skin, scholarly tradition favoured one method above all: limitation and control of the humours.

This method corresponded to the innumerable regimens which formed the basis of treatises of hygiene up to the seventeenth century: attention to the diet, because on that depended everything concerning the body. By determining the humours and their qualities, its composition determined what was healthy. To vary it was to act on the parasites by working on their source. 'Cacochymical bodies, which abound with sour humours, tend to have many such beasts. So to cure the itching which results, it is necessary to purge the cacochymy by appropriate medicines.'[10] To purge, but also to control; it was necessary to avoid those foods whose decomposition accumulated acidity and viscosity, and those which risked increasing the exhalations. Only the internal alchemy of the body could arrest the development of these parasitic creatures. Foods which were too 'humid', or too slow or difficult to digest, should be avoided. Was it surprising, for example, that in the sixteenth century the cells of Carthusian monks were not infested with bugs? Those of their

---

[8] G. de Chauliac, *La Grande Chirurgie* (fourteenth century) (Lyons, 1592), p. 471. This familiarity with vermin could be used in the great, gloomy, medieval debate about the frailty of man and the constant presence of death. The relationship between vermin and decomposition was what was stressed. Man was rotting while still alive. 'What are the fruits born of us? The agreeable and most useful fruits which we produce and which are born of us are the nits, fleas, lice and worms which are created by and in our bodies and are constantly growing there.' (Fourteenth century text quoted by J. Delumeau, *Le Péché et la Peur, la culpabilisation en Occident* (Paris, 1984), p. 57.)

[9] Ettmuler, *Pratiques de médecine spéciale*, p. 468.

[10] de Monteux, *Conservation de santé*, p. 275.

servants certainly were! To Cardan, it was obviously because the Carthusians knew to abstain from meat.[11] A cell free of vermin, in the sixteenth century, was something worthy of note, to be explained primarily by monkish humours. Such measures led to an empirical criterion of purified substances, which one of the first treatises on the art of 'bodily beauty' expressed in familiar terms in the seventeenth century. 'The way of life is crucial with this illness [ringworm], you should use only meats which engender good juices . . .'[12] These texts did not mean to argue that diet should receive excessive attention. But they did say that food was largely responsible for vermin.

Such a tradition belongs to the early phases of a history; it corresponds for us to a period of blindness and insensibility. By revealing perceptions which we cannot share, it demonstrates its utter remoteness, even rousing feelings of embarrassment, as if the threshold of the tolerable had been exceeded. Suggesting ideas now totally forgotten, these perceptions demonstrate a profound transformation of sensibility. Because it clearly is sensibility – even affect – which is at issue here, as much, possibly even more, than hygienic 'reason'. In this early history, a whole range of relationships later regarded as basic were not seen either as linking dirt and disease, or, more generally, as affecting perceptions which are today completely unconscious; they seem to lack the bodily references which to us are obvious.

The silence of these texts does not, however, permit us to assume the absence of all bodily cleanliness. This existed, but differently from today, governed by other rules. There was in this connection no absolute zero. A zone of total blindness was impossible. The civilising process, of which acts of cleanliness are a part, does not start from nothing. Once again, in order to understand the archaic forms of these acts, and the evolution of the successive thresholds, we have to abandon our own frame of reference.

HANDS AND FACES

On one theme at least, the first treatises on health show the existence in the Middle Ages of the 'ancient' criteria for bodily cleanliness: washing the hands and face, that is ensuring that what was seen was clean, removing the dirt from the visible parts. This was repeated in

---

[11] J.-B. Thiers, *Traité des superstitions* (Paris, 1692), p. 362.
[12] L. Guyon, *Le Miroir de la beauté et de la santé du corps* (Paris, 1615), p. 35.

the numerous translations of ancient medical treatises which were dominant for so long, and embodied in the classical verse:

Ta main soit au matin d'eau fraîche bien lavée
Et toute moîte encore sur tes yeux élevée.[13]

The analogy between water and the humid medium of the eye sometimes also encouraged washing. Water, said the doctors, sharpened the sight, especially if it was fresh and cold. It was as if there was an identity of substance, or a mechanical correspondence. Before fear of water as something which could penetrate and corrupt had gained general credence in the sixteenth century, this observation assumed a connection, premature but specific, with health. 'Wash your hands and face with freshly drawn water, as cold as you can get it, because such washing gives good eyesight, clear and keen.'[14] This comment on sharp eyes remained, however, allusive and subsidiary, asserted rather than explained. And washing the face was not invariably indicated and seems to have been less common than washing the hands.

Once again, the conception was not that of a danger to health. No demands were made on that score. The reasons for clean hands and a spotless face were not sanitary. The obligation, stated plainly and without comment, was moral. Its purpose was decency rather than hygiene. The rule owed more to the clerical than the medical tradition. Scholarly literature could only reaffirm the deep foundations of cleanliness and their primitive forms. The oldest criteria were those of good manners rather than health; it was appearance that mattered. The body was treated by means of its external coverings. The appearance that was created corresponded perfectly to the systematisation of courtly sociability in the Middle Ages; effort was devoted to appearance, and any fleeting allusions to cleanliness derived from good manners and operated only in the sphere of what was visible.

The practices and correct behaviour of the Middle Ages do not in themselves, obviously, constitute a beginning. They are not the commencement of bodily cleanliness. But they are interesting on two counts: their standards of cleanliness are systematic, and they are the forbears of our own, even though functioning very differently. In this

[13]   M. Le Long, *Le Régime de santé de l'école de Salerne* (Paris, 1633), p. 19.
[14]   Anon., *La Nef de santé* (Paris, no date, about 1490).

regard, they can be seen to constitute a sufficiently important example to be chosen here as a starting point.

Washing the hands and face formed part of the rules taught to pages at seigneurial courts. It was a matter of a social code, and indicated as such, the instructions brief and firm. The actions needed less justification because it was a question of morals; there was no explanation beyond that contrary behaviour was not 'becoming'. This was what was said by A. de La Sale in the fifteenth century when he advised Jehan de Saintré not to serve his lord with dirty hands 'because as with all the duties of serving at table, yours requires it'.[15] The seigneurial court, epitomising a ceremonial social life, inevitably strengthened this codification, and gave a new dynamic to correct practices. This directly visible cleanliness, combined with ancient observations about modest bearing and respect, was eventually taught as an undisputed code:

Enfant d'honneur lave tes mains
A ton lever, à ton dîner
Et puis au souper sans finir.[16]

To offer someone 'water for their hands' was a mark of civility and friendship. The gesture is found both in courtly romances and in the rules of numerous religious institutions. It was a sign of attentiveness and hospitality:

L'eau lui donnant à ses mains
Et la touaille à essuyer
Puis lui apportent à manger.[17]

It was also behaviour which was both regular and regulated. The sisters of the Hôtel-Dieu at Vernon, in the thirteenth century, had to 'go to the washroom' before 'assembling in the refectory'.[18] A special bell summoned the monks of Bec to the *ablutorium* where they washed their hands before meals (*sonare ad manus lavandas*).[19] Lastly, the rule of Saint Benedict, when it dealt with the upkeep of the

---

[15] A. de La Sale, *L'Histoire et Plaisante Chronique du petit Jehan de Saintré* (fifteenth century) (Paris, ed. of 1724), p. 62.

[16] Glixelli, 'Les contenances de table' (fourteenth century), *Romania* (1921), p. 37.

[17] Marie de France, *Lais* (twelfth century), in *Poètes et Romanciers du Moyen Âge* (Paris, 1979), p. 327.

[18] L. Le Grand, 'Statuts de l'Hôtel-Dieu de Vernon' (thirteenth century), *Statuts et Règlements de léproseries et d'hôpitaux du Moyen Âge* (Paris, 1903), p. 167.

[19] L. Moulin, *La Vie quotidienne des religieux au Moyen Âge* (Paris, 1982), p. 153.

possessions of the community, mentioned 'the cloths with which the brothers dry their hands and feet'.[20]

The frequent references to washing the hands and the frequency of 'bowls for washing the hands' in rich inventories in the Middle Ages give the act a quasi-ritual dimension, at least in noble houses. Guy, Count of Flanders, for example, had four 'silver bowls for washing the hands' in 1305;[21] there were two 'table wash-bowls' serving the same purpose, a century later, in the house of Clément de Fouquembert, canon of Notre-Dame;[22] there was only one in the house of the Rouen usurer, Jéhan Baillot, in the mid-fourteenth century,[23] but the royal inventory of the same date included a dozen, two of them 'enamelled with roses sprinkled with tiny coats of arms of France round the brim'.[24] The royal collection also included one or two bowls for washing the head or feet, indicating other possible uses for these objects. The vast majority of inventories, however, included only bowls for washing the hands. This practice was dominant to the extent of sometimes appearing exclusive, as, for example, when the procedure for getting up is described, and the morning wash confined to splashing water on the hands:

De mon lit tantôt me levai
Chouçai moi et mes mains lavai.[25]

The surfaces washed were restricted, and the old cleanliness expressed in these little discussed practices was primarily social – an act of seemliness confined to the visible parts of the skin (especially the hands). It was this double limitation, to decency and to parts, which constituted its specificity.

LINEN AND THE INVISIBLE

The body as a whole was hardly involved, hidden away inside clothes which were all that people really saw. The nature of the clothes,

---

[20] *Règle de saint Benoît*, in *Règles des moines* (Paris, 1982), p. 100.
[21] C. Dehaisnes, 'Inventaire de Guy, comte de Flandres' (1305), in *Documents et Extraits divers concernant l'histoire de l'art dans la Flandre* (Lille, 1886), p. 170.
[22] 'Inventaire des biens meubles de C. de Fouquembert', *Journal* of C. de Fouquembert (1431–6) (Paris, 1915), p. lxx.
[23] C. de Beaurepaire, *Nouveau Recueil de notes historiques et archéologiques concernant le département de la Seine inférieure* (Paris, 1888), p. 173.
[24] J. Labarte, *Inventaire du mobilier de Charles V* (Paris, 1879), p. 75.
[25] G. de Lorris, 'Le Jardin d'Amour', *Roman de la Rose*, 1st part (1240), in *Poètes et Romanciers du Moyen Age*, p. 550.

therefore, becomes all-important to an understanding of what constituted propriety. Their precise role in a strategy of good manners reveals the extent to which attention never went beyond the visible; but here, too, cleanliness was still not strongly emphasised. Though briefly mentioned in manuals of manners, it no longer found a place in institutional rules. In colleges, for example, dress had first of all to be respectable (*vestes honestas*), neither too long nor too short for decency. Only form and colour were important; what really mattered was the shape. 'They should not wear clothes which make them stand out, cut short, or too close fitting, or shoes cut away or laced. Let them maintain a respectable and decent exterior.'[26] The rules of hospitals, in their turn, insisted on an all-enveloping robe, and sometimes on grey or a dark colour.[27] What mattered in clothes was line, and this was almost all that mattered.

But clothing also had a structure, a relationship between outer and inner fabrics, for example, or an arrangement of materials. In this regard, medieval clothing began to include pieces of linen which contrasted with the material of the gown, that is, wool. And it is precisely in the play between these different layers that bodily cleanliness could be introduced, for example, by changing linen.

From the thirteenth century, the shirt had restructured dress, contrasting a fine texture, still hidden, with the texture of the cloth which covered it. The shirt was not seen, but with it, dress became tiered in its surfaces and its materials, ranging from lighter to heavier, and from the more intimate to the more visible. The shirt was flexible, a pliant lining between wool and skin. An illumination accompanying the French translation of the *Decameron*, in 1430, clearly illustrates the two layers of clothing.[28] A swindler armed with a long sickle robs his victim by a sunken path. The rascal is so greedy that he strips his prey down to his shirt; with the outer clothes removed, white linen hangs down to mid-thigh. The contrast is striking; no scrap of this linen emerges from the outer clothing. The witnesses to the scene provide the proof; only their all-enveloping outer clothes can be seen, presenting the observer exclusively with blocks of colour.

In daily life, linen remained concealed. But everything was in

[26] H. L. Bouquet, 'Règlement du collège de Harcourt' (1311), *L'Ancien Collège de Harcourt* (Paris, 1891), p. 73.

[27] L. Le Grand, 'Statuts de l'hôpital Comtesse à Lille' (1250), in *Statuts et Règlements de léproseries et d'hôpitaux*, p. 74.

[28] Boccaccio, *Decameron*, p. 122. For the shirt, see also F. Piponnier, *Costume et Vie sociale, la cour d'Anjou XIVe–XVe siècle* (Paris, 1970), pp. 134, 145, 168, etc.

position for it to serve a conception of cleanliness, by, for example, being regularly changed. However this seems not yet to have happened; at least it is never, at this period, clearly described. A series of episodes in a thirteenth-century lay of Marie de France revolved round its hero's shirt, assuming that it was normal for it not to be changed. The story only makes sense on this assumption. A unique item, recognisable by marks and signs inscribed on it by others, this shirt automatically accompanied him everywhere, in time and in space, glued to his back. He travelled, journeyed overseas, and returned to Brittany; the same piece of linen remained, always immediately identifiable. His lady, long separated, found in it the fold she herself had made.[29] Such a sign was only conceivable because this was the only shirt the hero wore. At Montaillou, at the beginning of the fourteenth century, Pierre Maury sometimes changed his shirt, but he did so infrequently. It was a sufficiently rare and striking event for him to mention it in passing when speaking of other things during the proceedings of the inquisition.[30]

The accounts of the very rich also reveal the still-ambivalent role of linen. A dozen gowns appear in the expenses of Etienne de La Fontaine, royal banker, between 1351 and 1352. Their material, chosen for appearance, included marbled cloth and cloth of scarlet, fur trimmings and rich linings. Miniver, in particular, from the stomachs of squirrels, edging silk collars and sleeves, was the essential indicator of magnificence. The person of the king was completely enveloped in materials designed above all to combine heavy opulence and variety of colour. Woollen cloth, elaborately furred, symbolised royal splendour. The outfit worn by Jean le Bon on Ascension Day 1351 was 'an ash-grey marbled cloth of Brussels', consisting of four pieces, and trimmed with miniver.[31] At the same period, the account devoted to the costs of linen (the '*chanevacerie*') recorded expenditure on the chapel and on the royal headgear, but nothing on making or purchasing shirts. For the most part invisible, the shirt remained an item rarely mentioned, and, presumably, rarely changed.

The early fifteenth-century accounts of Guillaume de Murol, a noble from the Auvergne, confirm this. We can distinguish in them purchases of robes, gowns and hose, but purchases of linen are less

[29]   Marie de France, in *Poètes et Romanciers du Moyen Age*, pp. 320–1.
[30]   Le Roy Ladurie, *Montaillou*, p. 207.
[31]   L. Douët d'Arcq, 'Comptes d'Etienne de La Fontaine', *Comptes de l'argenterie des rois de France au XIVe siècle* (Paris, 1874), p. 84.

clear. They existed, but it is not clear for what purpose, or on what scale. A reference to linen cloth bought for two francs in 1407, differentiated from woollens destined for outer clothing, contains no clues as to its future use. There is no indication as to who will wear the clothes made from it, or for how long.[32]

It is not that this 'body' clothing was generally despised or ignored, in fact, on the contrary. The quality of the material purchased often reflected social distinction. 'The ell of cloth of Rheims',[33] fine and costly, for a shirt for Mme de Rochefort, a noble lady of Forez, in the early-fifteenth century, was not the same as the linen cloth bought for the shirts of the servants. The former cost five times as much as the latter.[34] Also, the '*cotte*' (probably equivalent to a shirt) mentioned in an inventory from the Château des Beaux on the death of the Comtesse d'Alevin in 1426 was sufficiently precious to have gold thread woven into the linen. But it appears to be the sole item of linen, though the same inventory lists numerous dresses and furs of ermine.[35] Linen requires fine weaving, more complex than that of wool and costs more to produce. It was less common in the Middle Ages. Many inventories list no or only very few shirts: only one, for example, in that of the Parisian bourgeois, Galeran le Breton, in 1299,[36] and none in that of the Provençal bourgeois lady, Alicia Bonefoy, in 1400;[37] only one for a Parisian collegian who died in 1349;[38] only one for Jehan de Viersville, a childless craftsman who died in 1364, and whose estate passed by mortmain to the Duke of Burgundy.[39]

This paucity cannot be explained solely by cost. Those who owned linen, in particular many table covers, had little linen clothing, as if it served little purpose. The inventory of Jehanne de Presles, wife of the founder of the college of that name, included in 1347 several dozen ells of table covers and finely-worked fabrics. Linen cloth abounded. Some pieces were simply listed, with no specific purpose recorded;

---

[32] P. Charbonnier, *Guillaume de Murol* (Paris, 1973), p. 318.
[33] P. Peyvel, 'Le budget d'une famille noble à l'aube du XVe siècle', *Cahiers d'histoire* (Lyons, 1980), no. 1, p. 46.
[34] G. d'Avenel, *Histoire économique de la propriété, des salaires, des denrées et de tous les prix en général depuis l'an 1200 jusqu'à l'an 1800* (Paris, 1885), vol. 5, pp. 553–6.
[35] L. Barthélémy, 'Inventaire du château des Beaux en 1428', *Revue des sociétés savantes* (Paris, 1877), vol.6, p. 136.
[36] A. Goldmann, *Inventaire de Galeran le Breton* (1299) (Paris, 1892), p. 3.
[37] C. Arnoud, *Histoire d'une famille provençale* (Paris, 1884), p. 340.
[38] *Inventaire des biens de G. de Vernoit, étudiant de Sorbonne* (1347), AN, M. 74.
[39] B. Prost, *Inventaire des ducs de Bourgogne* (Paris, 1902), vol. 1, p. 37.

others were for the table or the bedroom. But this long inventory records only two '*doublets*' (also probably equivalent to shirts) and two '*cottes*'.[40] Linen for the body was counted in single figures, though there was no obstacle to its being plentiful. Wealth was not invested in an abundance of this type of clothing, as it was in table covers (though they were made of very similar material), or as it was, above all, in heavy external clothing. In the noble and bourgeois world, what mattered was the clothes' glowing colour, which fur seemed best to set off. It is clear that it was not the absence or shortage of linen cloth which limited the number of shirts. It was rather a cultural tradition, a particular attitude to clothes, one which favoured first and foremost formal lines and surfaces. It was also perhaps an attitude to the skin; frequent changing was not yet the rule. Certain physical manifestations, such as sweating, were mentioned in a therapeutic context, but consigned to silence in the context of cleanliness. Social norms here remain fluid, apparently neither fixed nor prescribed.

This does not mean, obviously, that linen was never washed or changed. But the frequency or the manner in which it was done are never clearly explained. They are occasionally mentioned, but without details. The practices remain vague, as if of little importance. Their significance is largely outweighed by the form and material of outer clothes. Rules for communities which are explicit about the frequency of certain acts of cleanliness are not so on the subject of the material in contact with the skin, even when they mention it. 'It is sufficient for a monk to have two tunics and two cowls, to change them at night and to have them washed.'[41] But how often such washing took place is never stated in rules drawn up in the Middle Ages.

The asceticism advocated by Saint Benedict apart, this was an employment of linen which became typical at this period in seigneurial courts and powerful monastic communities. Linen was rarely renewed, even when wealth was adequate to provide it in abundance. The shirts in the richest inventories were rarely counted in double figures. Still a functional item of clothing, the shirt was the quasi-nocturnal dimension. It was not ignored, but neither did it receive much attention. The focus of attention in clothes was their surface. It

[40] L. Douët d'Arq, *Inventaire de Jehanne de Presles* (1347) (Paris, 1878), pp. 16, 17, 26.
[41] *Règle de saint Bênoit* in *Règles des Moines*, p. 119.

was this which not only caught the eye, but held it. Richness and respectability were the two dominant qualities. The existence of the skin and the concrete conception of the body were largely forgotten in the presence of the coverings of wool and fur. It was as if everything should relate to the visible, as if material and form exhausted the potential qualities. The envelope assumed the role of the body.

As late as the end of the fifteenth century, when references are slowly becoming more complex, an episode in *Le Roman de Jehan de Paris* underlines the importance, for so long central and specific, of these surface indicators.

The English invitees to the marriage of the Spanish Infanta left home without a change of clothing. They wore the same clothes all the way, from London to Madrid; they journeyed over land and sea, from start to finish, in their ceremonial clothes, their shirts and their gowns. They had travelled bumpy roads and crossed dangerous rivers, been drenched by thunderstorms and downpours, and baked by the heat of the sun. By the time they arrived, their appearance was not impressive. Their appearance at the ceremony excited unfavourable comment. The French mocked these travellers without trunks or chests. They laughed to scorn their inability to preserve their wardrobes, and ridiculed their style. But when they described them, they mentioned hardly anything but their tired furs and ill-fitting, rain-damaged clothes. There was no reference to their possible physical discomfort, or even to their possible smell. The English were criticised for quite specific reasons; their clothes had lost their smartness, the colours had faded, they cut a poor figure. The explicit mockery of the French (and of the author) did not extend to matters of cleanliness or intimate sensations. The English had not offended against a code of bodily cleanliness. They had offended against a code of style and elegance.

And since the English wore their best clothes that they had had specially made for the wedding, because in their country they were ignorant of trunks and chests, you can well imagine in consequence what a state their clothes were in. Some were long, and some were short, others were trimmed with martin and fox and various other furs which had shrunk thanks to getting wet, and the next day you should have seen the cloth hanging over these furs, which were spoiled and shrunk.[42]

[42] *Le Roman de Jehan de Paris* (fifteenth century), in *Poètes et Romanciers du Moyen Age*, p. 721.

It was certainly crass to wear the same clothes for several weeks between London and Madrid, but mainly because they had lost their smartness; they had faded. It was the clothes and only the clothes which attracted the scorn of the other guests. The English error consisted in forgetting 'good form'. All that mattered, apparently, was the state of the clothes – the richness of the textures, the freshness of the furs and the right shape.

This lack of interest in the condition of the skin is typical of medieval attitudes. It is almost as if the existence of the body was delegated to the objects which covered and encased it. The concept of cleanliness was completely diverted to them. The quality existed, but it was concentrated in the visible parts of the body, or in the medium in which they moved.

BODIES AND SPACES

The rules of religious communities clearly reinforced these distinctions, insisting on the cleanliness of space and communal objects rather than on the cleanliness of persons and bodies. Kitchen linen, ecclesiastical plate and various utensils took priority, and Saint Benedict was more explicit about them than about anything else. 'If anyone is negligent or dirty in handling the monastery's property, he should be corrected.'[43] The body seemed only to be perceived indirectly, through the objects it touched, the places it inhabited and the tools it employed. Attention was concentrated on surfaces. The repeated references to certain objects show what it was that was seen. 'The weekly officers will, without shame, especially inside the monastery, wipe off all traces of dirt, also the stains on the cooking pots and cauldrons . . . , not to speak of the warmth of the fire, and the different types of kitchen dirt.'[44]

Silence surrounded intimate body space; it was a world of objects whose frontiers stopped where clothes began. In the case of religious communities, clothes were valued more according to decency than to richness – plain, grey colours, long all-enveloping tunics. The line and the material obeyed criteria of modesty. There was no place for furs or precious woollen cloth. But the surface was still all-important. 'If a brother exhibits vanity or excessive pride in his appearance, the

[43] *Règle de saint Benôit* in *Règles des Moines*, p. 98.
[44] *La Règle du Maître* (eleventh century) (Paris, 1964), p. 335.

provosts should at once take what he has away from him, and give it to another.'[45] It was always and exclusively the shape and the style of the enveloping garments which attracted attention and comment.

An immense gulf separated Benedictine monks from Parisian nobles. The vow of poverty was totally alien to the proliferation of costly woollen cloth. Clothing symbolised an extreme social disparity. But there were, nevertheless, several crucial similarities; a similar attention to hands and face, a similar concentration on vestimentary signs, and a similar absence of any reference to the possible existence of intimate space, gave to cleanliness a collection of similar norms. They were essentially social, and their bodily subjects essentially visible.

The dispositions adopted by other communities reveal even more clearly the coherence of this emphasis. In hospitals, for example, where the poor congregated and died, a cleanliness existed. But it was very definitely not that of the naked bodies crowded together in a confined space. These remained hidden, huddled within clothes and bed covers. The hands of the hospital staff did not touch the poor on their arrival, except to dispose them one beside the other, once they had received the Christian confession which symbolised their new status. 'Before the sick person is put to bed, he should be confessed . . . of his sins, and presently, if he is a craftsman, the body of our Lord should be taken to him, devoutly and decently and with great reverence . . . And soon after, he should be led or carried to bed.'[46] The reception remained moral, and cleanliness was not mentioned in the context of this accumulated suffering. Concern, in this connection, was felt, at the very most, for physical space. Accounts from the very early-fifteenth century mention brooms 'issued every Saturday'[47] and distributed round the various sections of the hospital. This cleaning was referred to more than it was described. But it cannot have been systematic; at least in those institutions dependent on charity or private initiatives, it was a matter of getting rid of clutter rather than of cleaning. In 1413 the Hôtel-Dieu in Paris still had a special account recording the cost of killing the dogs which wandered through the rooms and slept on the beds. Thirty-six 'stray dogs which had got inside and onto the beds of the sick' were killed in this way.[48]

[45] *Ibid.*, p. 333.   [46] Le Grand, 'Statuts de l'Hôtel-Dieu de Vernon', p. 153.
[47] E. Coyecque, *L'Hôtel-Dieu de Paris au Moyen Âge* (Paris, 1891), p. 71.
[48] Brièle, *Document pour servir à l'histoire des hôpitaux*, vol. 3, p. 47.

It was a fight against congestion; the disorder had to be contained before any real cleaning of bodies could be conceived of.

The problem was obviously not confined to hospitals. Those comments in fourteenth- and fifteenth-century rules of colleges which refer more or less directly to cleanliness, for example, deal primarily with the accumulation of rubbish. They aimed to prevent it piling up and taking over. 'No-one is to put rubbish in the courtyard, in the washrooms, in front of the doors or in front of the back entrance to the building.'[49] These rules do not address themselves to the frequency of washing. Their major preoccupation was keeping the passageways clear and stopping rubbish from accumulating. Cleanliness was a matter of space and rubbish. 'No-one is to place rubbish behind the walls of the house, except in designated places'.[50] Intimate bodily cleanliness, such as would escape view, was not referred to, though it would be at a later date in the same type of text. The dress of the collegians, on the other hand, was to respect formal decency.

The same problems were experienced with urban space. Here, too, it was a matter of clearing away an accumulation of rubbish rather than of cleaning. It was essential to keep free surfaces which were constantly under threat, to clear the ground by carrying away rubbish. 'Clearing' meant primarily carting away. But the absence of paving, the anarchy of the drains and the narrowness of the streets were all obstacles. The stone walls which surrounded towns aggravated the problem. Streams were stagnant and dirt piled up. The only policy was to repel the accumulation of refuse and waste; not, for example, to establish cess-pools or a system for the circulation of water, but to insist that owners 'got rid of their rubbish';[51] not to construct a drainage system, but laboriously to carry all the refuse to the river or to rubbish dumps; not, in fact, to wash, but to remove. Steam-baths existed, then, in the midst of barely-controlled accumulations of rubbish.

All these difficulties were increased by the nature of private and public latrines. Private latrines were very rare, and most had open drains: seats suspended in space, often between two houses, like those in Naples described in the *Decameron*, where Andreuccio, the young horse-dealer, balancing on the planks of an overhanging water closet,

[49] E. Coyecque, 'Notice sur l'ancien collège des dix-huit', *Bulletin de la société historique de la ville de Paris* (Paris, 1887), p. 182.
[50] Bouquet, 'Règlement du collège de Harcourt', p. 75.
[51] Delamare, 'Ordonnance de police de 1348', in *Traité de la Police*, vol. 4, p. 202.

falls into the ditch before the eyes of the passers-by.[52] Public lavatories were very similar. Where they were not installed by rivers, they ended up smelling out whole districts. 'The burgesses are thus, in the nature of things, compelled to relieve themselves [*de faire leurs aisements et souillures*] anywhere, to urinate [*lascher leurs eaux*] inside towers and casemates, or in the porches of private houses in the less frequented streets.'[53]

Paving the streets and stricter regulation of rubbish disposal did little to change such arrangements. It was only at the end of the fourteenth century that the Place Maubert was paved to make it easier to cart its rubbish away. The reasons quoted are revealing about what it was like.

We have received the entreaty of the inhabitants and residents living in or near the Place Maubert, stating that, as formerly the said Place was obstructed with many piles of dirt and other refuse which impeded the said inhabitants, and also the goods and merchandise taken there to be sold . . . the said Place has been emptied and cleaned, and afterwards paved at the cost and expense of those inhabitants.[54]

It was also at the end of the fourteenth century that the property-owners of Paris were threatened with a fine of sixty sols and even prison if they neglected to 'lift and carry to the accustomed places . . . the infected and rotten refuse and rubbish from in front of their houses'.[55] And it was in 1461 that the magistrates of Amiens resolved to establish a system for removing rubbish by means of dust carts.[56]

This urban landscape encumbered by filth and rubbish obviously does not by itself explain the criteria of bodily cleanliness prevailing in the Middle Ages. But it at least explains the struggle undertaken by certain institutions to organise a collective cleanliness. It also emphasises the renewed and only partly effective effort directed against the accumulation. This alone makes sense of the fact that the rules of hospitals and colleges remained almost silent on the principles of bodily cleanliness, but reserved, in contrast, a significant place for the essential removal of rubbish and filth.

[52] Boccaccio, *Decameron*, p. 147.
[53] Leguay, *La Rue au Moyen Âge*, p. 58.
[54] 'Ordonnance de police pour pourvoir au nettoiement de la place Maubert' (1374), in *Traité de la Police*, vol. 4, p. 203.
[55] 'Ordonnance de 1395', *ibid.*, p. 204.
[56] Quoted by B. Chevalier, *Les Bonnes Villes de France du xive au xvie siècle* (Paris, 1982), p. 224.

5. *The skin and white linen*

In a story by Bonaventure des Périers, from the middle of the sixteenth century, a master seeks a pretext for beating a servant. He wants to get him to strip, the better to maltreat, perhaps even humiliate, him. Unceremoniously interrupting one of the simple fellow's frequent games of tennis, he takes him to a nearby barber. His tone is kindly: 'My friend, lend me a shirt, if you please, for this young lad who is dripping with sweat and needs rubbing down'. The barber is in the know. 'They got Fouquet into the room at the back of the shop and had him undress in front of a fire they had lit to create a good impression. But the rods were ready for the unfortunate Fouquet, who had, of his own accord, removed his white shirt.'[1] The story in itself is unimportant and its crassness well-known. More significant for our purpose is the pretext it describes, though it remains marginal to the story. It seemed natural to change shirts after a game of tennis, just as it seemed natural not to use water to wash off the sweat. The barber himself, it appears, did not wash. Changing the shirt took the place of washing. This act, without being altogether ordinary, since Fouquet needed the assistance of a third person, was at least fairly common. In Rabelais, the circumstances are different, but the actions the same. 'After the game of tennis they refreshed themselves in front of a good fire, changed their shirts and enjoyed a feast, but with more enjoyment on the part of the winners.'[2] Changing was essential in the sixteenth century; the role of linen had altered. Its regular renewal had become a rule of cleanliness.

LINEN AND SWEAT

This rule came to be widely applied. If you felt sweaty, you changed your linen. 'If a man has sweated from working, he should change his

---

[1] Bonaventure des Périers, *Récréations et Joyeux Devis* in *Conteurs français de XVIe siècle*, p. 394.
[2] F. Rabelais, *Gargantua* (1540), *Oeuvres complètes* (Paris, 1955), p. 55.

shirt at once.'[3] It was the linen which 'washed'. At a pinch, wiping was the same as washing. Cleanliness was wholly concentrated in this act, and it applied to the parts of the body which were not seen.

These sixteenth-century texts seem to correspond to a gradual increase in self-discipline, a socialisation of the parts of the body which remained unseen. It was also a matter of physical sensibility. The discomfort which began to be formulated remained personal and, in a sense, intimate. It was released by a sensation, and it was this which underwent socialisation. This is what Joubert had in mind when, in 1578, he tried to redress 'the popular errors', recommending to a larger public the norms adopted in refined circles. Changing linen was expressed in terms of sensibility. 'So much so that if you are heedful of this, you will find that you are quite renewed, refreshed and invigorated by a change of linen and clothes, as if it renewed the spirits and natural warmth.'[4] Perhaps the clearest expression of how this sensibility had become habitual is found in Montaigne. He records it as something already firmly established, something which made, for him, certain acts essential. It was part of normal life, influencing everyday behaviour. 'I cannot sleep during the day, nor eat between meals . . . nor endure my sweat . . . and I can as ill do without my gloves as my shirt, or without washing myself when I rise from the table and get up in the morning, or the curtains round my bed, as very necessary things.'[5] Such juxtapositions may give an impression of confusion, but the importance of washing the hands is clear, and changing the shirt is recognisable as the crucial act of bodily cleanliness.

Precepts also changed, as is shown by the dialogue between the serving-maid and the scholar in the Colloques of Vivès, in 1575. Here, the maid enquires about the whiteness of the linen after the morning wash has been rapidly completed. '"Emmanuel, do you want a white shirt?" "I don't need one now. The one I have isn't too dirty, I'll take another one tomorrow. Pass me my doublet."'[6] These Colloques were pedagogic in purpose, and whilst the young boy's reply clearly shows the relativity of this whiteness, and the gradual establishment of the routines necessary to achieve it, it also equally clearly reveals that the ceremonial of getting up had changed. The shirt was not changed every day, but it had become a possibility to be considered.

[3] L. Joubert, p. 550.

[4] *Ibid.*, vol. 2, p. 28.

[5] Montaigne, *Essais*, p. 1217.

[6] J. Vivès, *Les Dialogues* (Paris, 1575), p. 4.

An additional element was operative; the shirt had broken through the surface of the clothes, enabling the physical body to be imagined, indirectly but clearly. It supposed a sensibility no longer confined to what was visible. Changing linen was also cleaning the skin, even if the skin itself was not touched by a cleansing hand.

A lasting principle had been established. It would be the sole criterion for cleanliness in classical France. Fresh, white linen removed dirt by its intimate contact with the body. Its effect was comparable to that of water. It was, furthermore, surer and, above all, less dangerous. To the unease aroused by bathing was added the conviction that it was unnecessary. Linen absorbed sweat and impurities; changing it was, in effect, to wash. Texts of hygiene laboured to explain what had become a shared sensibility amongst the aristocracy and the bourgeoisie, that linen absorbed body dirt. The shirt had become a sponge; it cleaned. 'We understand why linen removes the perspiration from our bodies, because the sweat is oleaginous or salty, it impregnates these dead plants [the linen] like the grasses which are composed of the same substances.'[7] This was a highly scientific formula to illustrate a practice which could exist without it. The hygienist was explaining what manners had already invented. At most, he added the aura of his metaphors and his weighty language. Linen continued to be regarded as the sole agent of cleanliness. 'The white linen, purifying the body, refines it and makes the emissions and greasy matters exhale more easily and adhere to the white linen.'[8] It transformed early modern hygiene to the point where all comparison with the ancients seemed pointless. When, in his work of 1626 on the construction of châteaux, residences and private mansions, Savot contemplated the possibility of including baths, on the pattern of certain ancient buildings, he had no doubts on this score. 'We can more easily do without than the ancients, because of our use of linen, which today serves to keep the body clean, more conveniently than could the steam-baths and baths of the ancients, who were denied the use and convenience of linen.'[9] The conviction grew that linen demonstrated the originality of the 'moderns'. It also proved their cleanliness, an immediate and sufficient testimony to their refinement. It constituted, in fact, the ideal testimony; no less, for Perrault in 1688 than the summit of 'modern' grandeur: 'We do

---

[7]   M. Bicais, *La Manière de régler la santé par ce qui nous environne* (Aix-en-Provence, 1669), p. 92.

[8]   P. Bailly, pp. 373–4.   [9]   Savot, *L'Architecture française*, pp. 102–3.

not make great baths, but the cleanliness of our linen and its abundance, are worth more than all the baths in the world.'[10]

It is clear that the explicit and conscious rejection of bathing, far from constituting a decline in standards, on the contrary corresponded to their raising. Requirements and controls had increased, and gone beyond immediate appearance. They gradually extended beyond clothed surfaces, though without being so demanding as to require the use of water. And it is equally clear that such standards constituted a new phenomenon. They can be depicted as a line, approaching close to the skin without actually touching it. It was only a moment in a long temporal dynamic. Its route can be traced: from the more external to the more intimate, from the more visible to the less visible. The concentration on linen seems to correspond to a transitory zone within the course of a trajectory; the surface of the skin was as yet only indirectly affected. All the same, this norm overturned many assumptions. The 'other' side of clothes had a new presence and role. Discussing clothes now meant discussing what they covered; attending to clothes became a sign of caring for the body. It signified whether this was done or neglected. The frontier between care and neglect had shifted. If cleanliness existed, it was through linen, and linen above all, that it was expressed.

LINEN AND LOOKING

These changes were all the more significant because of another major change, the restructuring of clothing. The emphasis on the whiteness of shirts and their frequent changing coincided with a new role in relation to the other clothes. Shirts became highly visible signs, no longer hidden beneath other clothes. The disappearance, in the second half of the fifteenth century, of the long medieval gown in favour of short clothes was accompanied by a gradual relocation of the shirt, which now showed at collar and cuffs. Till then concealed, its existence was now revealed.

The stages in this relocation can be traced. 'Les Heures d'Etienne Chevalier', painted by Fouquet between 1440 and 1480, shows the first stage. The Wise Man kneeling before the Virgin in the first miniature, whose features are those of Charles VII, is wearing doublet and hose. But the upper part of his clothing is edged and lined

---

[10] Perrault, *La Querelle des anciens et des modernes*, p. 80.

with fur, in the medieval manner. Only the fur appears, apart from the woollen cloth.[11] In contrast, the portraits of Bellini, for example the young senator[12] dating from after 1480, show the narrow white edge of the shirt at the neck, contrasting with the colour of the doublet. It is the same with the young man painted by Memling at the end of the fifteenth century,[13] and also throughout the series of paintings by Clouet dating from the beginning of the sixteenth century;[14] the finest example being that of François I, now in the Louvre,[15] where the shirt emerges at the breast and sleeves. It escapes from the narrow slits cut in the doublet as if to emphasise the existence of what it covers.

The visible shirt, which clearly demonstrated its intermediate status between skin and cloth, could play many roles. Its whiteness, obviously, was a sign that the clothes were clean. This last quality was added to those of richness and respectability hitherto rated most highly. The shirt allowed more varied combinations of materials and colours. It increased the diversity of clothes. Clothing was enriched by its new tier. It opened the way to more complex exploitation of contrasts and combinations. To variety of colour was added variety of fabric. But, above all, the white introduced depth to clothes, and testified to an 'underneath'. It was as if, through it, the existence of the skin was delegated to the surface of the clothes. What had been hidden now emerged. What was not seen became partly visible. The material which touched the skin became a witness, discreet or emphatic, on the borders of clothing. It revealed what clothes concealed. The white, in this case, signified a particular cleanliness, that of the inside. This additional attribute made it possible to evoke the intimate.

From the sixteenth century on, linen was subject to a double set of references: those of the sensations, which could ill tolerate being in a sweaty condition, and those of sight, which measured cleanliness of person by the whiteness of shirts. In social practice, the two themes were connected; collars and cuffs came to objectify the intimate. When bodily cleanliness was evoked, it was through them that it was expressed. Brantôme, for example, was shocked by the crudity of the

---

[11] J. Fouquet, 'Les Heures d'Etienne Chevalier' (1440–80) (Paris, 1971), pl. 2.

[12] G. Bellini, 'Portrait of a young senator' (about 1480), Padua City Museum.

[13] H. Memling, 'Portrait of a young man' (1475), New York, Lehmann Collection.

[14] J. Clouet, Gallery of portraits (early sixteenth century), Chantilly, Musée Condé.

[15] J. Clouet, 'Francois I' (1525), Paris, Louvre.

soldiers thrown onto the roads after the Wars of Religion. Their demeanour seemed to him coarse; they were uncouth, outcasts condemned to a life of brutality and opportunism. Their way of life was unstable, uncontrolled, and often violent. Their degraded condition created unease, and their dirtiness repelled. Brantôme picked on the latter, but not to claim that they failed to wash. The issue was not posed in those terms. Linen alone was relevant. 'God only knows how, dressed and got up more, in truth, for the gallows, as used to be said, than for cleanliness, they wore tattered shirts, with gaping sleeves, which lasted them for two or three months or more without being changed . . . showing their hairy, naked chests.'[16] It is easy to see the difference between the criticism of Jehan de Paris, describing the English travellers a century earlier, and that of Brantôme. Jehan de Paris evaluated an outfit by reference to the richness and brightness of the material of the clothes. The furs should impress by their splendour and brilliance. In this regard, noble and bourgeois values had only one register. Brantôme recognised a greater number of indicators, both visible and invisible. For him, cleanliness had become a specific attribute of clothing. It qualified it, and had other implications. Brantôme equated care of linen with care of the body. The cleanliness of the shirt extended well beyond its material. It had a further, internal dimension, whilst completing the qualities of the clothes, hitherto confined to richness and, in the case of the poor, to decency.

Cleanliness had thus penetrated beyond the surface of clothes, though the surface did not cease to dominate attention. It had merely diversified its qualities and significance. What lay beneath the clothes had reordered the frame of reference. This cleanliness remained essentially social, indeed had never been so visible. It opened up a new sphere of refinement to a court society of a new type, one which saw the appearance of the courtier. This highly centralised milieu, constantly revolving round the king, thus found an additional criterion for demonstrating distinction. It was at the very moment when this constellation surrounding the king was taking shape, with its network of relationships, its expectations and its watchfulness, and at the very moment when, along with it, the proprieties and the niceties were on the increase, that linen acquired these new connotations. It was with the invention of etiquette that linen became a

---

[16] Brantôme, *Les Femmes galantes*, vol. 5, pp. 302–3.

recognised sign of refinement. It emphasised manners. As a sign, it was all the more exploitable in that it had a quasi-symbolic meaning. Its very visible materialisation encompassed a spectrum ranging from clean clothes to clean bodies. Appearance thus acquired new connotations; it emphasised criteria of cleanliness, and it was deemed, in this regard, to suggest what was not seen. It was through it, in fact, that the sphere and the requirements of cleanliness were extended.

Treatises on manners, directly inspired by court practices, repeated throughout the sixteenth and seventeenth centuries, with ever greater insistence, this analogy: the cleanliness of linen was the cleanliness of the whole person. It was the hallmark of the courtier and the man of distinction. 'You must have the very best and finest linen to be found, you cannot be too careful about what comes so close to the person.'[17] For Faret, a man of the court was well-advised to make it his prime concern. Whiteness was essential, even if the whole outfit was not sumptuous. Heavy cloth and ostentatious rich furs declined in importance before the sophisticated refinement of white linen. 'It is enough if he always has fine linen, and very white.'[18] It was an essential criterion for Mme de Maintenon when she spoke of dress. The cleanliness of her pupils was entirely expressed in their linen. Along with hair and hands, it was the sole theme of personal cleanliness considered at Saint-Cyr. It was certainly the only one which the mistresses really had to supervise. 'I assure you that nothing would be so unseemly as to see you all well dressed and well turned out in white linen, while they were all dirty and negligent.'[19] If a 'dirtiness' of the body existed, only such objects were deemed to testify to it. It only existed through them, and could only be established through them. They gave it concrete form. Thus their role went beyond appearance; acting on them was acting both on what was seen, and on what was not seen.

These new emphases are also revealed in accounts and inventories. The change occurred in the sixteenth century. A record of expenditure on clothes at the Valois court in 1561 shows the extent of the changes. It lists the expenses of the Duc d'Anjou, the king's brother: purchases of cloth, leather and furs, with, in addition, payments to

[17]   C. Sorel, *Les Lois de la galanterie* (Paris, 1644), p. 12.
[18]   M. Faret, *L'Honnête Homme ou l'art de plaire à la cour* (Paris, 1630), p. 233.
[19]   Mme de Maintenon, *Education morale, choix de lettres* (letter written in 1711) (Paris, 1884), p. 157.

craftsmen making up clothes for the Duc, the future Henri III. An apparent continuity with the older accounts is misleading; the robes trimmed with fur of marten and lynx, the velvet doublets and the fabrics lined with white silk remain numerous, though lighter fabrics like silk and taffeta were much more common for outer clothing. The chief novelty lies in the distribution of expenditure – more was now spent on linen. It was the 'linen man', Pierre Amar, who was most highly paid. He received over £2,000 for purchases and for piecework, considerably more than the tailor, the embroiderer or the shoemaker. 'Cloths' were even specially made up to 'wrap the linen of Monseigneur'.[20] This account neatly epitomises the new vestimentary formulas; the interest in linen is expressed and revealed, exceeding, in some cases, expenditure on other cloth.

More modest, but equally significant, are the accounts of a young Breton noble of the same date. Purchases of linen are clearly recorded, with their intended purpose and their price, to which was added the cost of making them up. On average, four shirts of linen thread were made each year between 1573 and 1577. They were even despatched regularly from Brittany when the young seigneur of Lanuzouarn entered a Parisian college in 1576.[21]

The inventories reveal various nuances. At the very beginning of the sixteenth century, for example, shirts were still fairly uncommon, even rare, items, even in noble houses, whilst table covers and pieces of linen cloth were often counted in hundreds. This was the case at the Château d'Hallincourt, for example, where an inventory drawn up on the death of Pierre le Gendre in 1512 listed two isolated linen shirts in the middle of chests full of light materials, table cloths, bed covers and various other items. The list drawn up on the death of Jeanne d'Albret in 1514 presents a different picture; as well as several pieces of body linen, cropping up here and there, one chest contained shirts. 'A certain number of shirts for the use of the said lady with certain belts'.[22] Quantities increased during the sixteenth century. At the end of the century, the *doublets* of Gabrielle d'Estrées in the Château de Monceau alone 'were innumerable'.[23] And Henri IV – whose rustic

[20] M. Brossard, 'Etat de la maison du duc d'Orléans, frère du roi Charles IX', *Bulletin archéologique du comité* (Paris, 1890), p. 19.
[21] R. F. Le Men, 'Le livre de compte du sieur de La Haye', *Bulletin de la société archéologique du Finistère* (Rennes, 1877–9), pp. 102ff.
[22] E. Bonnaffé, *Inventaire de la duchesse de Valentinois* (Paris, 1878), p. 99.
[23] A. Descloseaux, *Gabrielle d'Estrées* (Paris, 1898), p. 271.

habits are a commonplace of history, Mme de Verneuil and many others, for example, accusing him of 'stinking like carrion' – had extremely fine linen.[24] The number of his shirts, much criticised by Louis XIII, exceeded several dozen, and they were 'made of fine linen, woven with thread of gold and silk, and many colours at the cuffs, collars and seams'.[25]

The form of inventories changes towards the middle of the sixteenth century. It becomes easier than before to see how each residence was organised, even, indeed, to attempt a reconstruction of the utilisation of internal space. In particular, however, they assemble and categorise objects better, bringing out the new importance some have acquired. Linen, for example, is always mentioned separately, at the end of the section devoted to clothes, confirmation of its special status. And shirts are counted consecutively, confirming their proliferation. Ownership of several shirts was more widely diffused. In 1570 the Parisian mercer, Cramoisy, left, along with many 'items of men's clothing' and others 'for women', an 'oak chest' containing linen, consisting of eighteen shirts, twelve of them woven of linen.[26] There were thirty-two linen shirts, including twelve with 'pleated collars' in the house of the Parisian doctor, Jean Lemoignon, in 1556, and thirty-four in the house of his colleague, Geoffroy Granger, in 1567.[27] Numbers fluctuated until the seventeenth century. The Marquise des Baux had ten shirts in 1580, for example.[28] Numbers then stabilised; members of the aristocracy and the bourgeoisie tended to have around thirty shirts. Molière had thirty at his death in 1672. Racine had thirty in 1699 and the provost of Anjou, seigneur of Varennes, had thirty-six in 1683, described as 'fine and delicate'.[29] Numbers alone, however, were no longer all that mattered.

[24] Tallemant des Réaux, *Historiettes*, vol. 1, p. 7: 'The late king Louis XIII, trying to be matey, said "I take after my father, I smell of armpits."' Cf. also the remarkable bibliography written by Jean-Pierre Babelon, *Henry IV* (Paris, 1982), p. 255.

[25] G. Baschus de Lagrèze, *Henry IV, vie privée, détails inédits* (Paris, 1885), p. 92.

[26] Y. Bézard, 'L'inventaire après décès du mercier Cramoisy', *Bulletin de la société historique de la ville de Paris* (Paris, 1937), p. 51.

[27] Lehoux, *Le Cadre de vie des médecins parisiens*, pp. 221–2.

[28] M. Mireur, 'Inventaire des habillements et parures d'une dame de Provence', *Revue des sociétés savantes* (Paris, 1874), vol. 2, p. 125.

[29] E. Soulé, *Recherches sur Molière* (Paris, 1863), p. 273; E. M. vicomte de Grouchy, *Inventaire de Jean Racine* (Paris, 1892), pp. 29–30; A. Joubert, *Les Constantin* (Paris, 1890), p. 237.

FREQUENCIES

Linen was handled, removed and washed. Accounts and inventories only imply this. They show that the amount of linen in use increased significantly from the middle of the sixteenth century amongst those who set standards and those close to them. But we need to establish the rhythms according to which these clothes, now visible, were changed and renewed. The court is again our best guide. When, in 1580, in *l'Isle des Hermaphrodites*, Arbus Thomas criticised the entourage of Henri III, he was implicitly condemning the behaviour of the prince, but he also described practices with regard to clothes. In particular, his astonishment that shirts were changed daily shows the novelty of this practice, and the resistance to it in circles not familiar with the court. Refinement of manners was seen by them as softness, even weakness. Hence the veritable outburst of Arbus Thomas on the subject of such frequent changing of linen. Thomas saw it only as peculiar delicacy or extreme sensibility. But it reveals also that norms were changing.

I saw enter another valet de chambre holding in his hands a shirt on which I saw all over the body and sleeves much cut-point work, but for fear that it might harm the delicate flesh of he who was to wear it . . . it had been lined with a very fine cloth . . . From what I hear, not content in that country with changing night and day, there are even some who never wear the same shirt twice, being unable to bear that what is going to touch them has been laundered.[30]

It seems that in court circles shirts were changed more or less daily from the end of the sixteenth century. This shows particularly when some obstacle prevented it from happening. Brichauteau, a young captain of the royal hunt, who had come briefly to Ollainville in August 1606 for a meeting with the king, said he could not stay a single night; he had neither change of linen nor nightshirt (which confirms incidentally the use of this last garment, and its frequent changing, amongst the aristocracy).[31] Being without linen seems here to correspond to not being able to wash at a later date, that is, a feeling of discomfort, veiled or explicit, and expedients designed to preserve at any cost an appearance which seemed to be threatened.

---

[30] A. Thomas, *L'Isle des Hemaphrodites* (Paris, 1724, 1st ed. 1580), p. 14.
[31] Cf. R. Ritter, *Henry IV, lui-même* (Paris, 1944), p. 403.

Wars and accidents provide frequent examples. In 1649, during the Fronde, Mlle de Montpensier had to flee the Louvre in such haste that she could not take her chests. At Saint-Germain, where she sought refuge, all those who had fled, including the queen, were in the same position. She waited ten days for a baggage cart, cautiously steered through the lines of the Prussian armies, to bring her her 'comforts'. In the meantime, her customary habits appeared threatened. She kept them up, nevertheless, and judged the episode sufficiently painful to record it in detail. 'I had no change of linen, and they laundered my nightshirt during the day and my day shirt at night.'[32] Even the avarice of M. de Louvigny, mocked by Tallemant, bowed before daily cleaning. 'It was miserliness without parallel . . . He had only one shirt and one ruff: they were laundered every day.'[33]

The king, obviously, constituted throughout the seventeenth century the most outstanding example, always visible, constantly copied, always revealing. For example, it is clear that the ceremonial of rising was not confined to a theatrical demonstration of the hierarchies, even if its prime purpose was spectacle. The etiquette established by the Valois, with its precise code indicating the rank of those who alone had the right to present the king with his shirt, was also a sign of royal distinction and royal cleanliness. With Louis XIV, for example, the ceremony was preceded by actions which emphasise how the employment of linen could be complex, while it remained, to all intents and purposes, the sole indicator of cleanliness. 'At eight o'clock the first valet de chambre, who had slept in the king's bedchamber, and who was dressed, woke him. The first doctor, the first surgeon, and his nurse, as long as she lived, entered at the same time. She embraced him; the others rubbed him down and often changed his shirt, because he tended to sweat.'[34] All these attentions took place without the use of water. The king's shirt, however, was changed even before he received his shirt for the day. Thus there might be two shirts a night. The rhythm had accelerated. The daytime rhythms accelerated further. The king changed all his clothes on returning from a walk or from hunting, sometimes even when moving from one activity to another, which greatly increased the use of linen. 'These changes of clothes, hats, shoes, wigs, and even shirts, two or

---

[32] A. de Montpensier, *Mémoires* (Paris, 1735, 1st ed. 1728), vol. 1, p. 157.
[33] Tallemant des Réaux, *Historiettes*, vol. 1, p. 534.
[34] Saint-Simon, *Mémoires*, vol. 28, p. 335.

three times a day, were the consequence of the king's love of comfort and fear of being uncomfortable.'[35] It was the structure of the norm which was specific, with a force of its own. The almost complete absence of bathing did not preclude reference to the feeling of the skin and the discomfort it could occasion. The reaction reveals a sensibility which exercised a constant effect on daily life. This sensibility applied a code with surprising rigour; the whiteness of linen reinforced by a particular relationship to sweat permeated all these practices. The king seems to push this logic to its limit. This norm mobilised domestic servants, time and objects, exactly as did luxury. The effect is all the more striking, in fact, because cleanliness is here allied to luxury in clothing. It existed through it and enhanced it. It functioned in a similar fashion, involving costs, services and signs.

But the example is also striking because it appears to be a furthest point. What further demands could be imagined? In fact, it was only a stage. It was not long before such exigence seemed purely relative. All that was needed was a change in the criteria. It was not, for example, always a question of renewing linen. The royal example is useful in this regard also in helping us to understand the future changes. It is not because the criteria employed by the classical code were subsequently made more demanding that standards have today become more restrictive. It is because they were changed. Their evolution came through their diversification and their complication.

A MATTER OF SURFACES

Linen continued to play a central role in the classical code. Its presence spread and diversified. A range of contrivances, in the seventeenth century, enhanced the play between the depth and the surface of clothes. Various pieces emerged as separate items, multiplying the intermediaries visible between clothes and skin; collar-pieces spreading over the shoulders emphasised collars separate from the shirt, canons let linen hang down over the tops of boots, removable cuffs extended right up sleeves. The fact that these pieces were handled and washed separately reveals even more clearly the desire for illusion. It is as if there was a deliberate intention to extend linen and increase its surface, even if it retained only an

[35] *Ibid.*, p. 357 (note).

artificial link with the hidden parts. Light fabrics escaped from clothes' every edge. They turned back over and partly covered them; they encroached on them. The shirt no longer simply peeped out from under the doublet, it overflowed and began to engulf it. It was no longer something underneath, but part of the surface. Linen was displayed to a far greater extent than in the sixteenth century, when it barely emerged. In the engravings of Abraham Bosse, for example, the collar falling over the shoulders comes close to the cuffs spreading up from the wrist; their edges almost touch. Whiteness was no longer confined to borders; it had spread. The underneath announced itself through clothing, it had itself became something to be displayed. The 1640 etching of the shops of 'La Galerie du palais'[36] shows this spectacle taking two distinct forms. It can be seen both in the clothes of the passers-by and in the merchandise displayed for sale. The clothing of these nonchalant shoppers is a picture in itself. The white has multiplied the layers, with linen spilling over and overlapping woollen cloth. Come from the skin, or assumed to, this fabric engulfed the other materials. It created patterns designed solely to please the eye. The surface of the intimate had become a completely external sign. It had established a new type of covering, whose relationship to the skin was ever more symbolic, all the more so, in fact, in that these objects had no contact with it. They were attached and removed, extraneous items fastened to the back of the clothes. By a development which pushed the logic of the visible to its limits, linen had become, in practice, an element of the surface. It is these itineraries over gowns and doublets which attract one part of our attention.

But the spectacle lies also in the shop, where collars, cuffs and canons are displayed on the walls, where they can be examined, and where they can dazzle. They are hung next to the bookshelves, the height of luxury in close proximity to learned tomes. Decorated containers, objects displayed around the royal coat of arms; linen was indeed noble stuff. Arranged at the back of the shop, it exhibited patterns both symmetrical and elaborate; it was displayed. Its surroundings definitively demonstrated its social promotion. These symbols of the body were now only expanses of white, fine and precious, designed to ornament costume. Laid out flat, they were reduced to what they were made for, no longer functional objects, but

---

[36]   A. Bosse, 'La Galerie du palais' (1640), Paris, estampe BN.

objects for show, juxtapositions of formal articles. They demonstrate, in fact, in these busy shops, all the ambiguity of classical linen.

The relationship of linen to sweat and ideas about the cleanliness of the skin had also changed. Linen washed without the use of water, but, at the same time, it displayed, and this role became crucial. The false pieces were no more than an exhibition of rare material, of fine weave and whiteness, but also of a more delicate texture. To colour was added the effect of lightness. Lace, in the sixteenth century, a border of threads spreading out into thin air from the edges of clothing, created a new material. It was increasingly used for collars and cuffs, rendering ever more ethereal these objects supposed to come from beneath the clothes. Certain portraits from the beginning of the seventeenth century provide excellent examples of this: the 'Jeune Prince' by Le Nain,[37] for example, or the 'Louis de Bourbon' by Michel Lasne.[38] Every linen surface is perforated. The holes are arranged according to a variety of patterns. Their delicacy added an extra cost to lightness. In this field, the lace of Flanders, Milan and Venice was unsurpassed. The people in the pictures of Cornelis de Vos,[39] in particular, with their long cuffs, delicate and perforated to the point of transparency, convincingly demonstrate the predominance of Antwerp.

It is hardly surprising that sumptuary laws, once concerned with furs, were now concerned with these embellishments of precious thread and lace. They emerged as almost the sole expression of wealth. In 1614 the Estates General recommended 'cutting back on lace decoration from Flanders and Milan, stuffs from China and other useless goods brought from the ends of the earth which remove from our kingdom much gold and silver'.[40] Sumptuary laws attempted generally and vainly to stem this ruinous expenditure. More subtly, they tried to control markets and prevent the collapse of local industries and manufacture, by driving out the work of Flemish or Italian craftsmen who had, since the sixteenth century, dominated the market. Colbert, as an economist, preferred to establish two hundred lacemakers from Hainaut and Brabant in the faubourg Saint-

[37] L. Le Nain, 'Jeune Prince' (1630), Nantes, Musée des Beaux-Arts.
[38] M. Lasne, 'Louis de Bourbon' (1632), Antwerp, Musée royal des Beaux-Arts.
[39] Cornelis de Vos, 'Portrait de famille' (1631), Antwerp, Musée royal des Beaux-Arts.
[40] Etats généraux de 1614; see L. Godard de Donville, *Signification de la mode sous Louis XIII* (Aix-en-Provence, 1978), p. 208.

Antoine, disperse thirty Venetian workmen about the provinces, and promote the techniques and crafts of Alençon.

But the sumptuary laws were above all discriminatory. Their attack on luxury was a paradoxical way of controlling access to it. It was a question of containing social mixing, fixing distance by means of clothes, and establishing a visible system of hierarchies of clothing. It ought always to be possible to distinguish 'a great lord, duke or count from a soldier or other with only a cloak and a dagger'.[41] And the denial of lace at the beginning of the seventeenth century only meant it was easier to determine the number who wore it. Clothes retained, at whatever cost, their ability to differentiate. A certain sort of white was distinctive, confirmation that the concept of cleanliness, gradually elaborated by means of this architecture of linen, was social. For a courtier in the seventeenth century to refrain from lace was a gesture of great significance. When Mlle Saujon left the Louvre, considering herself rejected and despised after her love affair with the king's brother, she also abandoned her splendid dress, her lace and her fine linen. Such an act created a deep impression. On her return, some months later, to assume duties proposed by the king himself, Saujon continued to demonstrate, by the form and the material of her linen, her former disappointments and rejection. 'She was offered responsibility for the women round Madame, which she accepted, and then she returned just like anybody else. Except that she was clothed only in serge, and wore only plain linen.'[42] At bottom a banal situation, Saujon was explicitly refusing certain attributes of wealth and knew how to show this.

Such a refusal could be even more significant. The sign could be internalised. Mme de Montespan, for example, in her disgrace, displayed a mortification which astonished Saint-Simon. She wore a hairshirt and belts studded with iron nails, and embraced charitable acts to the extent of herself making objects to give to the poor – on the one hand, a nobility which kept up appearances, on the other, a humility which admitted of manual work. And her linen concealed 'shirts of calico, of the hardest and coarsest'.[43] They were, in fact, well hidden; the visitor was in complete ignorance, and appearances were maintained. To do other would have signified an immediate change

---

[41] A. du Verdier, 1576, quoted by H. Aragon, *Les Lois somptuaires en France* (Paris, 1921), p. 69.
[42] De Montpensier, *Mémoires*, vol. 1, p. 184.
[43] Saint-Simon, *Mémoires*, vol. 15, p. 96.

of condition, which was unthinkable. It was a question of secret mortification, a moral turn-round by the former 'queen', a more or less affected contrition. Mme de Montespan suffered in secret. What she concealed, nevertheless, retained all its significance, that is a certain 'sullying'. For her, hemp was degrading, too drab and too coarse. To wear it was in itself to stoop. It was what was worn by the people and some of the bourgeoisie. Madeleine Béjart, the companion of Molière, 'contented' herself with several precious cloths and '15 shirts of hemp, 7 white and 8 yellow'.[44] It was a question of price, obviously; in 1610 the fine shirts of Isabelle de Tournon, made of linen cloth, were worth eight livres each, equivalent to a labourer's wages for a fortnight.[45] Those of the queen, who had an average of two shirts a month made for her in 1642, were worth seven livres.[46] Hemp was more accessible; shirts made from it were worth about two livres in the middle of the century, two days' pay for a tailor, or three or four days' for a labourer.[47] The difference in cost was, of course, greatly increased by the addition of lace.

In the case of Mme de Montespan, then, hemp was equivalent to haircloth. It demeaned, it was coarse and drab. But it showed indirectly the extent to which the insistence on white linen had a special significance in the seventeenth century. Linen alone, by its material and its method of manufacture, could in reality pretend to this colour. It alone signified a certain cleanliness. To mention linen, then, and associate it with whiteness, was to associate it with a certain condition. This cleanliness had from the start a social and distinctive significance. When seventeenth-century treatises on manners insisted that linen should be clean, regularly changed, and of fine quality, they were confusing, to a considerable extent, material and cleanliness. It amounted to more or less the same thing. The effect of washing and the effect of the material were the same. Together they exuded a cleanliness which was not accessible to all. At a pinch, rich clothes could even be dispensed with, as long as the linen remained of good quality. Keeping it white was a way of keeping up appearances. 'If the clothes are clean, and, above all, if the linen is white, you do not need

[44] Soulé, *Recherches sur Molière*, p. 252.
[45] B. de Montbrison, *Inventaire des habits, bagues, joyaux et habillements de Mme Isabeau de Tournon* (1610) (Paris, 1910), p. 13.
[46] *Maison d'Anne d'Autriche*, AN, K. 203.
[47] D'Avenel, *Histoire économique*, vol. 5, pp. 553–6, and vol. 3.

to be magnificently dressed.'[48] Mme de Maintenon displayed identical criteria when, recalling her youth, she remembered her strenuous efforts to keep up appearances at all costs. 'If the quality of the material was simple, if the clothes were well chosen and ample, if the linen was white and fine, there was nothing to fear.'[49]

These criteria relegated various other practices to obscurity. The spectrum they suggested was not lacking in nuance. The fact that the quality of clothing to some extent defined what was clean could not but have consequences. Thresholds were inevitably expressed through objects. In this regard, 'cleanliness' could not exist for the poor. It was not even to be mentioned. Nor, for that matter, was body dirt. Seventeenth-century charitable institutions, those which, for example, in accord with the well-known centralising impulse, had begun to take in orphans and poor children, took little interest in their appearance or clothes. Drugget, fustian or other such coarse cloths did not attract the eye. Such materials could not evoke the image of cleanliness. Special material for shirts did not exist in this context. The clothes of the children confined in the General Hospital show this clearly. 'The said children, boys and girls, will be clothed in coarse cloth and will wear clogs.'[50] When Démia sent some of his teachers to visit the lodgings of the pupils to whom he gave initial instruction, his interest did not extend to their physical surroundings or their appearance. The creatures to be visited remain shadowy. Their penury and squalor could not emerge from the questioning of their interrogators. The questions were moral, prolonging the designs of the Counter-Reformation and the internal colonisation inaugurated by Saint Vincent de Paul. On arrival, the teacher 'should recommend parents to take great care of their children, not to encourage them in their vices, and to offer a novena to the Holy Infant Jesus so that their children would be good . . .'[51] If the bedroom was opened, it was only to ascertain that a place was set aside for prayer. It was never to assess the physical condition of the surroundings. Establishing control over these children on the verge of vagrancy and vagabondage meant ensuring their regular presence

---

[48] A. Courtin, *De la civilité qui se pratique en France parmi les honnêtes gens* (Paris, 1671), p. 100.
[49] Mme de Maintenon, *Education morale*, p. 179.
[50] M. dom. Félibien, *Histoire de la ville de Paris* (Paris, 1725), vol. 4, p. 266.
[51] C. Démia, *Règlement pour les écoles du diocèse de la ville de Lyon* (1716), p. 39.

and their observance of moral rules. Or even, in the case of the General Hospital, exercising on them direct physical pressure.

The rules of the little schools were more complex. They might apply to the children of craftsmen or to all those who had crossed over the poverty threshold. Here precepts about cleanliness existed, referring to hands and faces, inevitably, in the tradition of the treatises on manners, but also to clothes. However, many reservations emphasise the limits of this cleanliness. Clothes are referred to only briefly and negatively; anything which might be too showy was to be avoided, various prohibitions were to be observed – no coloured linen or, above all, showy materials. It is as if modesty and discretion implied a purely formal allusion to cleanliness. It was indicated, but with the analogy to the drab which characterised their clothes. 'Let the children be clean in their clothing, without any vanity or affectation, and without giving them rich clothing above their station; they should not wear feathers in their hats or caps; but they should be cleanly clothed, with their hair combed but not powdered or curled, and they should be free from vermin.'[52] Clothes had to be clean. For this intermediate category, cleanliness and sobriety tended to be confused.

There remain the groups closer to those who set standards, and all the anonymous behaviour which was clearly evolving at this period. Certain communities, because they echoed the transformation of court practices, but from afar, toning down their rhythm and their rigour, are in this regard very enlightening. The Jesuits, in particular, reveal what has changed.

Appearance was a major preoccupation of the Jesuits. Regular inspection of the scholars was laid down for the first time, in particular of their rooms and their clothes.

The prefects should take great pains to see that the scholars are clean in their room; and to this end they should take care, with the lower classes, that the servants comb their hair twice a day, that they attend to their clothes in the evening and particularly in summer, that they never allow them to appear before them in clothes which are torn or dirty or in poor condition.[53]

But the cleanliness of the scholars and boarders was in the seventeenth century primarily that of their linen. This is repeated and

[52] Bétancourt, *Instruction méthodique de l'école paroissiale* (Paris, 1669), pp. 67–8.
[53] C. de Rochemonteix, 'Règlement du collège de La Flèche' (seventeenth century), *Un collège de jésuites aux XVIIe et XVIIIe siècles* (Paris, 1889), vol. 3, p. 192.

emphasised. Such insistence implies specific acts, a rhythm, and the establishment of regular cycles, a range of actions assuming a new organisation. The communities demonstrate most clearly the content and scope of these changes. It was a question of confirming criteria, of designating tasks and frequencies. In 1620 the rules of the Jesuits established for a long time to come both rhythms and responsibilities. The role of 'he who looks after the clothing', for example, consisted of keeping written records of the movement of linen, of collecting it to be washed, distributing it, and verifying its condition. 'The handing out of linen is to be recorded in the launderer's account, whether internal or external, and its return in the same manner.'[54] Shirts were marked to prevent mistakes or losses. A 'circuit' was organised, with clearly indicated frequencies; a cycle was established. 'On Saturday night he should distribute clean linen to all the rooms and on Sunday morning he should collect the dirty linen from the same rooms, being careful to get back all he handed out.'[55] Obviously, practices were not the same everywhere. It was necessary, for example, for the regent of the college described by Sorel in 1623 to fall in love before he discovered a rhythm that the Jesuits had already outgrown. 'Instead of being accustomed to change his linen only once a month, he changed it every fortnight.'[56] But the linen cycle became in general more regular and more widespread in the seventeenth century, with rules and specific tasks. Within religious communities, especially, it was institutionalised. And frequencies accelerated during the course of the century. At the Oratory of Troyes, for example, a paragraph of the regulations was specifically devoted to cleanliness. 'Shoes are changed every day, and linen twice a week, usually on Sundays and Thursdays. Stockings are changed as often as possible.'[57] The Ursulines described at length the responsibilities of the linen maid. 'She should hold the key to the chests of those who are incapable of caring for their linen: she should give them clean linen twice a week or more often if the Mother Superior thinks it necessary, and she should put it on their beds on Wednesdays and Saturdays; in winter she should first see that it is aired.'[58]

These religious communities clearly express the change in sens-

[54] *Règles de la Compagnie de Jésus* (Paris, 1620), p. 386.   [55] *Ibid.*

[56] C. Sorel, *Histoire comique de Francion* (1624) in *Romanciers du XVIIe siècle*, p. 189.

[57] G. Carré, 'Règlement de la pension de l'oratoire en Champagne' (seventeenth century), *L'Enseignement secondaire à Troyes du Moyen Age à la Révolution* (1882), p. 361.   [58] *Règlements des religieuses ursulines*, vol. 1, p. 96.

ibility; the cleanliness of persons was that of their linen. Its criteria were, therefore, expressed in objects. The body had delegated representatives. Reading the regulations of educational institutions, in particular, confirms a double dynamic: a speeding up in the frequency with which linen was changed, and a diversification of the objects involved. The acceleration in frequencies is very marked between the sixteenth and the seventeenth centuries. A gulf separates the recommendation of Father Maggio to the Parisian Provincial in 1585: 'It is desirable to change the shirt every month',[59] and the twice-weekly cycles of many colleges at the end of the seventeenth century.[60] Standards and self-discipline are revealed by these rhythms. And these changed in classical France, the court remaining a central example, whilst at the same time a little apart. To these frequencies was added a diversification of objects. The norm required the integration of new tools, and the areas affected extended and multiplied. The shirt for long remained the essential point of reference. But many regulations from the end of the seventeenth century show that shoes, stockings and collars (washed once a week by the Ursulines) were all subject to the supervision of the prefects. Cleanliness was expressed in a world of things. What counted was to display these things. And amongst the aristocracy and their imitators, linen allied with fashion to take over clothing.

The intimate had well and truly acquired a new position. Changing a sweaty shirt, for example, can remain a private act, by oneself, for oneself. It need have no witnesses, arising from private sensibility. What is essential is what its author feels. The norm had created this space and regulated it with increasing rigour. But at the same time, linen and lace made cleanliness into a spectacle. It was what caught the eye of others that mattered, and what held it; hence the operation of strategies of illusion.

[59] *Ratio Studiorum* ms BN, 1585.   [60] See above, note 57.

6. *Appearances*

With the advent of linen, cleanliness became to an even greater extent a matter of appearance. This became more explicit and its code grew stronger, encompassing not only hands and face, as was traditional, but also cuffs, collars, veils and various bands. A cartography was established, traversed by 'lines of force', with a number of corresponding focal points. There were, in fact, both more indicators and more sites.

THE CLEANLINESS THAT DISTINGUISHED

It was in the seventeenth century, with the language of Louis XIII and Louis XIV, that the word 'clean' (*propre*) changed its meaning. It was more often used as a judgement in portraits and descriptions. It gave point to profiles and nuance to comments. It was even sometimes extended to attitudes and behaviour. It was sufficiently notable for its use always to be significant, and sufficiently important not to be used lightly. Tallemant, for example, employed it as a concise and pointed judgement: 'I have thousands of times seen a deaf-mute quite well made as to his person and quite clean';[1] the Marquise de Sablé, on the other hand, 'is always in her bed, which is never made, and the bed is as clean as the lady';[2] whereas the wife of the chancellor, Séguier, 'was never beautiful, but she was clean'.[3] Saint-Simon demonstrated the same scale of values. He emphasised the 'extreme cleanliness of Mme de Contie',[4] and the 'noble and clean'[5] appearance of Mme de Maintenon. He, too, offered no explanation. The word was enough in itself. Its meaning was clear. The fact that the word was thought worth employing and that it was used sparingly confirms once again that cleanliness distinguished. It was not universal, but the mark of a seemliness which was not general. Its more frequent and more precise

---

[1] Tallemant des Réaux, *Historiettes,* vol. 2, p. 827.
[2] *Ibid.*, vol. 1, p. 519.   [3] *Ibid.*, p. 615.
[4] Saint-Simon, *Mémoires*, vol. 13, p. 284.   [5] *Ibid.*, vol. 28, p. 253.

literary use confirms its stronger hold on consciousness. Its employment was immediately discriminatory.

It revealed, in one word, something which could not be assumed. In her journey across France at the time of the Fronde, for example, Mme de La Guette, received at the Château de Beauvilliers, asked for the services of a woman for the night. Her host thought this must be some sort of trick; he suspected the visitor of being a 'very great seigneur', forced into disguise and deception by the troubled times. He complied with all the more rapidity. 'Madame, there is but one woman here that you would find at all acceptable. I will send her to you.' A young woman appeared; she was elegant and well cared for. 'The young woman came, very neat and quite clean.'[6] Enough had been said. This one word told all. The young woman was more distinguished than Mme de La Guette could have expected, and mentioning that she was 'clean' recorded her surprise. It is as if this particular word was enough in itself to indicate immediately an appearance and an urbanity which was by no means universal. It signified a specific and notable seemliness. It was distinctive.

But it is precisely in this that the meaning of the word really changed. Cleanliness in the seventeenth century was so often associated with distinction that it became assimilated to it. The association was so insistent that it eventually affected the word itself. Because what was clean was partly defined by appearance, the terms became interchangeable. One could be substituted for the other. The distinction was blurred. By dint of qualifying a distinguished external appearance, the word *propre* also qualified distinction. It was this confusion which gave a quite new dimension to the tedious and traditional questions about the 'vanity of ornaments'. This was not only because a court society challenged the suggestion of vanity; it could not, in the nature of things, readily accept it. It was because the argument itself shifted its ground. The absence of ornamentation could now be denounced as the absence of *propreté*, which rendered it even less acceptable. Dirtiness (*malpropreté*), simplicity and austerity in clothes lost a possible justification. An assimilation had taken place. The interlocutress of Mme de Maintenon expressed this clearly. It was impossible, for this reason, to neglect one's clothes; was it necessary 'to be dirty [*malpropre*] to be esteemed'?[7] The reply admitted of no doubt; 'cleanliness' was also good manners. To

6   Mme de La Guette, *Mémoires*, p. 116.
7   Mme de Maintenon, *Education morale*, p. 334.

conform to these, clothes had to be well-cut and in fashion. Elegance must be added to cleanliness; they went hand-in-hand, and, in the end, the same adjective qualified them both. When Tallemant described the entourage of Marshal de Grammont as 'always *propre* and in good condition', the word had obviously also acquired connotations of order and decency.[8]

The evolution of treatises on etiquette is revealing in this respect. After Erasmus, works on manners for children, and especially manuals designed for courtiers, devoted more and more attention to clothes. Clean clothes gradually came to equate with clean linen, and decency came increasingly to require respect for fashion and custom. 'I wish the courtier to be always clean [*propre*] and elegant in his clothing, and to conform to honest and decent behaviour.'[9] It was all of this which was soon to be encapsulated in one word. That the courtier was 'clean' signified a whole range of attributes.

'Cleanliness' being a certain correctness in a person's clothes, just as good manners are correctness of a person's actions as regards other people, it is necessary, if we wish to be 'clean', to tailor our clothes to our figure, to our condition, to our age . . . The one law which is indispensable to this is fashion, it is under her absolute mastery that reason should be deployed.[10]

This 'cleanliness', completely equated with manners, that is, this 'propriety' could be applied to both people and objects. When Colbert inaugurated his Château de Sceaux with a royal feast followed by fireworks, *Le Mercure galant* was soon bogged down in pompous formulas. 'The decorations and the furniture were of that marvellous "propriety" [*propreté*] which catches the eye as much as exceptional magnificence.' The village girls, in their turn, gave of their best on the approaches to the castle. They donned their most beautiful clothes and danced. They, too, showed themselves to be 'proper'. 'The paths were covered with leaves. The peasant girls danced on top of them; they had forgotten nothing which might render them "proper" [*propre*].'[11] For apartments and modest women alike, the description was the same. Both presented their very best appearance.

The word was used in the same way during the visit to Saint-Cyr made by the bishop of Chartres in 1692. And with the same

---

[8] Tallemant des Réaux, *Historiettes*, vol. 1, p. 531.
[9] B. Castiglione, *Le Parfait Courtisan* (sixteenth century) (trans. Paris, 1624), p. 214.
[10] *Le Mercure galant* (Paris, July 1677), p. 274.   [11] *Ibid.*, p. 280.

amalgamation; everything was 'proper' in Mme de Maintenon's institution. Everything was in order. One could only admire both rich objects and symmetry in design. The worthy bishop wanted to see everything. For three days he progressed round offices, gardens and dormitories. He opened the linen-cupboard and lingered in the church; the linen there was of the very finest, the wood mouldings were most imposing, and all covered by the same term – an inimitable 'propriety'. The cells were visited one by one, they were all, of course, very 'proper'; the furniture consisted only of water-jug and cup. It was not noticed, however, that these utensils were lacking in the dormitory of the pupils. It was not, in fact, a real 'lack', the question did not arise. What mattered was style; the desirable qualities were regularity and elegance. Correctness even took precedence over simple cleanliness. Each example shows this in its own way. 'On both sides of the first gallery there were two oratories constructed of wood with windows overlooking the church, in one of which, very properly [*très proprement*] adorned, there was an iron grill, very proper [*très propre*], about two and a half feet wide and three in height.'[12]

In the case of clothing, fashion and this new 'cleanliness' ended by merging. The latter meant first and foremost respect for the canon Such a coincidence of meaning between style and cleanliness could only happen because appearance played a central role. There had to be a systematic priority accorded to the external for the definition to begin to change. Cleanliness had to apply essentially to clothes for the word to focus on clothes to the extent of changing its meaning. The success of the new definition only confirms the seventeenth-century view of 'cleanliness'. It became an element in an art of performance. More generally, it was integrated into a specific social model – the court as example and spectacle. It was not only a matter of visible vestimentary signs. It was a matter of cultivating, almost consciously, a practice of illusion. The art of the court was essentially an art of performance.

The fête at Sceaux and the opera at Versailles belonged to the same world. Their value lay in their display, their tactics were those of the theatre; as in Baroque art, where to display was at the same time a way of concealing. It was the theatrical gesture, the show, that mattered. It might even, at a pinch, be said that the peasant women of Sceaux were

---

[12] 'Procès verbal de la visite de l'évêque de Chartres à Saint-Cyr', (Versailles, 1692); see T. Lavallée, *Histoire de Saint-Cyr* (Paris, 1866), p. 309.

more 'proper' for having transformed their streets into theatre. Their order, more or less contrived, had been able to sustain the illusion. Effort went into deception.[13] The best example of this is linen, which served as a sign of the internal. It stood for, and represented, something else. The code was so strict that each element in dress came to correlate to the others. Only what was visible counted. But this, at least for those who dictated the norms, formed a whole. The details were never unimportant. The effect was that of a picture, considered and studied, where no piece could be seen in isolation.

Given this inter-dependence, many elements were interchangeable. From the positioning of the hat to the cleanliness of the clothes, did it not, in some sense, amount to the same thing? 'Let everything be done properly [*dans la propreté*]. Do not wear the hat too high on the head, or tipped too low over the eyes, like a braggart or a show-off . . . Do not wear your clothes dirty or unstitched, or dusty or showing wear, and clean and brush them as a general rule once a day.'[14] Thus advise descriptions where the word *propre* to describe clothes meant style as much as simple cleanliness. It described the shape as much as the material. It confirmed that double criterion which only time would change, an accepted assimilation of cleanliness and the visible, and a demonstration by this means of distinction.

The art of display eventually went beyond dress; the picture grew more complex. The face, in particular, was redrawn. Make-up had, since the sixteenth century, redefined its features. The very pale whites of Clouet, and the even whiter whites of Bronzino, gave flesh the appearance of alabaster.[15] The red of the lips stands out from a smooth, milky surface; the outlines have a wax-like clarity. A few decades later, the picture was enriched by rouge accentuating the contrasts. The noble children painted by Largillière in the seventeenth century have cheeks like cherries embellishing their starch-white faces. And make-up was no longer confined to women. In Largillière's 'Louis XIV et sa famille', painted effigies pose side by side, eyebrows emphasised, cheeks rouged, their theatrical pose only echoing their contrived features.[16]

[13] P. Beaussant, *Versailles opéra* (Paris, 1981).
[14] Anon., *La Civilité nouvelle*, p. 103.
[15] Bronzino's painting, 'Lucrezia Panciatrichi' (1550) is a good example. See, on this theme, the recent work of P. Perrot, *Le Travail des apparences ou les transformations du corps féminin, XVIIIe–XIXe siècle* (Paris, 1984): 'The Renaissance and the Classical Age, so dirty, made up lavishly', p. 33.
[16] A. Largillière, 'Louis XIV et sa famille' (1711), London, Wallace Collection.

Illusion was accentuated by a new and decisive practice: powdering the hair. Appearance was recomposed as if artifice must always be increased through the use of objects. Hair was no longer combed but powdered. This practice was not completely new. Powder had long been used for its drying properties. It made it possible to dispense with washing the hair whilst retaining its softness. It was substituted for water, the latter feared as a means of cleaning.

When it is a question of cleansing the hair of the head, washing should only be employed with the greatest caution . . . Instead, rub with bran stewed in a pan, changing it frequently; or spread over and between the hair some drying and cleansing powder before going to bed, and remove it in the morning with a comb.[17]

Powder had, in fact, already enjoyed a lasting success at the court of Henri III. Sweet-smelling, it was no longer only a means of washing the hair, but had become a hair cosmetic.

If, some decades later, the use of powder was more or less universal amongst the aristocracy, it was because it added another way of enhancing appearance. It controlled, while partially colouring, the hair. It was a further extension of artifice in appearance. The intention was to mask nature, as if to erect a screen between the body and the onlooker. It was part of a determined policy of artificiality which gradually nibbled away at the visible. Along with the cut of clothes, powdered hair became an element in 'propriety'. It completed the picture; it, too, was immediately included in the evaluation of physical cleanliness. It was adopted by those whose way of life was by no means confined to the court. Beaufort, for example, opponent of royal power and turbulent and unruly captain, shows that this practice gradually became normal amongst the aristocracy in the middle of the seventeenth century. His appearance was often deplorable – his collars neglected, his hair unkempt. But Beaufort was not ignorant of the code. He had only to adopt it for everyone to exclaim at this rediscovered 'propriety'. 'He was turned out quite differently from normal. He is the dirtiest man in the world; his beard and hair were powdered, he wore a leather collar, a blue scarf, a white handkerchief at his neck: his "*propreté*" astonished the company, and he made excuses.'[18] The practice was increasingly widely adopted. One of Scarron's matrons could not receive a woman friend until she

[17] J. Liebault, *Trois Livres de l'embellissment et de l'ornement du corps humain* (Paris, 1632, 1st ed. 1582), p. 215.   [18] De Montpensier, *Mémoires*, vol. 2, p. 196.

had 'done her hair, curled and powdered it'.[19] Scarron mocks the old woman's clumsy and tremulous gestures. But propriety ruled in matters of form and colour. The norm prevailed. When Furetière ridiculed the bourgeois for their 'black and filthy'[20] hair, he was obviously implicitly contrasting it to powdering, which, for him, was no longer simply a refinement. The contrast was also with the wig, the ultimate in artificiality.

Powdering played the same role as lace and linen. Its absence signified impropriety and at the same time a public renunciation. It was during her bitter periods that Mlle de Montpensier, Louis XIV's cousin, paraded certain austerities: no longer powdering, wearing different clothes, and abstaining from certain practices. The story of her impossible marriages is also the story of her social retreats. After each deception and each sorrow she abandoned for a while certain vestimentary signs as so many signs of 'propriety'. The absence of powder inevitably featured in all these negative gestures. 'I no longer went to court, I no longer put on my beauty-spots or powdered my hair; I neglected my hair until it got so dirty and long that I was quite unrecognisable.'[21]

THE PERFUME THAT 'CLEANSED'

Powder, in fact, had another purpose – its perfume. It did not yet, in the seventeenth century, have that silvery appearance presented by the white film plastered onto wigs a century later. Its whiteness could be detected, but remained faint and indistinct. It was as much a question of smell as of appearance.

> Une dame ne peut jamais être prisée
> Si elle n'a son chef de poudre parfumé.[22]

The dried and pounded substances used in its manufacture[23] produced a scent as well as a rather muted colour. The illusion was complex, its signs more subtle and more elaborate. It was also disguise, but of a different sort. This was remarked on by various

---

[19] Scarron, *Le Roman comique*, p. 560.
[20] A. Furetière, *Le Roman bourgeois* (1666), in *Romanciers du XVIIᵉ siécle*, p. 1048.
[21] De Montpensier, *Mémoires*, vol. 1, p. 119.
[22] Anon., *Discours de la mode* (Paris, 1613), quoted by J. Quicherat, *Histoire du costume en France* (Paris, 1877), p. 463.
[23] J. de Renou, *Institutions pharmaceutiques* (Paris, 1626), p. 185.

pamphlets stimulated by the new fashions of the early-seventeenth century. 'They taint everything with their false wigs, sprinkled with powder of Cyprus to combat even worse smells.'[24]

Perfume was an ideal tool in this art of appearance, all the more deceptive in that it was invisible. It was employed in chests, which were saturated with powder so that the linen retained its smell. This practice even made it possible, under certain conditions, to dispense with daily changes of linen. 'You make containers for linen in the form of little chests just big enough to hold the fine linen that a man of quality might need in two days; you garnish them both within and without with the same fragrant materials and substances as wig-boxes.'[25] Cinnamon water was 'held in the mouth' to give the breath 'a sweet smell'.[26] And scent-boxes gradually released their aromatic vapours; as for example at the 'magnificent reception'[27] given to Don Carlos in *Le Roman comique*, or in the galleries of Saint-Germain for the fastidious ambassador of Suleiman Aga.[28] The perfume was sometimes so heady that opening a chest could turn into an ordeal. Onlookers choked when her servants unpacked the queen's chests at Saint-Germain in 1649. They fled or held their breath, not daring to breath until the chests had been aired. This was the logic of a perfume so overwhelming that it became unbreathable.[29]

Perfume was not, of course, a discovery of the seventeenth century. It is often mentioned in medieval inventories. Queen Clemence of Hungary, the wife of Jean le Hutin, owned several amber apples, one of them 'ornamented with gold and precious stones',[30] at her death in 1328. The inventory of the Château des Beaux, a century later, records a 'little silver box holding musk'.[31] Royal accounts had for a long time recorded purchases of rose-water and honeysuckle water, even 'vine-branches, roses and lavender . . . to put with linen'.[32] And at Brocéliande, finally, mythical site of the thirteenth-century romance of Chrétien de Troyes, ladies-in-waiting at the court drew their prestige from possession of a particular, highly-regarded skill,

[24] Anon., *La Mode qui court à présent et les singularités d'icelle* (Paris, 1622), p. 3.
[25] S. Barbe, *Le Parfumeur royal* (Paris, 1691), pp. 112–13.
[26] Guyon, *Façon de contregarder la beauté*, p. 338.
[27] Scarron, *Le Roman comique*, p. 560.   [28] Beaussant, *Versailles opéra*, p. 88.
[29] De Montpensier, *Mémoires*, vol. 1, p. 158.
[30] Douët d'Arcq, 'Inventaire et vente après décès des biens de la reine Clémence de Hongrie' (1328), in *Nouveau Compte*, p. 80.
[31] Barthélémy, 'Inventaire du château des Beaux', p. 134.
[32] Douët d'Arcq, *Nouveau Compte*, p. 214.

knowing how to distil rose-water,[33] proof both of the importance the practice had already acquired, and of its relative rarity.

The real change came, once again, with the ostentatious use of linen, its burgeoning out over the clothes, and the heavy emphasis on its lightness. Lace, in particular, should be perfumed, as with the scented shirts of the characters of Margaret of Navarre,[34] or the scents impregnating the 'collars and cuffs' of the gallants of Dupont de Drusac,[35] or the 'imperial oil serving to wash the linen of some great prince' described in successive editions of the *Secrets* of Alexis Piémontais in the sixteenth century.[36]

The seventeenth century at first simply inherited these practices, along with the use of linen and manners. Certain sensibilities were no longer explained, so firmly were they embedded in the culture of the privileged, too obvious to need justifying. The protracted debate about strong smells, in which garlic, amongst other things, figured as a necessary stimulant against tiredness and certain illnesses, was a thing of the past. Bouchet, though not without a trace of irony, remained close to popular culture when, in the sixteenth century, he praised those smells already rejected by people who knew how to behave. 'Garlic is the true meat of the soldier, giving him heart for the fight, as good as onions . . . And, as our ancestors used garlic, they were not ashamed to smell of it.'[37] In the seventeenth century the rupture was complete. A gulf developed between refined and other smells; the debate was over. 'Garlic eaten with vinegar every morning'[38] was a stimulant of the people. 'A little good myrrh in the mouth'[39] for the same purpose was quite a different matter. The two solutions were no longer comparable. The distinction was one of sensibility and of cost. The treatises of perfumers and apothecaries fostered certain distinctions, depending on their public. Lemery, in 1709, proposed the ultimate classification, distinguishing a 'royal perfume', a 'perfume for the bourgeoisie' and a 'perfume for the poor'. But this last was not aesthetic; composed of 'common oil' mixed with soot, it served only to 'disinfect the air'.[40]

[33] C. de Troyes, *Perceval le Galois* (twelfth century) (Paris, ed. 1866–7).
[34] Margeurite de Navarre, *L'Heptaméron* (1548), in *Conteurs français du xvie siècle*, p. 789.
[35] G. Dupont de Drusac, *Controverses des sexes masculins et féminins* (Paris, 1536), p. 62.   [36] A. Piémontais, *Les Secrets* (Paris, 1567).
[37] G. Bouchet, *Les Sérées*, (Lyons, 1618, 1st ed. 1570), p. 140.
[38] Anon., *Préservatifs contre la peste*, p. 19.   [39] *Ibid.*, p. 18.
[40] N. Lemery, *Recueil des plus beaux secrets de médecine* (Amsterdam, 1709), pp. 360–3.

The seventeenth century also inherited the therapeutic connotations of perfume; it was good for you. Its use served to strengthen the body and 'marvellously refreshed the brain'.[41] It counteracted corrupt and dangerous air. The development of measures against the plague provides the best example. Chauliac recommended fire as well as flight during the Great Plague of 1348 in Avignon. Fire purified; it 'improves the air'.[42] But the burning of fragrant substances gradually came to be considered even more effective. Purification and perfumed emanations combined. Similarly, smells with a sweet and 'fragrant'[43] perfume were gradually preferred to the penetrating and long-lasting smells meant to preserve the mouth in times of plague. Gum benzoin, storax, myrrh, musk, and rosewood, made into pastilles held in the mouth, came gradually to be preferred to sharper tastes. Vinegar was another matter. Its sharp fresh quality counteracted the decay assumed to accompany the plague and people walking in the streets sniffed impregnated pads. The acid contained active principles. Perfume, however, gave better protection from the contagion by correcting the corruption of the air. Its role went far beyond the merely social. Attractive smells were, by their very composition, opposed to decay. They added a protective dimension to the simple pleasure of the senses. They had a psychological effect, by 'marvellously assuaging the sensual and cephalic faculty'.[44]

The role of perfume in the art of disguise and appearance was thus a complex one. It was not confined to concealment or pleasure. It was also, in a very concrete sense, purification. Appearance even assumed the force of reality. When the men of Rabelais' *Thélème* drenched themselves with perfume before meeting their lady-friends, they believed they were actually changing their bodies. There was no use of water, simply impregnation with perfumes; washing was subsumed in a strategy of perfume. 'At the doors to the rooms of the women's

---

[41] De Renou, *Institutions pharmaceutiques*, p. 181.

[42] De Chauliac, *La Grande Chirurgie*, p. 181.

[43] Piémontais, *Les Secrets*, p. 146.

[44] De Renou, *Institutions pharmaceutiques*, p. 184. There was an almost medical view of purification in the seventeenth century: in a recent thesis (*Sang et Encens. Anthropologie de l'odeur*, University of Paris VII, 1984), Annick Le Guerer very subtly emphasises a possible parallel between the handling of urban rubbish and attention to individual evacuations. Waste matter remaining too long in the body risked becoming dangerous in the same way as rubbish lying around in towns. Fevers and epidemics were associated with both; hence precautionary purgings and bleedings. Le Roy Ladurie has also recently emphasised the social importance of purging: 'The higher one is placed in society, the more one is bled and purged'. See his introduction to Claude Grimmer, *La Femme et le Bâtard* (Paris, 1983), p. 13.

lodge were the perfumers and hairdressers through whose hands the men passed when they visited the ladies.'[45] In other words, perfume effaced as much as it concealed.

Classical France not only inherited these images, but elaborated them. The array of objects thought to be fortifying because they were perfumed continued to grow. There were, for example, medicinal caps, whose linings, saturated with powder, exercised a stimulating effect by 'manifestly restoring the animal spirits by virtue of [their] smell'.[46] Sachets of scent were carried between linen and doublets. Even utensils in everyday use were adapted and altered. The linen which held toilet articles such as combs, mirrors and powders might be put between perfumed linings. 'You sprinkle over coarse powder of violets, then you cover the whole with tabby. Before putting on the tabby, you should rub it gently with a little civet.'[47] The royal inventories from the end of the seventeenth century record over forty items of this type, including a dozen specially perfumed by Martial.[48] The perfume in this case was playing two roles. It was directly associated with a cleansing article and appealed to the sense of smell. But at the same time it purified. It was the complete opposite of dirt and counteracted it. All the values of appearance were subsumed in the operational. Perfume cleansed, repulsed and erased. Illusion had been turned on its head to become reality.

Wearing perfume when in the streets was therefore not simply an aesthetic gesture, and walking with an amber apple in the hand was more than a matter of fashion. And the scene, common for several decades, as described by an Italian visitor to Paris at the time of Henri IV, became, in a sense, symbolic. 'A stream of fetid water coursed through every street of the town, into which ran the dirty water from each house, and which tainted the air; consequently it was essential to carry sweet-scented flowers in the hand to allay the smell.'[49] Equally significant is the distinction between certain Parisian hospitals drawn by Locatelli, a Bolognese traveller of insatiable curiosity, who, in 1664, traversed the France of Louis XIV. He contrasted the 'stinking' atmosphere of the Hôtel-Dieu, for example, where the sick lay four or

[45] Rabelais, *Gargantua*, p. 178.
[46] De Renou, *Institutions pharmaceutiques*, p. 184.
[47] Barbe, *Le Parfumeur royal*, p. 109.
[48] J. Guiffrey, *Inventaire général du mobilier de la couronne* (seventeenth century) (Paris, 1885–6), vol. 2, p. 103.
[49] G. d'Ierni, *Paris en 1596 vu par un Italien* (Paris, 1885), p. 6.

even five to a bed, and the constant danger of plague at the Quinze-Vingts, which was swamped with incurables, with the apparent calm at la Charité, where a distinctive smell assailed the visitor. The perfume of scent-boxes wafted through the rooms day and night. This aroma, noticeable in every room, fascinated the Italian priest. Surely this agreeable smell protected the body? For Locatelli, it was what made all the difference between the hospitals. It drove away contagion, giving a special strength to the most worn-out organs. 'Near each bed there was a little altar decorated with flowers, with a brazier, onto which, from time to time, the attendant threw fine perfumes.'[50] Locatelli's fascination was so great that he momentarily longed to share the life of these unhappy people, even though they were as crammed in here as elsewhere.

The recourse to 'anti-smells' completed the range of classical cleanliness. It even added a protective, quasi-therapeutic element. But it, too, was first and foremost a matter of 'spectacle', extending the image of linen and of the visible parts of the skin. The sachets placed in the armpits or between the legs, or slipped into the folds of gowns or behind doublets were, indeed, sachets of cleanliness. They served as supplementary instruments in the vital game of appearances.

Of central importance in the cleanliness of the classical period, however, was the limited employment of water. The actions of the princess Palatine at the end of a taxing journey are highly revealing. One day in August 1705, the princess had travelled far on roads baked dry by the sun. She arrived at Marly exhausted, her make-up ruined, her body bathed in sweat. Her face was so stained by dirt from the road that she agreed to wash it. 'I had to wash my face, it was so dusty; I looked as if I was wearing a grey mask.'[51] This was an exceptional occurrence. Otherwise, the princess changed her shirt, her dress and her 'finery'. She was 'clean' again. But it was the linen which had been washed. Water flowed in profusion in the gardens of Château de Marly, but liquid hardly touched the skin of those who lived there. Cleanliness existed, but it was the cleanliness of what was visible.

[50] S. Locatelli, *Voyage en France* (1664–5) (Paris, 1905), p. 144.
[51] Princesse Palatine, *Lettres* (Paris, 1982, 1st ed. 1843), p. 244.

Part 3 *From water that penetrated to water that strengthened*

7. *A pleasant sensation on the skin*

When he describes the bath taken in 1746 by the Marquise du Châtelet, Longchamp, then her valet,[1] may surprise the modern reader; their relationship did not permit of modesty. The valet was responsible for the temperature of the water and supervised the boiler. From time to time he poured the contents into the tub, taking care not to burn the marquise. In short he was there in the room, in attendance, attentive. The lady felt no embarrassment as she undressed and bathed, felt no inclination, even, to render the water opaque. The conditions of mistress and valet were too far apart for decency to be threatened. The servant was not yet a person. As 'neutral' as an inanimate object and as 'familiar' as the household furniture, he was completely assimilated into the background. He handled the familiar utensils, but was a creature apart. What Longchamp might see was irrelevant; he did not belong to the same universe as the young woman. She did not see him. He hovered somewhere between childhood and domestic service, too far away, at all events, to affect the bathing lady.

Longchamp was conscious as he described the scene that he was recording customs that would change with the end of the Ancien Régime. He emphasised the detachment of the marquise, her cold familiarity, her extreme but quite unconscious remoteness. The valet was entirely defined by his function, that of intimate yet trivial services. Another similar man (or woman) could just as well perform these insignificant acts. Longchamp admitted his unease. The body of the marquise troubled him so much that his hand trembled as he poured the water. This conscious emotion, and this surprise, are a sign that customs were changing. Only female servants attended great ladies in their baths from the end of the century.[2]

---

[1] S.-G. Longchamp and J.-L. Magnière, *Mémoires sur Voltaire* (Paris, 1826), vol. 1, p. 120.

[2] Marie-Antoinette and Joséphine de Beauharnais had female servants to assist them when bathing. Cf. Mme de Campan, *Mémoires* (Paris, 1979, 1st ed. 1823), p. 60, and Mlle M. Avrillon, *Mémoires* (Paris, 1969, 1st ed. 1833), p. 224.

On the other hand, Longchamp makes no comment on the bath itself. He found it quite normal, which implies another change. A bath no longer occasioned surprise, but had become part of daily life. The episode is therefore doubly revealing; it shows a transformation of private decencies, and a transformation of attitudes to water, at least amongst the privileged. The bath had reappeared in this social milieu since the second third of the eighteenth century. This is not to say that it had become common, or that cleanliness was its expressed purpose, but at least a transformation in this field had become a possibility. With it, washing gradually spread, and immersion, till then extremely rare, began to be acceptable. Water was integrated into new circuits; this tentative practice could expand. It was probably still very restricted, perhaps even rare, when the marquise took her bath. It was certainly confined to a very narrow elite, and it did not correspond to any heightened concern with matters of hygiene. But in promoting what was almost a new practice, it had its consequences; for certain people in the middle of the eighteenth century changing linen could no longer be all that was needed to care for the skin. A new treatment, using water, existed. Very slowly, within the closets of the great nobility, new criteria were elaborated. A particular sort of bathing, in specific surroundings, and with specific attentions, emerged. It was also specific in that it remained infrequent, and in the ideas about the body which it supposed; we need to define this special character. It suggests, once again, that there will always be many different ways of using water. But we need to look at this aristocratic and still uncommon bathing in order to understand how, by successive stages, and not without changes of direction, the use of water came to be transformed.

A NOVEL AND RARE TYPE OF BATH

Various indications of this new practice exist. A series of building works was undertaken at Versailles, for example, to construct special rooms to accommodate baths, to install them in several of the main apartments, or to change their position during the frequent phases of rebuilding.[3] Luynes thought it worth mentioning the queen's request to use the king's baths temporarily when building works rendered her own inaccessible.

[3] P. de Nolhac, *Le Château de Versailles sous Louis XV* (Paris, 1898).

The queen bathed the day before yesterday. The baths in her apartment had been changed at the time of her journey to Fontainebleau . . . The baths previously in her large green closet being temporarily out of use, she had someone request, or herself requested, the king for permission to bathe in his bath. The king granted his permission with the best possible grace.[4]

The scene might even be made into a spectacle. In 1742, when the royal mistress took a bath, she spun the episode out into a series of stages which were followed by the courtiers.

Mme de Chateauroux obliged the king to be present at her baths, and the prince brought with him the courtiers, he alone entering the salon, leaving them in the chamber with the door half-open, and continuing to talk to them. When Mme de Chateauroux got out of the bath, she retired to her bed, dined there, and everyone then entered her chamber.[5]

This pretentious behaviour was primarily a demonstration of the newly acquired power of the favourite, but it also confirms the change in the status of bathing towards the middle of the eighteenth century.

Allusions begin to appear in letters, memoirs and in many learned texts. References are at first rare, but become frequent from 1740 on, with, for the first time, mention of the royal example. 'When it pleased the king to bathe . . .'[6] The prejudices of Louis XIV were forgotten and outmoded, though certain precautions persisted; his successor, for example, chose 'water drawn from the middle of the Seine in preference to water carried in pipes'.[7] Water taken from the beds of great rivers was believed to conserve greater purity. Water, in fact, remained an equivocal substance. It needed to be pure because it diffused. It was still assumed to penetrate the body, and affect its organs and functions. It disturbed, and produced numerous mechanical effects. 'It insinuates itself into every interstice, which it enlarges by the slackening produced by its warmth.'[8] A body immersed was a body impregnated. The flux exercised an irresistible pressure. 'The force with which water enters the pores is immense. Its limits are unknown.'[9] But, above all, as in the past, it left behind open and fragile pores. It logically followed, therefore, that there was always a risk of a bath doing harm. It was still essential to take precautions: a

[4]   L. C. de Luynes, *Mémoires* (Paris, 1865–7), vol. 10, p. 180.
[5]   Maréchal de Richelieu, *Mémoires* (Paris, 1793), vol. 6, p. 119.
[6]   *Avis concernant les nouveaux bains de la Seine* (Paris, 1761), p. 1.   [7]   *Ibid.*
[8]   H. Maret, article on 'Bain' in the *Encyclopédie* (Paris, 1751), vol. 2, p. 21.
[9]   F. Raymond, *Dissertation sur le bain aqueux simple* (Avignon, 1756), p. 19.

purge before immersion so that the infiltration did not increase surfeits; rest and bed afterwards to give maximum protection to the body and ward off fatigue. But fears of plague, of various diseases and of obscure weaknesses were a thing of the past, lost and forgotten. This was not only because the major plagues were over. The consequence of bodily openings itself no longer seemed to have sufficient power to occasion acute anxiety; it seemed that the body could react in other ways than by a passive openness. Immersion became a possible and acceptable practice, for some even familiar, as shown by the Marquise du Châtelet. Very slowly, bathing established itself amongst the upper classes of eighteenth century society.

This new practice did not, however, overthrow tradition at one go. It is clear that in the middle of the century bathing remained very rare, even amongst the aristocracy. In J.-F. Blondel's *l'Architecture française* of 1750, which recorded the plans of seventy-three private Parisian mansions, only five had a bathroom.[10] Out of twenty or so luxurious mansions described by Marot at the same period, two had bathrooms.[11] In the middle of the century, then, fewer than one in ten great mansions had a special space for a bath. Bathtubs were probably more common. In 1751 the *Encyclopédie* included a definition and a description of this item of furniture which testifies to its actual use. The object even had a more or less standard shape: four and a half feet long by two and a half wide, and twenty-six inches high. It might be made of copper or of wood bound with iron. It was, therefore, no longer round, and already close in shape to that of today.[12]

Also, such bathrooms as existed were by no means used consistently. At Commercy, for example, during Louis XV's visits in 1755, the bathroom became the apartment of the Marquise de Boufflers.[13] The tub was covered over and concealed. The room lost its special function, and was turned into living quarters. The marquise held entertainments and dinners there. Other examples confirm that the practice was still by no means general. The Duc de Croÿ indirectly shows this when he describes the marriage of his daughter to the Duc d'Havré in 1762. The bath taken by his daughter is reminiscent of those of the seventeenth century, reserved for life's

[10]   J.-F. Blondel, *L'Architecture française ou recueil de plans* (Paris, 1752–6), 4 vols.
[11]   J. Marot, *L'Architecture française ou recueil de plans* (Paris, 1750, 1st ed. 1727).
[12]   Article on 'Baignoire' in the *Encyclopédie* (Paris, 1751), vol. 2.
[13]   Longchamp and Magnière, *Mémoires sur Voltaire*, vol. 2.

great occasions, in particular the day before important marriages, and taken in bath-houses. By their explicit reference to this bath, the Duc's memoirs emphasise its rarity. Why insist on it if the young lady regularly bathed? 'The 17–18–19 were spent in making visits, for my daughter in being purged and bathed and preparing her body and her soul.'[14] Similarly, when, in 1769, Condorcet remarked that he occasionally bathed, Julie de Lespinasse did not immediately associate this act with cleanliness. 'Is it for the sake of your health, or is it by choice that you take baths, and were you born under the sign of the fishes?'[15] Even more significant are some scenes of arrivals and halts whilst on journeys. A few years later, Gauthier de Brecy, leaving Paris for his Provençal Intendancy, spent the first night at the house of a relative in Dijon. He refers to cleanliness as a necessity, but not to bathing. 'I arrived at his house in travelling clothes. I needed to clean myself up: he gave me a room . . . They lit a good fire in the Prussian fireplace. I shaved, I really needed it.'[16] Resuming his secretaryship with a Roman cardinal in 1754, Casanova got a reception which both surprised and delighted him – water and a tub, but not a bath. 'I was shown into an apartment consisting of three rooms, including a bedroom hung with damask . . . A servant came to give me a light dressing-gown, went out and returned a moment later with a second carrying linen and a large tub of water. It was put down in front of me, they took off my shoes and washed my feet.'[17] Cleanliness was clearly involved here, but not actually a bath.

This tentativeness, a taste still uncertain but nevertheless real, is explicable in terms of the novelty of the practice, the hesitancy of any new beginning. A new practice is inevitably fragile, inconsistent and slow to become established. It does not achieve immediate geographical and social victory; it needs time. The bathroom and the bathtub were the preserve of a small section of the nobility before gradually spreading and becoming more common.

SENSIBILITY

But this gradualness and hesitancy had other causes. The situation was complicated by a continued preoccupation with the mechanical

[14] E. de Croÿ, *Mémoires, 1727–1784* (Paris, no date), p. 178.
[15] J. de Lespinasse, *Lettres* (1769–76) (Paris, no date), p. 45.
[16] C. E. Gauthier de Brecy, *Mémoires véridiques et Imprévues de la vie privée* (Paris, 1834), p. 146.
[17] G. G. Casanova, *Mémoires* (Paris, Livre de Poche), vol. 1, p. 244.

effects of water. The new interest in bathing even reinforced this. The body, agitated and shaken by a water which was alien to it, was inevitably profoundly affected. Immersion corresponded to a series of actions whose effects on the body extended far beyond cleanliness, and some of which were considerably more important. These effects continued to dominate the imagination in the middle of the century. Hot water, the most penetrating, extended its emollient influence to every part of the body; warm water tempered over-heating, calmed nerves and malaise during hot weather; cold water, by causing contractions, could firm up the muscles and invigorate. It was precisely when water seemed better accepted that the multiplicity of its actions was quoted in its favour. The new interest in bathing and the insistence on the variety of its effects for long went hand in hand. The temperature of the water, in particular, seemed to be crucial. Oppositions were established: the regular as opposed to the seasonal bath, for example, and, most important of all, the cold as opposed to the hot, but also the strengthening as opposed to the softening. The choice was all the more important because water was a subtle medium, and it was by exploiting this subtlety that warmth could vary its effects. But water was still a medium of waves and shocks, of movement and pressure. It created a condition for the submerged body. It affected it more than climate; as it enveloped, it controlled. It was not a neutral substance. How could bathing be imagined without reference to these effects?

These physical activities were all the more important in that they soon acquired social significance. The people who, from the middle of the eighteenth century, basked in warm water, were not the same as those who, a decade or two later, discovered the virtues of cold. A refined and sensual practice can be contrasted with an austere, even ascetic, one; luxury contrasted with the severity the cold methods contrived. A significant divergence emerged between a very aristocratic softness and an asceticism of successful ambition; ostentatious luxury against ambitious vigour.[18] Water had to be seen as an active substance for such applications to be suggested, to conjure up turbulent, dynamic images. These, by fusing with hygienic criteria, further complicated the picture.

The first eighteenth-century baths, taken in private mansions, were hot, and apparently for the purpose of cleanliness. But the attention

---

[18] See chapter 8, 'Cold and the new vigour'.

devoted to the mechanics of water already hinted at a greater complexity. Richelet's distinction in 1728 suggested certain nuances: 'Young people bathe for pleasure, and others take baths for the sake of their health.'[19] Pleasure, then, came first. As far as health is concerned, he probably did not have in mind care of the skin; the dynamic effects of water on the system were probably more important. In any case, the bathroom was a luxury, one which was rare, certainly, but also a conscious choice. It needs to be understood as such. It implied a specific practice. In mid-century at least, cleanliness was probably not the dominant motive.

There can be no doubt that a bathroom added distinction to noble houses. The story published by Bastide in 1753, *La Petite Maison*,[20] provides an illustration of this which is all the more interesting in that it is so blatant. To seduce Mélite, a reluctant lady-friend, the Marquis de Frémicour suggests that she visits the house he has recently built on the banks of the Seine, at the gates of Paris. The young woman hesitates, teases, but finally accepts. The inevitable happens. The visitor is conquered bit by bit as she proceeds through the rooms. The growth of her sentiment is closely in step with her discovery of the new house. It is not, however, its magnificence which wins her over, but rather its convenience and elegance, taste, rather than grandeur, cleverness and utility rather than ostentation. 'It was a question of the conveniences with which we have become enamoured and which our ancestors rather neglected.'[21] It was a question of a harmonious arrangement of rooms, many and concealed services, a studied profusion of paintings, engravings, stucco and perfumes; a prestige of techniques, then, and a refinement of physical surroundings. Progress lay in comfort and aesthetics. The seduction of Mélite had its origin in this double impact. It was not by chance that the visit ended in the bathroom. 'She walked on and entered a new room more delightful than any she had yet seen... This new room was a bathroom. Marble, porcelain, muslin, no expense had been spared ... At one side was a small washroom, with panelling painted by Houet ... I can't bear it, she said, it is too beautiful. There is nothing like it on earth.'[22] Cleanliness, aesthetics and refinement united in one single emotion.

[19] P. Richelet, *Dictionnaire de la langue française* (Paris, 1728), vol. 3, p. 287.
[20] J.-F. Bastide, *La Petite Maison* (Paris, 1758).
[21] J.-F. Bastide and J.-F. Blondel, *L'Homme du monde éclairé par les arts* (Paris, 1774), vol. 1, p. 146.   [22] Bastide, *La Petite Maison*, pp. 18–19.

The publication of Bastide's story in the economic journal in 1753 is significant. In line with the policy of this journal, started in 1751, the story brought together the themes of technical advancement and sensibility, of luxury and progress. It repeated the arguments of Voltaire and Montesquieu: the refinement of the arts was the precondition for the refinement of the senses. And economic matters governed both themes. For the arts, far from 'weakening the people',[23] caused sensibility to blossom and produced wealth. Bastide extended this new consciousness of the early eighteenth century: the arts, as they affected the senses, also multiplied resources. They had a dynamic effect on industries. The 'superfluity' extended beyond the purely economic. Wealth determined the power of nations. By his pleasures, Voltaire's *Mondain* 'in fact enriches a great state'.[24] It is his desires and tastes which stimulate craftsmen and manufactures, before being adopted by them. Old moral rigidities could, more than ever before, be cast aside. Pleasure, and sometimes 'even softness'[25] found other formulations. A new and insistent relationship to the economy gave them their justification.

With this new relationship, the bath, too, found a new place. It was an additional refinement for the worldly. It was a further subtlety of the senses and of taste:

> Il court au bain: les parfums les plus doux
> Rendent sa peau plus fraîche et plus polie
> Le plaisir presse: Il vole au rendez-vous.[26]

When Casanova described the apartment in Venice which had been lent him in 1754 by the French ambassador to further his amorous encounters, he saw in the marble bathroom adjoining the 'boudoir prepared for the mother of loves'[27] a rare luxury. But it was a luxury of a very special sort, mingled with an eroticism and a sensuality which pushed into the background any idea of a functional purpose. The bath was a necessary, almost a superfluous, extra. It was in no way a basic or routine practice in the middle of the eighteenth century. It was the affirmation of a wealth in which sensuality was dominant. There was a similar ambiguity when Le Sage's devil

---

[23] C. L. Montesquieu, *Lettres persanes* (1721), in *Oeuvres complètes* (Paris, 1956), vol. 1, p. 288.
[24] F. M. Voltaire, *Le Mondain* (1736), in *Mélanges* (Paris, 1965), p. 208.
[25] *Ibid.*, p. 203.   [26] *Ibid.*, p. 205.
[27] Casanova, *Mémoires* (1744–56) (Paris, 1977), p. 433.

allowed the scholar to enter in succession every house in Madrid – a social and cultural survey in the scope of a few pages. There is only one bathroom scene in all these visits, but a very significant one: 'The second part of the building was inhabited by a beautiful woman who had just that minute bathed in milk and got into bed. This voluptuous woman was a widow . . .'[28] It was, no doubt, the desire for a delicate, white skin which motivated this unusual practice. But it was the voluptuous refinement which attracted the attention of the observer.

And when, for the first time, in 1759, a text on the art of beauty was introduced by a long eulogy of bathing, the example was borrowed from contemporary images of the oriental harem – lascivious connotations and female space. In the bath of the odalisque, pleasure always predominated over utility, and titillation of the senses over cleansing. The decor of the seraglio, as described by the author, indicated sensual delights: mother of pearl and pearls, aromatic plants, the bathtub itself transformed into a shell, creating more than just an ambience. Such objects pointed to a particular milieu. Every act had other connotations than washing. Caught up in a image of refinement and preciosity, bathing could not be simply a functional practice. The acme of refined culture, it acted on the senses. Once bathed, the odalisque could 'surrender into the arms of a soft and voluptuous sleep'.[29] She was at the same time siren and languor.

Mme de Genlis will tell us later the extent to which this practice induced a 'state of body'. The potency of water quickly overwhelmed the senses, a mixture of relaxation and idleness, and worship of artifice. Bathing, in the middle of the eighteenth century, prospered by the indolence of the rich. 'Baths were a necessity in warm countries, a fashion in others; they have never been so common and so widespread amongst us as recently. Laziness and idleness have done much to establish and maintain them. The afternoons are so long for those without work since they dine at six o'clock.'[30] More than ever, the hot baths taken in noble bedrooms were an affair of women. But beyond the connection with femininity and languor, the

---

[28] A. R. Le Sage, *Le Diable boîteux* (1726) in *Romanciers du XVIIIᵉ siècle* (Paris, 1966), vol. 1, p. 284.

[29] A. Le Camus, *Abdeker ou l'art de conserver la beauté* (Paris, 1754), p. 94.

[30] Mme S. F. de Genlis, *Dictionnaire critique et raisonné des étiquettes de la cour* (Paris, 1818), vol. 1, p. 64.

practice gained ground as an additional pleasure authorised by wealth.

And it was this very wealth that the first architects of bathrooms in the eighteenth century originally exploited. They did not necessarily design with constant or even regular use in mind. The new spaces were often places for refreshment and relaxation. They were chosen for moisture and shade. Plants and lawns were rarely far away. When the chosen site was an orangery with its northern wing exposed, it was because the bath was put there for hot days, not for cold spells. The attention to greenery, to sheltered gardens, and to hidden nooks, bespeaks, as if self-evident, a preferred time of year. 'The purpose of this apartment demands freshness, which is why it is usually placed on the ground floor of a building, shaded by a wood and near to a fountain; so that, on leaving such places, you can breathe cool air in the shade of some agreeable verdure.'[31] These were bathrooms expressly designed for the warmth of summer.[32] There was the same emphasis, if more furtive and less direct, when Diderot wrote to the Volland sisters on 10 August 1769. 'Oh, how hot it is, I seem to see all three of you in your bathing wraps.'[33] The practice is also directly associated with warmth in the writings of Diderot. Bathing seems not yet to have been sufficiently frequent or familiar to be independent of times and seasons. Immersion was consistently linked with warmth, with the ambient atmosphere. Such immersion was intended primarily to create a 'condition'. The same emphasis appears again when the Prince de Ligne recalled the baths he took after reading on the island in his sunny park. It was a luxurious place, associated 'with fresh, sweetly scented air'.[34] *Le Médecin des dames* summed it up in 1772 – a seasonal practice, largely confined to an elite, vaguely sensual: 'Baths for reasons of health, or for voluptuousness, or cleanliness, are hardly ever taken in winter. Spring and summer are the most suitable seasons.'[35]

It was a complex practice, then, in which cleanliness combined with other motives. The nature of water meant that the impregnation of

[31] J.-F. Blondel, *Traité d'architecture dans le goût moderne* (Paris, 1737), vol. 1, p. 172.

[32] Cf. also C. E. Briseux, *L'Art de bâtir des maisons de campagne* (Paris, 1743), p. 7; 'As a general rule, the bathroom is put in the building housing the orangery'.

[33] D. Diderot, *Lettres à Sophie Volland* in *Oeuvres complètes* (Paris, 1969), vol. 8, p. 877.

[34] Prince de Ligne, *Mes adieux à Boloeil* (c.1770) (Brussels, 1914), (unnumbered pages).

[35] *Le Médecin des dames ou l'art de conserver la santé* (Paris, 1771), p. 318.

the body and the effects on its condition dominated. To bathe was perhaps primarily to experience an atmosphere, undergo influences, feel an affect. Substances were interchanged, and pressures deployed. The bath roused the 'impressionable' system. It was the quasi-internal sensibility of the body which was involved. It was a luxurious practice, at all events, confined to a tiny minority in the mid-eighteenth century, but a practice sufficiently important to give birth, almost at the same time, to new initiatives.

A first establishment breaking with the tradition of the bath-house was built on the Seine in 1761: hot baths with water pumped from the river to supply little cabins distributed about a boat. This novel arrangement was designed to facilitate the circulation of the water. The project was both therapeutic and hygienic at the same time. 'I see all the time the sick comforted and healed with the aid of the baths; equally, they come here to safeguard their health.'[36] Commended by the Faculty of Medicine, praised in various quarters, and benefiting from an 'exclusive privilege',[37] the Poitevin baths remained the only ones of their kind until 1783.[38] Luxurious (a bath cost three livres in 1761, when the daily wage of a craftsman was then half a livre, and that of a day-labourer about a quarter),[39] they were intended for a restricted public, confirming the minority status of a hot bath. But, above all, the establishment wavered between being a therapeutic and a hygienic institution. Poitevin repeatedly asserted that it was necessary 'to give the rich the chance to be healed more quickly than if they had to seek the necessary help far from home'.[40] He also stressed, even delighted in, the showers designed to enhance the mechanical effects. 'The cures operate by displacing by a greater force the strange humours which form stoppages in the painful membranes and in the muscles swollen by their presence.'[41] It was hydropathy, in fact, which dominated. In its arrangements, if not in its practices, the

---

[36] J.-J. Poitevin, *Lettre à messieurs les doyens et docteurs régents de la faculté de Médecine* (Paris, 1776), p. 1.

[37] *Ibid.*

[38] Cf. *Décret de la faculté de Médecine sur les nouveaux bains établis à Paris sur les quais de la Grenouillère* (Paris, 1723). This establishment, the Albert Baths, like that of Poitevin, had hot baths. It is described by Mercier, and also in Thierry's *Guide des amateurs et des étrangers voyageurs à Paris*, published in 1787 (vol. 2, p. 597). Several cold baths were already in existence, but posed a different problem (see chapter 8).

[39] Poitevin, *Lettre à messieurs*, p. 14.

[40] For the price of baths, cf. *ibid.*, p. 15. For the wages of craftsmen in 1760, cf. M. El. Kordi, *Bayeux aux XVIIe et XVIIIe siècles* (Paris, 1970), pp. 256–7.

[41] Poitevin, *Lettre à messieurs*, pp. 11–12.

establishment was the forerunner of the baths of the nineteenth century.

Finally, the new interest in bathing was expressed in the mid-eighteenth century by a marked increase in medical monographs on the subject. The question posed by the Dijon Academy in 1755 ('the virtues of the simple water bath')[42] attests to the importance of the theme. The practice, therefore, had its theoretical aspect. And the first texts emphasised unequivocally the effects of the disturbance created even inside the organs. Attention was primarily concentrated on phenomena of sensibility. The body was soothed as much as taken over by the bath. 'Hot water causes a pleasant sensation on the skin which it bathes: the sensitive faculty delightfully relaxes the fleshy system.'[43] The first intention was to describe this; it was a matter of restoring a condition. The hot bath was basically enjoyable because it affected the senses by its very substance. 'This gentle relaxation which produces a sort of delectation on the skin, passing thence into the whole nervous system, renders the bath calming. It makes people somnolent.'[44] Looked at more closely, it was once again the logic of fluxes and shocks which was dominant. When Guillard, in 1749, tried to justify, in one sentence, baths for his 'happy citizen', it was the internal phenomena which consistently prevailed. Once the states had been described, interest was concentrated on the profound mechanism set in motion by the bath. The text is revealing because it marks the revival of the bath, and probably also already the beginnings of a new cleanliness, whilst remaining largely concentrated on the constitution of the body. 'He bathes and rubs himself with oil to preserve the suppleness of his nerves, to facilitate sweating, to prevent the humours from settling too abundantly in any part of his body and causing sharp pains, often fatal, which could easily have been avoided.'[45] The hot bath soothed because it made the humours circulate, and that was its chief virtue.

THE 'CONVENIENCES'

Other more physically limited uses of water testify to a more profound transformation of hygiene amongst the elite in the second

---

[42]   This was the dissertation of Raymond (*Dissertation sur le bain aqueux simple*), who won the prize.
[43]   Raymond, *Dissertation sur le bain aqueux simple*, p. 25.
[44]   J.-P. de Limbourg, *Dissertation sur les bains d'eau simple* (Liège, 1757), p. 43.
[45]   G. Guillard de Beaurieu, *L'Heureux Citoyen* (Lille, 1759), p. 22.

third of the eighteenth century. A new item appeared, especially after 1740, visible both in noble inventories and the accounts of the great cabinet-makers; it was called a 'chair of cleanliness', or, already, a 'bidet'. It was first being used a little before the 1730s. One day in 1726, d'Argenson was received by Mme de Prie as she made her toilet. Polite words were exchanged. The scene was quite normal. Then, Mme de Prie, without more ado, sat 'on her bidet'[46] and engaged in an intimate wash. D'Argenson wished to withdraw. Mme de Prie insisted he stay. The scene turned into a flirtation. The deed astonishes by its gracelessness; but it is the date which concerns us here. There is no trace of such an object in the Malmaison inventory of 1713, though one had appeared by 1750.[47] In 1739, Remy Pèverie, cabinet-maker and turner of the Rue aux Ours, at the sign of the 'Belle Teste', could conceive bizarre double bidets, set back to back.[48] For a long time the bidet indicated social distinction. Usually consisting of a wooden frame with a bowl of tin or earthenware, they were often of elaborate and luxurious appearance. The back-rest and the folding lid which concealed the bowl made a sort of chair often to be found in the chambers of the nobility. The one given to Mme de Pompadour by Duvaux in August 1751 was typical in its elaborate workmanship. 'A bidet with a back of rosewood veneer and floral mouldings, its feet and fittings of gilded bronze'.[49] Mme de Talmont's bidet at Saint-Germain-en-Laye was equally typical: mounted 'in cherrywood with kingwood mouldings, above a footstool covered with red morocco studded with gilded nails'.[50] Some of these elaborate objects had crystal flasks incorporated into the seat-back. When, in 1762, he made a metal bidet with feet which unscrewed to make it portable, J.-B. Dulin provided an indirect demonstration of the importance the object was beginning to assume.[51] It was not exclusively used by women; a commode and a bidet are recorded in the closet of M. de Hérault, and in that of the owner, in the inventory of the Château de Montgeofroy in 1775.[52] Similarly, a commode and

[46] Le Voyer, marquis d'Argenson, *Mémoires et Journal inédit* (Paris, 1867), vol. 1, p. 205.
[47] B. Chevallier, 'Les inventaires mobiliers du château de la Malmaison', *Bulletin d'histoire de la Ville de Paris* (1979), pp. 105–7.
[48] Cf. Havard, *Dictionnaire d'ameublement*, vol. 1, p. 313.
[49] L. Duvaux, *Livre journal* (1748–53) (Paris, 1873), p. 94.
[50] J. Deville, *Dictionnaire du tapissier* (Paris, 1877), vol. 1, p. 515.
[51] Cf. Havard, *Dictionnaire d'ameublement*, vol. 1, p. 313. Cf. also R. H. Guerrand, 'L'âge d'or du bidet', *L'Histoire* (Paris, 1983), no. 157, p. 84.
[52] P. Verlet, 'Inventaire du château de Montgeofroy' (1755). *La Maison au XVIIIe siècle en France* (Paris, 1966), p. 262.

a bidet were found in the closets of both the Prince de Condé and his wife in the inventory of the Palais-Bourbon in 1779.[53]

The engravings of G. de Saint-Aubin are revealing about this particular luxury. 'Les Papilloneries humaines' of 1770 manages to illustrate a wealth of social situations by endowing butterflies with slender and anthropomorphic forms, a play on the image and a witness to customs. The toilet scene is that of the great noble houses – elegant furniture, rich materials, attentive and busy servants. An 'insect' has her hair done, adopting a nonchalant pose. The whole range of goods in use in mid-century ornaments the scene: engraved mirror, embroidered handkerchiefs, lace table covers, delicately shaped holders protecting flasks, and, finally, a bidet, placed on one side, behind a screen of painted cloth.[54]

The bidet remains, however, a very rare object in the middle of the century, hardly ever found in the bourgeois world. There was, for example, no bidet in the house of J.-L. Tamisier, a merchant who died at Apt in 1767 in possession of more than 100,000 livres of rent.[55] He knew, nevertheless, how to enjoy his wealth: he had over sixty fine embroidered shirts. Mme Tamisier's closet, situated on the first floor, contained a dressing-table with mirrors, creams and flasks of perfume. There is nothing here to suggest any modification of seventeenth-century hygiene, even though the 'toilet-table' is now fitted with mirrors, drawers and perfumes.[56] This inventory provides all the indications of classical hygiene: plentiful linen of good quality, objects emphasising attention to external appearance and to smell. Similarly, Rousseau's accommodation at Montmorency was without a bidet in 1758.[57] So was the accommodation of Collin, Mme de Pompadour's steward, at her death in 1764.[58] The distribution of bidets within châteaux is also significant; in mid-century and for some decades after, they were found only in the bedrooms or closets of the owners. This was the case at Malmaison in 1750,[59] and at Montgeofroy in 1775.[60]

[53] 'Inventaire du Palais-Bourbon' (1779), *ibid.*, p. 274.
[54] G. de Saint-Aubin, 'Les Papillonneries humaines' (1770), Paris, estampe BN.
[55] O. Teissier, *La Maison d'un bourgeois du XVIIIe siècle* (Paris, 1886).
[56] See E. Dumonthier, *Mobilier national de France, le meuble toilette, style Louis XV, Louis XVI, premier et second Empire* (Paris, 1923).
[57] 'Inventaire de J.-J. Rousseau à Montmorency, rue Mont-Louis', in the *Mémoires* of Mme D'Epinay published by F. Boiteau in 1884, p. 435.
[58] J. Corday, *Inventaire de Mme de Pompadour* (Paris, 1939), pp. 111, 113.
[59] Chevallier, 'Les inventaires mobiliers du château de la Malmaison', p. 109.
[60] Verlet, 'Inventaire du château de Montgeofroy', p. 262.

A more or less obvious sign of distinction, the existence of the bidet supposes a more intimate practice of cleanliness, modifying actions and attentions. The appearance of this item of furniture merits all the more interest in that it was neither preceded nor accompanied by any modification of the manuals of hygiene, even less of the manuals of manners, from which classical cleanliness had till then drawn its norms. It was after 1760, for example, that certain texts began to evoke a sectional cleanliness, according to the part of the body. The treatise of Jacquin (1792) remains fairly euphemistic. It indicates local washing. The 'secret' zones of the body exist in it, but it is still impossible to identify precise actions. The principle of such washing did not extend beyond generalities. 'Cleanliness requires that you wash various parts of the body fairly often, especially those where sweat, if left, produces a disagreeable smell. It is a matter of delicacy as much as of health.'[61] *Le Conservateur de la santé* (1763), on the other hand, very deliberately named parts. It dwelt on smells, and on overheating. It described the risks run by not washing all these particular hidden surfaces.

If perspiration or sweat remain on these parts (the armpits, the groin, the pubic area, the genitals, the perineum, between the buttocks or 'the furrow) the warmth inflames them, and, apart from the unpleasant smell which results and is spread about, part of these exhalations, and of the substance of which they are formed, is taken up by the absorbent vessels and carried into the circulation where it can only do harm by disposing the humours to putrefaction.[62]

The image of a body which absorbs (in this case, sweat which can 'flow back' into the pores), persists, but with the use of water to care for certain parts; these should be bathed regularly with a damp sponge, advised *Le Médecin des dames* in 1772. For some parts, washing was necessary. 'The care of the natural parts is an indispensable necessity. They must be washed every day, and aromatic plants or some spirit put in the water to be used for this purpose.'[63] The insistence on feminine cleanliness was for the first time very explicit. The use of the bidet preceded these texts. It was, in fact, contemporaneous with another transformation, more important because it concerned space and the intimate, that of closets for the 'conveniences'.

[61] N.-J. Jacquin, *De la santé* (Paris, 1762), p. 290.
[62] A. G. Le Bègue de Presle, *Le Conservateur de la santé* (Paris, 1763), p. 345.
[63] *Le Médecin des dames*, p. 302.

What differentiated the great residences of Blondel in 1737[64] and 1752[65] from those of Le Muet a century earlier,[66] was a more precise distinction between the various parts of the building; to the state and public apartments where noble social life was mainly lived were added more secluded areas designed for more intimate use.[67] Offices with specific purposes were installed next to bedrooms: various closets, large and small, each with its specified function, for example for books or for washing (*réchauffoir, serre livres, toilette, garde-robe,* etc.). The rooms of the great seventeenth-century residences, usually multi-purpose, had, a century later, gained annexes. When Michel de La Jonchère transformed Malmaison in 1737,[68] he increased the number of small closets (*chambres de garde-robe*) in a residence which had hitherto had only ground-floor passages and ante-chambers. The improvements effected at the residences of La Vrillière in 1752, of the Baron de Thiers in 1747, and of Armini in 1748,[69] involved similar changes. Rooms retained their proportions and their monumental scale. But round about them, between one room and the next, numerous places appeared. At the Hôtel de La Vrillière, a room in one wing had attached to it a wash-room, a closet and a back-stairs.[70] At the Hôtel de Belle-Isle, built by Bruant in the Rue de Bourbon in 1721, one room had attached to it a wash-room, a 'convenience room', a closet and a privy.[71] Comparing the buildings of the seventeenth century with those of his own times, Blondel emphasised their lack of 'closets' and 'conveniences'.[72] At the end of the seventeenth century, for example, Mme de Maintenon had no special place where she could make her toilet. She slept in a room where the king continued to chat to his ministers. Her women came to 'undress'[73] her at the foot of the bed. They then helped her slip into the bed, whose heavy hangings alone isolated her. It is this very intimacy which was affected by the changes to large mansions from 1730 on, and by the separation of state bedchamber and private

---

64 Blondel, *Traité d'architecture.*   65 Blondel, *L'Architecture française.*
66 P. Le Muet, *Manière de bien bâtir pour toutes sortes de personnes* (Paris, 1623).
67 C. Oulmont, *La Vie au XVIII*ᵉ *siècle, la maison* (Paris, 1929), p. 31.
68 Chevallier, 'Les inventaires mobiliers du château de la Malmaison'.
69 Blondel, *L'Architecture française*, vol. 1, p. 239; vol. 2, p. 200; vol. 3, p. 111. For the earlier condition of some of these residences, see P.-J. Mariette, *Architecture française* (Paris, 1727), 2 vols.
70 Blondel, *L'Architecture française*, vol. 1, p. 239.
71 *Ibid.*, vol. 2, p. 86.   72 *Ibid.*, vol. 3, p. 84.
73 Saint-Simon, *Mémoires*, vol. 28, p. 250.

rooms. And it is this which was affected by the creation of rooms specially for the toilet; rooms so specific that, by the 1760s, complete sets of bathroom furnishings were being sold, with walls and ceilings of painted cloth.[74]

These luxurious residences of the second third of the eighteenth century did not, however, change all individual relationships. The apartments of master and mistress generally remained separate. The familial ties between them were not necessarily closer. Men and women continued, for the most part, to occupy separate wings of the residence.[75] This space oriented towards state bedchambers and public apartments did not yet affect familial intimacy. Its real originality was to make possible greater personal intimacy. By their specialisation, the closets encouraged private attentions. The individual now had time to himself. His actions were less directed towards external display. Other relationships, of oneself to oneself, became possible. A privacy was established within noble existence.

In practice, the various models, those of the traditional aristocracy and those of the great financial bourgeoisie, fused, the latter importing into noble life a privatising dynamic quite new to it. The great residence of the 1730s, such as that of a Receiver-General of Finances like de Meulan,[76] or a minister like Rouillé,[77] was inspired by the norms of the court at the very time it was displacing them. Ostentation gave way to a less demonstrative luxury. A larger space was set aside for private functions. Conveniences, boudoirs and closets were not constructed simply for show. Private man enjoyed there a new space. Nothing was more important to the financial elite than ennoblement and imitation of the men of the court, but nothing was more inevitable than a mutual influencing of their values. 'Thus, while noble pleasure tends to become privatised, a private person, once arrived, tries to conceal his origins by copying an aristocratic way of life.'[78] The Hôtel d'Evreux, which Mme de Pompadour had altered by Lassurance in 1752, and the Hôtel d'Armini, which

---

[74] One was sold, amongst other things, on 3 October 1765: 'A pretty "*cabinet de toilette*", or boudoir, about nine feet high by six feet wide and eleven feet deep, with a ceiling and panelling, the whole painted on canvas by M. de Machy.' See Havard, *Dictionnaire d'ameublement*, vol. 4, p. 1356.

[75] The remarks of Norbert Elias on this point (*La Sociète de cour* (Paris, 1974, German ed. 1969), p. 29), remain fundamental.

[76] Blondel, *L'Architecture française*, vol. 3, p. 111.　　　　[77] *Ibid.*, p. 60.

[78] J. Starobinski, *L'Invention de la liberté (1700–1789)* (Geneva, 1964), p. 16.

belonged to the financier, de Meulan, ended up by resembling each other.[79]

The washroom (*cabinet de toilette*), the 'room of cleanliness' (*cabinet de propreté*),[80] the convenience room (*cabinet de commodité*) and the privy (*lieux à l'anglaise*), all of which were to be found in rich Parisian mansions from the second third of the eighteenth century, seem to originate in this privatisation. The privies, clear signs of wealth, are particularly significant. They transformed the use of the commode by establishing a fixed and enclosed place for the natural functions. They applied the first technology to comfort, for example a valve to close off the hole to prevent smells spreading. Special places for intimate functions – a new space had been created.[81] The washroom, on the other hand, signified a new cleanliness, localised, certainly, but going beyond what was seen, and rendering reliance on clean linen alone inadequate. A new, and above all a private, practice; the place counts here as much as the actions. And this whole range of activities was primarily based on personal sensations, developing without any theoretical justification. Intimate washing had begun. A more private space favoured its appearance. Particular objects indicated its presence. The bidet was the prototype of these innovations, but pottery bowls and jugs also helped to furnish these private places.[82]

Though important in that its cleanliness, though localised, achieved an intimate dimension, this transformation was nonetheless extremely limited. Not only was it confined to a few privileged people, but it had not yet completely emancipated itself from its traditional connections with appearance and good manners. The fact that the toilet could still for a long time to come be made in public emphasises that the crucial element in it remained the metamorphosis achieved by doing the hair and attending to the face. The dominant role of the visible had not been overthrown. The Duc de Croÿ, present at the toilet of Mme de Pompadour, was fascinated as much by the aesthetic effect as by the proximity, quite institutionalised, such a situation

---

[79] Corday, *Inventaire de Mme de Pompadour*, pp. 20ff.; Blondel, *L'Architecture française*, vol. 3, p. 111.

[80] The term is used after 1770; cf. Verlet, 'Inventaire du château de Montgeofroy', p. 262.

[81] This theme can only be touched on here. For a more direct approach, see L. Wright, *Clean and Decent* (London, 1960), and H.-G. Guerraud, 'Petite histoire du quotidien: l'avènement de la chasse d'eau', *L'Histoire* (Paris, 1982), no. 43.

[82] See Chapter 11, p. 156.

authorised. 'Nothing more delightful could be seen.'[83] The operation was designed for visual effect. The toilet consisted above all of a patient transformation of the appearance. Its appeal was visible. Intimate cleanliness, discreet and little discussed, was tending in other directions. But this cleanliness still remained largely captive to the classical preoccupation with appearance. The essential aim was still display. Change would come elsewhere. It was by becoming more functional, for example, by finding other legitimations, in particular those of health and strength, and above all by confronting the mechanical images that water still bore, that cleanliness would change its meaning. Paradoxically, some of these changes were achieved by questioning the luxury which was still dominant, by establishing a hygiene opposed to the values of appearance, though not, it must be emphasised, lacking in social connotations.

[83] de Croÿ, *Mémoires*, p. 33.

8. *Cold and the new vigour*

Bathrooms, bathtubs and washrooms show that the use of water gradually changed in the middle of the eighteenth century. For a privileged minority, at least, this meant a new cleanliness. But it remained very uneven, and the number of people affected very small. It remained allusive, even obscure; water itself was not seen as it is today. Its warmth, its infiltration and its pressure all emphasised its uniqueness. It was an active substance, a dynamic milieu, acting on and traversing the body rather than washing it, stirring up its physiology and activating hidden energies.

Interest in these mechanical effects was not confined to warmth and penetration. Many other effects could be imagined and other images were possible. Shocks and disturbances, for example, might be caused by the physical mass of water. Its mechanical effects seemed multifarious, and it was to these that curiosity and speculation were directed. Agitation of the body's parts, disturbances and internal movements remained the chief preoccupation. One particular idea was to play a role of especial importance since it reconciled numerous attractions, that is the shock effect of cold water. There was firstly a simple constant: cold contracted the body. Speculation about consequences ensued: such contractions might have a therapeutic effect by acting on the humours, or a quasi-moral effect by acting on the energy. Once again, hygiene became confused with preoccupations which went beyond it. The coldness of water became its most important quality, and interest was initially concentrated on the internal movements which contact with it set in motion. For many people in the second half of the eighteenth century, bathing and the use of water were dominated by the demand that it be cold. 'Does it not make men stronger and more robust?'[1] The concept rarely corresponded to actual practice, but it occupied an important role in theories and debate.

---

[1] Brouzet, *Education médicinale* (Paris, 1754), vol. 1, pp. 82–3.

These speculations supposed the transformation of many other assumptions. They required, for example, a quite new confidence in the reactions of the body; a liquid as inhospitable as cold water, after all, submitted the body to an apparent evil in order to strengthen it. This belief in cold water, which seduced a new generation of hygienists from the middle of the eighteenth century, could only be arrived at after a long theoretical and cultural journey.

IDEAS ABOUT COLD BATHS

At first, before 1750, it seemed to be exclusively a question of therapeutic effects. There were strange cures and edifying histories. A certain Capuchin, for example, was reputed to restore life to dying bodies by applications of iced water. The unnatural convulsions helped to renew energy, death retreated before the shocks of life. The *Mercure* of 1724 described this worthy ecclesiastic's activities. Summoned to attend a dying man, he strove valiantly with the aid of the coldest of compresses. 'He applied towels dampened with ice; death still mocked the good Capuchin and hung onto the patient. Eventually, the Capuchin called angrily for a block of ice weighing eight pounds and rubbed the man's stomach and belly with it; upon my word, death let go, the patient revived, from top to toe; he opened his eyes, recognised everybody and drank some water without more ado.'[2] Such mechanical reactions are pre-scientific curiosities. There was clearly no shortage of credulity in the *Mercure*'s tale, and a barely concealed taste for the bizarre. Nature astonished; its defiance seduced reason. The laboratories of the early eighteenth century, with their fumbling and their crude investigations of marvels, are not far away. Cures of this type, at all events, were widely publicised.

The deeds of the Duc de La Force, who saved a poor wretch from dying from sunstroke, belong in this same category. Two travellers, come from afar, were crossing his lands during a terrible heat wave. The summer was exceptional; it was boiling hot. They succumbed. One died some distance away, the other fell almost at his feet. The Duc de La Force ordered the sick man to be bathed in the stream flowing below. He put him to bed, covered him up, and waited: 'The patient came to, and well rested overnight, the next day recovered

---

[2] *Mercure Galant*, Paris, September, 1724, p. 1913.

enough to say that he felt very well.'[3] The coldness of the water had triggered off the return to life. Noguez, who reported these events in 1730, offered an explanation: the cold tempered. It calmed excessive agitation and contracted vessels dangerously dilated. It strengthened the parts by constricting them. 'The coldness of the water and its weight moderate and stop these prodigious movements, constricting the vessels and restoring their tone.'[4] The explanation was extended, diversified, and applied to a multiplicity of ills; the therapy gained in variety. Contracting the body in its deepest zones (or so it was supposed), the cold conjured up images of the circulation of humours, the evacuation of viscera, and the reduction of tumours. It acted on solids and on fluxes. It caused masses to retract, compressed by its pressure. Organs contracted and quickened. And their abrupt distortion could be controlled.

There is no method as effective as cold when it is a matter of dissolving blood or evacuating glutinous matters attached to the linings of the vessels; when you want to cleanse the glands and procure a more abundant filtration of animal spirits or make them run more rapidly in the nerves, when you need to induce urine or dissolve obstructions in the liver, the spleen, etc. . .[5]

This therapy exploited a series of images: conflict between what relaxed and what contracted, between what softened and what made hard. The role of the cold, in this case, comes as no surprise. 'It fortifies and contracts the fibres where they are too weak.'[6] The cold bath thus orchestrated the movement of fluids and solids. In 1763, Pomme immersed patients who were suffering from vapourish complaints. He wanted, by the cold, to combat their softness, 'to restore strength to their solids'.[7] In his single-minded application of the logic of hardening, Pomme sometimes went to extremes. He prolonged baths to eight hours a day. His enfeebled invalids spent their days in icy water. There was no trace here of earlier concerns. The discontinuity is all the more striking in that tradition favoured warmth; it was hot water which had formerly been employed to expel the humours.

But the implications went far beyond these new cures. The cold

[3] P. Noguez, *Explication physique des effets de l'eau*, Hoffmann, *Les Vertus médecinales de l'eau commune* (Paris, 1730), vol. 2, pp. 437–8.
[4] *Ibid.*, p. 439.
[5] L. de Préville, *Méthode aisée pour conserver sa santé* (Paris, 1762), p. 368.
[6] J. Huxan, *Essai sur les différents espèces de fièvres* (Paris, 1752, 1st ed. London, 1750), p. 36.
[7] P. Pomme, *Traité des affections vaporeuses des deux sexes* (Lyons, 1763), p. 18.

bath in the eighteenth century was not only a therapeutic technique which broke with tradition, it became a technique of radical hygienists. Constricted and consolidated fibres, it was argued, were as likely to reinforce sick as healthy bodies. Because the code of vigour and resistance was directly concerned, so inevitably was health. The bath, for the first time, had an explicitly hygienic role, though less because it cleansed than because it strengthened, so powerful was the image of the mechanical actions of water. It was the effect on the bodily machine which counted, rather than its effect on the cleanliness of the skin. Many texts of hygiene from the second half of the eighteenth century promoted a vision of increasing toughness. They promised a world of hard physique. Water was perpetually confronting the functioning of the body. Its coldness consolidated.

Considerable advantages are attributable to cold baths: the sudden effect of cold on our bodies rapidly contracts the external parts and those which adjoin them; by this means, the vibrations of the fibres become tauter, and the blood and the spirits circulate more rapidly. This is why cold baths are good for rarefying the blood and rendering it more fluid, for arousing the animal spirits and causing them to circulate more rapidly . . . for facilitating the digestion and giving an appetite; lastly, for rendering the body agile and vigourous.[8]

Filaments and fibres grew hard, stiff and compressed. The whole 'hard' structure of the body contracted, and was, as a result, consolidated. Books on health, formerly dominated by attention to régime (in any case largely dietary), increasingly insisted on the stimulating virtues of cold; cold water, along with lighter clothes, favoured frequent muscular tensions and reactions. Without it, 'the fibres will lose tone and the cellular tissue slacken'.[9]

Certain practices already in existence acquired a new significance. River bathing, for example, till then reserved for sport or a handful of cures, was seen, in the second half of the eighteenth century, as a means to health. It was both a strengthening exercise and an invigorating technique. The few Parisian baths, crudely installed next to boats equipped with ladders,[10] received renewed attention. They were mentioned, described, even recommended. The *Descriptions de*

[8] Jacquin, *De la santé*, pp. 286–7.
[9] J. Ballexserd, *Dissertation sur l'éducation physique des enfants* (Geneva, 1762), p. 152. France was late in discovering certain principles of Locke on education through 'cold'. Cf. *L'Education des enfants* (trans. Amsterdam, 1695, 1st ed. 1693), pp. 8ff.
[10] Cf. the article on *Bains* in the *Encyclopédie*, vol. 2 (1760), pp. 20–1.

Paris and the *Guides des voyageurs*, which had hitherto ignored such places, now indicated their locations, and even risked passing judgement. Jèze, for example, whose *Etat de Paris* was re-edited almost annually between 1754 and 1765, adopted the thesis of the hygienists. Such baths could not but be 'the healthiest',[11] even if their appointments seemed crude. 'The places called baths consist of a boat completely covered by an awning near which there are fixed in the river twenty or so stakes in a circle about twelve fathoms long and two wide, enclosed with planks and also covered by an awning. You get down by a ladder.'[12] The space was constricted and even cramped, no luxury, but invigorating actions.

It was after 1760 in particular that this idea, fixed and unvarying, circulated amongst the hygienists: 'The cold bath, by condensing the solids, makes them resilient and strengthens them'.[13] The body was subjected to the regime of hardened steel. The fibres were the focus; their 'convulsive movements'[14] induced hardening. The repeated references to this demonstrate the definitive abandonment of a medicine of humours, even though the action of the solids hardly passed beyond the threshold of elementary physics.[15] But Maret set about calculating the shrinkage of a strip of animal skin exposed to the action of cold water,[16] whilst others immersed themselves in rivers and counted the acceleration of their pulses, or recorded certain physical reactions,[17] actions which go beyond a vague curiosity.

These scientific aspirations, however, would have had little effect if they had been confined to simple physiological images. But the

[11]   Jèze, *Etat ou tableau de la Ville de Paris* (ed. of 1757), p. 187. Slightly earlier works such as those of the abbé Antonini, *Mémorial de Paris* (1744), or of J.-C. Nemeitz, *Séjour de Paris* (Leiden, 1727) do not mention these establishments. Some fairly basic arrangements designed primarily for sport had existed for some time. Cf. G.-F. Saint-Foix, *Essais historiques sur Paris* (Paris, 1777), vol. 7, p. 96.

[12]   Jèze, *Etat de Paris*, p. 187.

[13]   de Limbourg, *Dissertation sur les bains d'eau simple*, p. 35.

[14]   P. Fabre, *Essais sur différents points de physiologie, de pathologie et de thérapeutique* (Paris, 1770), p. 317.

[15]   Eighteenth-century medicine focussed attention on the 'solids' of the body, endowing them with particular qualities, including irritability, which was not without its consequences for the image of a system 'reacting' to its milieu. Cf. on this point, M. D. Grmek, 'La notion de fibre vivante chez les médecins de l'école iatrophysique', *Clio Medica* (Oxford, 1970), vol. 5.

[16]   H. Maret, *Mémoire sur la manière d'agir des bains d'eau douce et d'eau de mer* (Paris, 1769), p. 48.

[17]   de Limbourg, *Dissertation sur les bains d'eau simple*, p. 59. Le Monnier had already, in 1747, measured the acceleration of his pulse according to different degrees of warmth of water. Cf. *Mémoires de l'académie des Sciences (1747)*, p. 271.

cultural dimension was in practice equally important. Texts did not deal exclusively with the mechanics of fibres. For some, cold water was above all an austere substance. The practice of the cold bath was above all an ascetic practice. The toughening induced was as much moral as physical. This hardening was intuitive rather than really explained; it was a matter of mobilising energy and affirming firmness.

Tronchin, for example, the doctor of the encyclopedists, followed by some of his Genevan admirers, did not explore the details of organic functioning, but made the cold bath a quasi-moral theme. 'As long as the Romans, on leaving the Champ de Mars, went and plunged into the Tiber, they ruled the world. But the hot baths of Agrippa and Nero reduced them gradually to slaves ... The conscript fathers were, therefore, quite right to oppose public baths, but the gilded company, infected with Asiatic luxury, triumphed over the opposition and the virtue of the conscript fathers.'[18] Tronchin, too, confidently prescribed long cures of cold baths, as warmth could only 'soften'. His argument was ethical; softness was opposed to virtue, and physical weakness to moral force. Physiology was subordinated to the Antique reference, as in Plutarch's *Lives*,[19] with their celebration of primitive virtues. Rome, after all, was lost by a youth which 'disdaining to bathe in cold water, abandoned to softness, almost resembled our little masters in forsaking the physical exercise responsible for its strength and virtue'.[20]

The savage played the same role in this type of text. He, too, provided excellent educational material. 'The inhabitants of the American Isthmus plunge into cold water when they are in a sweat and their health does not suffer.'[21] Travel stories provided further

[18] T. Tronchin, *Manuscrit de 1764*, quoted by H. Tronchin, *Un médecin du XVIIIe siécle, Théodore Tronchin* (Paris, 1906), p. 59.
[19] A common example was that of the laws and education of Sparta (as, in particular, in Plutarch's *Vie des hommes illustres*) where enduring the cold in a simple tunic was regarded as strengthening. This virility had an ambiguous relationship with cleanliness, the latter being always a possible sign of weakness. In ascetic Sparta, to be clean meant to be 'tender'. Plutarch says clearly what Tronchin, obviously, no longer says, but he at any rate emphasises the early significance of cold. 'They were always dirty and never either bathed or used perfume, except on certain days of the year when this softness was permitted' (vol. 1, p. 92 of the 1838 edition of Plutarch). Cold meant above all simplicity.
[20] Tronchin, *Un médecin du XVIIIe siècle*, p. 59.
[21] C. A. Vandermonde, *Essai sur la manière de perfectionner l'espèce humaine* (Paris, 1756), vol. 2, p. 215.

ammunition for such theories. The savage was not invariably idealised, but he was frequently made an example of rude habits and robust physique. Baths taken in the Amazonian or Canadian rivers provided a dramatic illustration of an energy and a resistance which could be transposed. 'It is a scientific fact that the American Indians plunge their children into rivers the moment they are born.'[22]

It is Rousseau who best expresses the essence of these voluntarist references. The Romans and Spartans of Plutarch, the Indians of La Hontan and Le Beau[23] all appear as examples of rustic habits, their practices as examples of strength. Above all, they very obviously became polemical instruments. 'Multitudes of people wash new-born children in rivers or the sea as a matter of course. But ours, softened before even being born by the softness of their fathers and mothers, bring into the world a temperament already spoiled.'[24] References to ancient heroes and to savages are interchangeable. Cold water was exploited till it came to symbolise a water which rendered invulnerable. The image of the Styx added its cultural and symbolic allusions, with its old Achillean models burdening college courses. The new hygienists all remembered their classical studies and exploited them in their own way. 'Harden their bodies . . . Dip them in the Stygean water.'[25] Thus, Emile was washed in ever colder water till he was accustomed even to water which was 'icy'.[26]

This idealisation of strength had a social function: the ancient citizen as opposed to the present victim of despotism, simple habits as opposed to corruption, regeneration as opposed to decadence. Criticism of softness was also criticism of a city. 'We no longer have citizens.'[27] Simple habits were deemed to offset the etiolation of the 'little masters'. Romans and savages signified an 'elsewhere' of liberty and strength. They were opposed to an aristocratic luxury now become 'enfeeblement', and to an arbitrary power which was implicitly denounced. They played, in fact, the role of counter-example. This critique dominated much thinking after 1789. Antiquity offered a

[22] J. Mackenzie, *Histoire de la santé ou de l'art de la conserver* (The Hague, 1761), p. 172.

[23] L. A. La Hontan, *Nouveau Voyages du baron de La Hontan dans l'Amérique septentrionale* (The Hague, 1709); C. Le Beau, *Aventure parmi les sauvages de l'Amérique septentrionale* (Amsterdam, 1738), 2 vols.

[24] J.-J. Rousseau, *L'Émile* (Paris, 1951, 1st ed. 1762), pp. 37–8.

[25] *Ibid.*, p. 20.   [26] *Ibid.*, p. 38.

[27] J.-J. Rousseau, *Discours sur les sciences et les arts* (Paris, 1931, 1st ed. 1750), p. 34.

model of liberty. 'If we imitate these free peoples . . .'[28] It also offered a model of strength, with education assuming responsibility for training for war. 'I want fights, games, exercise, races and movement, far more than books and lessons.'[29]

Frugality as against luxury, energy as against feebleness, were coded references. Weakness, delicacy and effeminacy were the reflection of aristocratic artifice. Their meaning was obviously social. And it was this meaning which rendered the cold bath a complete counterpoise to the baths of noble mansions. These, with their enfeebling warmth, became, for the enlightened bourgeoisie, a sign of degeneracy. They had their 'origin in our taste for softness, an inevitable consequence of the luxury which is conquering all estates'.[30] A useless and dangerous privilege, the hot bath was condemned as the practice of a decadent class. It, too, was symbolic, of the excess which corrupted and softened. Quite simply, it 'debased nature',[31] by inculcating a useless refinement of habits. The idle youth, submerged in the 'vapours' mocked by Mercier, who 'dawdled from bath to dressing room and from dressing room to bath',[32] personified aristocratic laziness. Similarly, 'the delicate people who spend hour after hour in tepid baths and almost invariably pay for their perseverance by aches and pains, feebleness, or even total prostration',[33] were obviously victims of their 'delicacy'. But this was primarily a sign of their social background. There was thus on the one hand a refinement which weakened, on the other a simplicity which strengthened, a debilitating softness contrasted with an invigorating rigour. In each case, the words went far beyond their physiological meaning. Bourdieu has noted the beginnings of these changes in Montesquieu. Warm practices tended towards feebleness. 'Relaxation [relâchement] of the fibres, relaxation of habits, relaxation of vital strength and manly energy, cowardice [lâcheté]: to engender

---

[28] Daunou, quoted by D. Julia, 'Le brouert noir des enfants de la patrie', *Raison présente* (Paris, 1981), no. 59, p. 115. On the same theme, cf. also, Mona Ozouf, *La Fête révolutionnaire, 1789–1799* (Paris, 1976): 'La déhistorisation de l'histoire ancienne primitive utopisée en vie simple, frugale et équitable', p. 330.

[29] Jeanbon de Saint-André, 1792, quoted by Julia, 'Le brouert noir', p. 114.

[30] J.-L. Fourcroy de Guillerville, *Les Enfants élevés dans l'ordre de la nature* (Paris, 1774), p. 90.

[31] Vandermonde, *Essai sur la manière de perfectionner l'espèce humaine*, vol. 2, p. 219.

[32] S. Mercier, *Tableau de Paris* (Paris, 1783), vol. 3, p. 98.

[33] Vandermonde, *Essai sur la manière de perfectionner l'espèce humaine*, vol. 2, p. 212.

socially acceptable myths, it is enough, we can see, to let the words have their effect.'[34]

A new class, in the face of aristocratic models, invented a strength. It did so by reactivating vigour and dynamism. It justified itself. It definitively separated a new asceticism from conspicuous indolence. By the austerity of coldness, it signalled its superiority over pleasures judged too indulgent. It emphasised rigour the better to increase cultural and social distances. Lack of sensibility and energy became the dominant lessons. It was these that Grimm's correspondence said should be learned from Tronchin. 'He has reminded us of Republican habits and the moral philosophy of the ancients.'[35]

Cold was only a sign of a major shift in values. What mattered was the discontinuity in physical codes and moral values; at a deeper level, it was a transformation of a whole social frame of reference, with strengths imagined where they did not exist and decadence limited to a defined milieu. The references to bathing were only a pretext. Their impact was primarily on the imagination; they conjured up visions of manifest powers and impressed by heroic examples. But the cold bath was usually an exclusively literary conviction; it did not abruptly invade bourgeois habits in the wake of these hygienic arguments. It remained for the most part a rhetorical reference, an abstract rule, an intellectual argument, not an actual practice.

Millot, still, in 1801, displaying the utopian spirit of certain revolutionary debates, conceived the idea of an establishment which would be 'regenerating'. He proposed that a circular place should be constructed in the Seine, with a series of steps to allow the regular immersion of children of all ages and sizes. Frequent periods in the river would ensure that they grew progressively stronger. It was not a question of swimming, but simply of a spell in the cold. The pedagogic and public application of the cold bath would at last be achieved.

Whenever the government wishes, it can change the feeble constitution of our Parisians, and make them as robust as our German neighbours: all that is needed is the construction of a bath at the edge of the Seine, near the Invalides; this bath would consist of an elipse cut into the waste land on the bank which would be dug out to four feet only, and constructed like an

[34] P. Bourdieu, 'Le Nord et le Midi, contribution à l'effet Montesquieu', *Actes de la recherche en sciences sociales* (Paris, 1980), no. 35, p. 25.
[35] F. M. de Grimm and D. Diderot, *Correspondance littéraire* (Paris, January, 1782 (ed. of 1813)), vol. 1, part 3, p. 314.

amphitheatre, in stages each raised only four or five inches above the next, to seat children of all ages after teething.[36]

In 1801, Millot saw his arguments as still innovatory. He thought little had been achieved. Nothing, it seems, had changed in the militant and persuasive tone, except the appeal to public authority and an obviously institutional and political purpose. 'This bath would introduce throughout the whole of France the practice of the cold bath, and within fifteen years, the government would begin to see the beneficial effect of such baths.'[37] Explicitly evoking Rome and Sparta, and proposing quite unrealistic demands, Millot's formulas were doomed to failure. This sort of general and compulsory bath could never be imposed. It did, however, affect a limited public who were sensible of its value as an example, and of the social demarcation on which the idea was based.

WHAT PRACTICES?

Mme de Maraise, associate of Oberkampf and enlightened woman of the world, was an admirer of the hygienists. This friend of Tissot,[38] who had read his texts with passion, and who invited him to Jouy in 1780, reveals both her convictions and their limits. She entertained no doubts, for example, about the value of cold baths, but was cautious about taking one. For this sociable and dynamic member of the bourgeoisie, who said she had never bathed, the cold bath long remained theoretical. She appreciated its logic rather than its practice. She spoke of it in the future rather than the present. 'Your experience should be a better guide than my poor little theory, which only I can vouch for, never having tried any sort of bath, and when my health permits, it will be in the Seine that I start.'[39] She bathed for the first time over a dozen years later, in the Seine. She took two or

---

[36] J.-A. Millot, *Art d'améliorer et de perfectionner les hommes* (Paris, 1801), vol. 1, p. 92.   [37] *Ibid.*

[38] Cf. S. A. Tissot, *Avis au peuple sur sa santé* (Paris, 1765), 2 vols. Tissot's work is a good example of the images evoked by cold, that is, acceleration of perspiration and strengthening. Cold is essentially a factor of dynamisation in which fibres, fibrils and nerves participate: 'The cold bath re-establishes perspiration, restores strength to the nerves and thus dissipates all the disturbances which these two causes occasion in the animal economy' (vol. 2, p. 66). Water is well and truly, in this case, a 'disturbing' medium.

[39] Mme M. C. R. de Maraise, *Correspondance* 27 May, 1780, quoted by S. Chassagne, *Une femme d'affaires au XVIIIᵉ siècle* (Toulouse, 1981), p.106.

three baths a year there, though still sometimes abstaining for several seasons. Thus practice followed genuine conviction, but remained irregular and infrequent. On 12 September 1812, Mme de Maraise alludes incidentally to this irregularity. 'The 28 of last month, you came to my house just as I was going out on various errands, and in particular for my third river bath this year, which I hadn't found time for since 1809.'[40] This friend of Oberkampf was more pressing where children were concerned. She believed in baths which completely submerged the body, head included. She promoted them, described them and praised them to the skies. But she reveals indirectly some reserve and some difficulties. 'I would like our little ones to be plunged into cold water like English children, but they must not have a maid like the one they have for this operation, nor, I am inclined to say, a father like theirs, albeit he is quite capable of making prejudice bow to experience; but when I myself was about to take a cold bath, he was absolutely insistent that my head should be excluded.'[41] The insistence on total immersion reveals that cleanliness was not the main object. In fact, Tissot, from whom Mme de Maraise proudly drew her asceticism, implied this. One of his statements is particularly revealing. 'Weak children are the ones most in need of washing; the very robust can do without . . .'[42] Cold water, it is clear, washed less than it strengthened. It was primarily an ordeal. Furthermore, it was tempting to treat it as pure theory, which, to an extent, it was. Merely to refer to it caught the imagination by creating new visions of physical qualities. It was not always necessary to go further.

Nevertheless, actual examples of cold baths are by no means entirely lacking. Mercier noted a tangible change. It particularly concerned children, and those of the enlightened bourgeoisie, soon influenced by this new code. This infatuation paralleled that which simultaneously condemned swaddling clothes and corsets. Children 'are better raised than formerly. They are plunged into cold baths, we have adopted the happy custom of clothing them lightly, and without binding.'[43] And the practice spread beyond a narrow enlightened circle. Exiled to Louveciennes after the death of Louis XV, Mme du Barry embraced this new behaviour. She took a cold bath every day, changed her diet and wore fewer clothes. This asceticism on the part

[40] *Ibid.*, p. 141.   [41] *Ibid.*, p. 74.
[42] Tissot, *Avis au Peuple*, vol. 2, p. 63.
[43] Mercier, *Tableau de Paris*, vol. 5, p. 77.

of the former favourite is the exact opposite of that which Mme de Montespan had inflicted on herself a century earlier;[44] not in this case a rigour which mortified, but a rigour which strengthened and served different ends. When the citeziness of Louveciennes explained herself, her statements remained allusive and intuitive, but an 'acquired' robustness was at the heart of her assertions. Dufort de Cheverny recorded her enthusiasm, not to say her ingenuousness, after a chance meeting. 'Her pretty face was rather flushed. She told us that she took a cold bath every day. She showed us that under her long cloak she wore only a shirt and a wrap. She absolutely insisted that we touched her flanks to prove to us how little the cold affected her.'[45]

A different example, but also evidence of actual practice, was the invention of the Comte de Milly, member of the Academy of Sciences, who in 1776 proposed a complicated mechanical bathtub. In this, the water was set in motion to produce a current comparable to that of a river. This flux added its pressures to those caused by the cold; it accelerated the series of shocks. The expectations of mechanical effects had never been so great. It reveals the prominence recently acquired by the image of the river, with its coldness, its movement, and its vaguely idealised dynamic pressures. This bathtub 'augments the action of the water on the surface of the skin by producing, after only a few moments of immersion, a greater effect than is obtained in many days by the ordinary method'.[46] The word 'method', and the calculation of length (from several minutes to many days) show, without it being explicitly stated, that it was a matter of causing physiological effects as much, if not more, than of washing.

Yet another example is provided by the passion with which Benjamin Franklin could speak of the river-baths and 'tonic' immersions which he regularly enjoyed after 1760. The example is particularly interesting because Franklin emphasised both a veritable infatuation and a substitute practice. Nothing equalled the virtues of the cold bath, but the resulting shock might disturb and unsettle the body. It might even harm certain constitutions. Franklin dealt with this difficulty by resorting to a very simple alternative: the air bath. Rising early each morning, he opened the windows, and worked and

---

[44] See chapter 5.
[45] J. N. Dufort de Cheverny, *Mémoires* (1731–1802) (Paris, 1886), vol. 2, p. 22.
[46] Advertisement in *La Gazette de santé* (Paris, 1776), p. 107.

moved around naked inside the house for 'an hour or a half-hour, according to the season'.[47] Cold air apparently had the same effect as cold water! The relationship between cold and cleanliness, it must be said, was in this case very tenuous.

Certain institutions, finally, employed cold water for its strengthening properties. The rules of the royal military schools, for example, consequent upon the reforms of the Comte de Saint-Germain, introduced it in 1776. It was a seasonal practice, still, but one which paved the way to more regular local ablutions. The future soldier was to be toughened by exploiting the virtues of water. 'The pupils of all ages should be accustomed to washing their hands and faces daily in cold water. If there is a river or a stream near to the college, where they can bathe without danger, they should be taken there from time to time in good weather.'[48] Cold water had its equivalents in clothes, the way rooms were arranged and in light bed-covers – the mania of a milieu which regulated everything: 'To this end, they should often be let go bare-headed and lightly covered . . . The pupils should be given only one bed-cover even in the coldest season.'[49] This explains the several buckets installed for foot-baths, about 1780, in the courtyard of Mans-Neuf in the Collège Louis-le-Grand.[50] The use actually made of them, however, is difficult to discern, as it escapes the rules of the civil colleges. All the more so, as at Brienne, for example, though a military college, the inventory of 1788 mentions only 'two bath-containers for the legs'.[51]

It was, nevertheless, chiefly the outlook of educational institutions which had been transformed. In his comments to accompany the proposal and programme for the establishment he created in 1777, and which he wanted to serve the 'important employees of the State', Verdier enthused about river-baths and swimming. They promoted health and vigour. But they were too risky for the pupils. 'In Paris, the pupils should never be taken beside the water, or onto the ice, or to any dangerous place.'[52] At the Collège Sainte-Barbe, on the other

[47] B. Franklin, *Correspondance choisie* (trans. Paris, 1818), 2 vols., (letter of 28 July, 1768).

[48] *Règlement concernant les nouvelles écoles royales militaires, du 28 mars 1776*, Archives historiques de l'armée, Ya 145, art. 9.   [49] *Ibid.*, art. 10.

[50] G. Dupont-Ferrier, *Du collège de Clermont au lycée Louis-le-Grand* (Paris, 1920), p. 186.

[51] *Inventaire de l'ameublement de Brienne* (1788), Archives historiques de l'Armée, Ya 158.

[52] J. Verdier, *Cours d'éducation à l'usage des élèves destinés aux premières professions et grands emplois de l'Etat* (Paris, 1777), p. 232.

hand, as at several other institutions towards the end of the century, the pupils were taken to bathe in the Seine at the onset of the summer.[53] Meanwhile, a new establishment had seen the light of day: the school of swimming, opened on the Pont de la Tournelle in 1785 by Turquin.

Many abortive attempts to found similar schools had been made since that of Arnaud in 1777.[54] They had run into financial obstacles or failed to gain approval. Turquin obtained the endorsement not only of the provost of the merchants, but of the Academy of Sciences and the Royal Medical Academy. The concept had gained acceptance. The quest for so many guarantees confirms his ambitious designs; Turquin wanted to create a hygienic establishment. Neither technical apprenticeship nor the utilitarian role of swimming were neglected, but the aims of the institution were more ambitious, and other objectives dominant. What mattered most was movement in cold water, and, once again, the organic reactions which accompanied it. Turquin had been an apt pupil; swimming accentuated the effects of cold.[55] It was an additional instrument to accelerate the mechanical effects of liquid; it facilitated the stimulating action of the bath. The theory had become a commonplace. It appeared in the *Encyclopédie* of 1765,[56] and other texts expanded and developed it. Swimming gave the water more force, while reconciling suppleness and tension. The organs, in consequence, were more thoroughly massaged, even pummelled. The agitation completed the mechanical action.

Swimming has an advantage over a simple bath, because the vigorous, repeated movements made to overcome the resistance of the water are more conducive to making it penetrate the interior and give suppleness to the muscular activity of all parts of the body, to promoting the easiest and most

---

[53] *Ibid.*, p. 368.
[54] Cf. abbé Arnaud, 'Etablissement qui intéresse l'utilité publique et la décoration de la capitale', *La Gazette de santé* (Paris, 1777). Arnaud revealed, in a text with the same title and dating from 1790, his approaches to various academies, and to the royal entourage. The refusal seems to have come from M. de La Michaudière, provost of the merchants, and the minister, de Breteuil. The plan was for the establishment to be attached to the piles of one of the Parisian bridges. The reasons for the refusal are obscure, connected, it appears, with the cost of the establishment, fears of hindrance to traffic on the Seine, and a lack of conviction of its usefulness (text of 1790, pp. vii–x). Cf. also L. C. Macquart, *Manuel sur les propriétés de l'eau* (Paris, 1783), p. 349.
[55] Turquin, *Avis au public sur l'établissement d'une école de natation* (Paris, 1786), p. 1.
[56] Article on 'Natation' in the *Encyclopédie*, vol. 2, pp. 54ff.

favourable secretion and excretions, in a word, to setting the seal of health on the finest constitutions.[57]

Swimming, Turquin insisted, accentuated 'the salutary effects of the river-bath'.[58] It was its culmination. The school of swimming was, in fact, primarily a place for toning up the body.

Opened in July 1785, the establishment was an instant success. Turquin planned a new and supervised space: four boats, firmly anchored, together bounded an enclosed rectangle, the first Parisian swimming-bath. Cabins were provided. The clientele was select. This is shown by the cost of individual subscriptions: ninety-six livres a year, first class, forty-eight livres for the second.[59] The price was high. Comparing it with taxes speaks volumes: in 1790, for example, the patriotic contribution was claimed from those with incomes higher than four hundred livres a year, reckoned to mark the threshold of easy circumstances. The subscription alone amounted to a quarter of such an income. The school's clientele could not be drawn from the common people. This is confirmed by some of its private customers.[60] The Duc d'Orléans sent his sons there in 1788, a significant decision in that the Duc had for long adopted the sensibility of the enlightened bourgeoisie. For purely political reasons, the policy of the Orléans, a cousin and rival branch of the royal family, had been to oppose aristocratic standards. The cultural terrain was all the more important in that it could appear 'innocent'.[61] The future Philippe-Egalité knew how, in this regard, to make a public demonstration of certain attitudes. Tronchin and Desessarts,[62] for example, were the Orléans family doctors, and Mme de Genlis, governess to the three sons, scrupulously applied the rules of the hygienists. Attending the school of swimming was a clear sign of an adherence. And the cold bath, though limited, was no longer simply a matter of theory.

---

[57]   Macquart, *Manuel sur les propriétés de l'eau*, p. 347.

[58]   Turquin, *Avis au public*, p. 1.

[59]   *Ibid.*, p. 3.

[60]   General Thibault, in his *Mémoires* published in 1893, records several anecdotal scenes from the swimming school, where he came into contact with the Orléans children (vol. 1, pp. 198ff.). Cf. also Arnaud: 'Master Turquin, without consulting me, created a swimming school for the rich, not for the children of the people' (text of 1790, p. x).

[61]   Cf. J. Defrance, 'Esquisse d'une histoire sociale de la gymnastique', *Actes de la recherche en sciences sociales* (Paris, 1976), no. 6.

[62]   Tronchin, *Un médecin du XVIIIe siècle*, p. 86.

VISIONS OF INVIGORATED BODIES

Such practices, though still rare, confirmed the status of cold water after 1760. Though an element in a new type of bathing, it was not really a question of cleanliness. Too many other aims were involved, and too many justifications. It was not a neutral substance, but something still surprising and strange, which set in train multiple effects, and was difficult to control. An almost unnatural milieu for the body, it had to be tamed. At this point, actual practices are significant. They emphasise that the hygienic recommendations had gone beyond simple literary references or rhetoric. What is more important, they emphasise how the public concerned was directly influenced by an enlightened bourgeoisie, exploiting concepts of vigour and robustness. It is the social significance of these concepts which best enables us to understand how they were viewed and evaluate their impact. It is they which express most clearly the birth of an entirely new image of the body. They are its most suggestive expression. The cold bath was primarily, and in essence, the indicator of a code, hitherto unknown, of bodily efficiency.

The transformation in bathing children is particularly revealing and provides the clearest expression of the new code. Baths for children were rare in France in the sixteenth and seventeenth centuries, though they existed (they were common, in particular, immediately after birth). They involved two procedures, both of which were expressly affected by the changes of the second half of the eighteenth century, that is, washing in a warm and protective liquid, then stopping up the pores with sticky substances to give better protection and strength. Concern with the bodily openings was dominant. Ambroise Paré expressed it unequivocally: 'The child [at birth] should be cleaned with oil of roses or bilberries to remove the dirt and excrements which it bears on its skin; also to close the pores so that afterwards its constitution will be rendered firmer.'[63]

The complex relationship between bathing and firmness was not new. It was not the concept of strengthening which was original in the arguments of Tronchin and his friends. There was a long tradition of wishing to strengthen children's bodies, which were manipulated in the desire to achieve hardness. The body itself, however, was passive, and submitted to the protective hand. To make it firm meant

---

[63] Paré, *Oeuvres*, p. 947.

primarily closing the pores; strengthening it meant coating it or stopping up the holes. The analogy was with objects which needed to be closed. An alien hand worked on the skin, hardened it, and managed it. It did not lack tools: thick oils, waxes, salts, even dross of saltpetre. Once the pores had been treated, the flux of the humours, by their movement, made possible new strengthening, thickening or fluidity. The hand manipulated the skin and controlled its outlets.

The myth of the cold bath, however, turned this picture on its head. It supposed a body endowed with a pre-existing power, not an inert mass. It possessed innate resistance, internal resources, hidden strengths. 'There exists no other natural warmth for a child than its own, and that is enough.'[64] To plunge it into cold water, then, was to trust in precisely that obscure energy which the preceding century had denied. The body was no longer a passive substance; from its first day, it possessed an inherent strength which only had to be liberated. The ways of augmenting this were equally new. There was, for example, no longer recourse to an alien hand; strength came from within. It came from the repeated reactions of the organs themselves. It was these repeated contractions which fortified, not external manipulation. Strength came from within the body.

The image was sometimes intuitive, giving priority to hidden strengths, or dreaming of Roman toughness; physical and moral designs combined to confront hostile matter. The image was sometimes more concrete, detailing how cold instigated this vital force. It was a matter of discovering particular organic reactions, playing on the originality of the living being, recognising a physiological autonomy, describing this 'reactive' place. Already, according to the *Encyclopédie*, the cold bath instigated a precise physical response. 'By keeping the vessels in a highly constricted state, and by thus achieving an increased strength, the cold bath occasions more action and more effort in consequence on the part of the motor power to conquer them, hence the augmentation of the progressive movement of the humours.'[65] The same ideas are found in Maret; the irritability attributed to muscle by Haller enabled him to evoke an autonomy of physical reaction. Cold had become a stimulant. It worked through soliciting. It challenged. The mechanical metaphors only emphasised the importance of the sequences. 'The effect of these actions is proportionate to the force of the stimulants which set them

---

[64] Fourcroy de Guillerville, *Les enfants élevés dans l'ordre de la nature*, p. 107.
[65] Article on 'Froid' in the *Encyclopédie*, vol. 7, p. 323.

going . . . The effect of the cold in condensing the solids and fluids increases their force.'[66] Similar ideas are found in Hufeland, who even divided the dynamic polarities between 'external' and 'internal', those which assisted the body, and those born of it. Bodily strength came not from the hand which sustained it, but from an invisible internal energy; it was a question of interpellation rather than assistance. Cold was simply an appeal to these latent strengths. 'I know nothing so pernicious, nothing which encapsulates so perfectly the idea of weakness and infirmity as the characteristic of human nature become almost general in our time, of acting from the exterior on the interior . . . We must remember that, by constant and often excessive warmth, we do everything, from the beginning, to relax the skin and deprive it of its strength.'[67] The cold bath, in contrast, provoked response and innate strength. It replaced the actions designed to reinforce. External assistance was succeeded by internal action, management of something inert by a challenge to the living.

The reversal of the image also makes it easier to understand the possibility, even the success, of inoculation in the second half of the eighteenth century. Inoculation, after all, worked through bodily 'resistance'. This practice, in which the skin was cut open for some purulent fragments of smallpox spots to be inserted, supposed a confidence just as obscure, but also just as real, in a reactive organic strength. The hygiene of the cold bath closely resembled this new preventive practice. All the defences that the body opposed to sickness had to be re-thought. Operating through the openings, or through the mechanics of the coverings, was no longer all that was possible. Attempts to make clothing into a barrier against unwholesome air were in part out-dated. The body was no longer simply a passive machine. Other strategies existed. It became possible to make use of the body's own strengths, to solicit, once again, internal and active dispositions. This did not happen by chance; the hygienists of the cold bath and those of inoculation were often the same people. It comes as no surprise that Tronchin inoculated the Orléans children in 1756. Inoculation, like cold, supposed an initial resistance to illness, and it was operating on this resistance that produced strength.[68]

The concept of the cold bath thus only illustrates a profound

[66] Maret, *Mémoire*, p. 21.

[67] G. G. Hufeland, *Avis aux mères sur les points les plus importants de l'éducation physique des enfants* (Paris, 1800, 1st ed. in German, 1796), pp. 19–20.

[68] For inoculation at the end of the eighteenth century, cf. J.-F. de Raymond, *La Querelle de l'inoculation* (Paris, 1982).

transformation of the images regulating the employment and the strength of the body. The real change was social: the belief in an autonomous strength, invented by a bourgeoisie confident of its own physical power, and confident, above all, of powers totally independent of the ties and codes of blood. This strength was present in all bodies; it should therefore be solicited, trusted and put to work. It had to be believed in. It hardly mattered that it was more in the mind than a matter of actual practice. The belief grew and spread. The body concealed powers which could be utilised. It was this same dynamic, finally, which in the second half of the eighteenth century discredited the aristocratic code of appearance and manners. The process was all the more important in that cleanliness now derived from that which liberated. To be clean was soon to mean removing whatever fixed and constrained the appearance, in favour of whatever freed it.

9. *Nature and artifice*

The rupture which, especially after 1760, dissociated the new 'vigour' from aristocratic 'softness', was accompanied by an antithesis with greater significance for cleanliness: the contrast between nature and artifice. A nature itself contrived, certainly, but whose success, especially by the end of the century, extended well beyond the ranks of the bourgeoisie. When the Baronne d'Oberkirch left Versailles in the small hours of the morning of 9 June 1782, after the ball given for the future Tzar of Russia, she emphasised almost in spite of herself, how prevalent was this theme in aristocratic culture. The description she gave of the peasants encountered on the road to Paris, and her caustic comments on the powder and paint of her companions, are shot through by an image of nature.

Day had broken and the peasants were starting on their daily labour. What a contrast between their calm and contented faces and our tired visages: the rouge had fallen from our cheeks, the powder from our hair. The return from a party is not a pretty sight, and can inspire many philosophical reflections in those with a mind to it.[1]

The 'natural' reference here is without social implications. The Baronne was far from calling into question her milieu. She was quite capable, on occasion, of mocking the *philosophes*. She detested Rousseau. She laughed at the education given to the Orléans children by Mme de Genlis. But, on the themes of the body and of appearance, the memoirs she left in 1787 are hopelessly ambivalent; there is an obsessive interest, for example, in the tools which traditionally composed noble faces, but denigration of these same tools; a fascination for powders, starch and wigs, yet a denunciation of their role, even a fear of their effects: of cosmetics damaging or clogging up the skin, of artifices 'serving to spoil what nature has made'.[2] The gradual transformation of attitudes towards the materials employed

[1] Baronne A. d'Oberkirch, *Mémoires* (Paris, 1970, 1st ed. 1787), p. 199.
[2] *Ibid.*

to produce classical appearance had, by the end of the century, reached even court circles.

There can be no doubt that this critique had originally possessed social significance. It had long mocked 'the little masters, elegant and elaborately got-up'.[3] It was against them that the crescendo of accusations against artifice, and against appearance deemed too elaborate or affected, had been directed. It had been through them, also, that the aristocratic code of manners had been perceived. The opposition between vigour and delicacy could only play variations on these emergent themes: simplicity as opposed to affectation, spontaneity as opposed to disguise. Wigs, powdered heads and coloured substances on the cheeks all fell into disfavour in their turn because of their excessive artificiality. The 'pyramids of curls'[4] were inconvenient as well as changing the hair. 'Nature' was deemed to be lost to the point of degeneracy. They were all reprehensible signs of luxury. Only weakness and vanity were to be found in these 'scented powders and pomades which fatuity has unfortunately seen fit to invent and which the sensuality of the rich employs in their toilet with a profusion as dangerous as it is reprehensible'.[5] It was because they were also the subject of a social critique that cosmetics signified softness and debility.

These themes were all the more important in that by restoring a distance between nature and artifice, they overthrew cleanliness's frame of reference. Calling into question the code of appearances and dress, for example, denouncing the primacy of vestimentary values, was to affirm other values, issuing from within. The condition of the skin, for example, was more important than the substances which coloured it, and natural hair than the various contrivances which substituted for it. It was in polemicising against worldly sophistication that Rousseau insisted on Sophie's cleanliness. He made it an alternative to artificial coquetry, a sign written 'on her person' itself.[6] He elaborated on it, insistently extending his own dreams of trees and gardens, playing on the metaphor of sap and roses, exhausting analogies with the countryside and the fields: 'Sophie knew only the perfume of flowers and her husband breathed nothing so sweet as her

[3] Mercier, *Tableau de Paris*, vol. 1, p. 94.
[4] A. Riballier, *De l'éducation physique et morale des femmes* (Brussels, 1779), p. 38.
[5] A. Ganne, *L'Homme physique et moral* (Strasbourg, 1791), p. 43.
[6] Rousseau, *L'Emile*, p. 500.

breath.'[7] Cleanliness was opposed to 'vain affectation'.[8] It was not at this point contrasted with loathsome dirt. There was no question, in 1762 or for many years after, for example, of attacking the deficiencies of the poor, or of assessing the danger of a 'filthy' peasantry. A whole range of practices had yet to be defined as deficient. It was not in opposition to this that militant cleanliness was born. It was a paradoxical response to excessively elaborate dress and over-refined artifice. It stood against superficial appearances, and, above all, against the status of display. The issue, it must be remembered, was one of distinctions. It was here that there began a very special rapprochement between hygiene and cleanliness.

HEALTH VERSUS COSMETICS

Before even being a simple critique of fashion, the denunciation of the excess of powder and pomades raised questions of health. By preventing the issue of the humours, for example, certain artifices might constrain them into unnatural journeys. The explanation was mechanical; the natural fluxes might be impeded inside heads plastered with diverse substances. The congealed powders might act as a barrier. The fluxes might be compelled to search out different outlets, or corrupt the blood, or swamp other organs, or induce pain, or multiply ills. They might cause unexpected swellings and spread inflammations. There was no telling where they might travel, and poison:

> The perspiration intercepted by the accumulation of powder congealed with pomade and sweat flows back into the neighbouring parts and causes catarrhs, disorders of the throat, the ears, the eyes . . . I have seen a boy of ten die from an abcess on his throat caused by his dirtiness. It had been so long since he had been combed . . . The humour had flowed back into his throat and he died of the abcesses it had formed.[9]

The accumulation of cosmetics upset the internal relationships. In consequence disequilibriums were created and strength sapped; they

---

[7] *Ibid.*

[8] Cf. Riballier, *De l'éducation physique at morale*, p. 64: 'I shall certainly be criticised for taking my examples only from the class of rich people, which I freely admit. But do I need to say that I have chosen this class deliberately because it is the class which gives a lead to all those below it. The whole world is today infected and degraded by the contagion of their bad example' (pp. 64–5).

[9] Jacquin, *De la santé*, pp. 291–2.

disturbed. They could produce 'a thick layer of filth whose effect was to prevent sweating'.[10] As with coldness, there was an affirmation of forces and functions which artifice seemed likely to stifle, and a simultaneous emphasis on the danger of a concern limited exclusively to appearance. Beyond appearance, other issues and, in particular, other forces, were at stake. 'The mass of pomades and powders that most wig-makers employ . . . weigh down the head, block the pores and frequently cause migraines and disorders of the head which turn the hair white or soon cause it to fall out.'[11] To suppress or reduce artifice was thus to permit a liberation, a less constrained attitude; it was to enfranchise, to refuse a constraint. The 'pound of powder and pomade which the least movement caused to fall onto the shoulders', for example, became too much of an encumbrance.[12] These criticisms joined forces with those of corsets and stifling clothes.[13]

A chemistry still in its infancy also influenced these ideas. The argument was one of substances which corroded, their 'acridity can irritate the nerves'.[14] The very composition of the artifices employed gave cause for concern. Might they not attack the skin and cause it to suffer irreparable damage? One should fear, in particular, substances 'made of lead, ceruse, lead vinegar, magisterium, flowers of bismuth or other such, which are, in truth, the most beautiful of all whites, but which, by their saline, poisonous, arsenical, indelible constituents incurably impair and spoil the complexion'.[15] Cinnabar similarly 'wore away' the skin.[16] There were 'sulphurous substances'[17] alleged to threaten the chest and the eyes. Chemistry came to the aid of nature. In 1789, the *Encyclopédie méthodique* was unequivocal. 'Most cosmetics are made of minerals which are more or less harmful, but always corrosive, and disastrous effects are inseparable from their use.'[18]

Eventually, at the end of the eighteenth century, the arguments of

[10] Le Bègue de Presle, *Le Conservateur de la santé*, p. 340.
[11] *Le Médecin des hommes depuis la puberté jusqu'à l'extrême vieillesse* (Paris, 1772), p. 413.
[12] Marquise de La Tour du Pin, *Mémoires* (Paris, 1979, 1st ed. 1907), p. 39.
[13] The two themes emerge at the same time, especially after 1760. Cf. the authors already quoted, and, among others, Desessarts, Tronchin, Riballier, Jacquin and Rousseau.   [14] Mercier, *Tableau de Paris*, vol. 4, p. 125.
[15] L. de Jaucourt, article on 'Cosmétique' in the *Encyclopédie*, vol. 4, p. 292.
[16] L. de Jaucourt, article on 'Fard' in the *Encyclopédie*, vol. 6, p. 410.
[17] de Jaucourt, 'Cosmétique', p. 292.
[18] Article on 'Art du parfumeur' in the *Encyclopédie méthodique* (Paris, 1789), vol. 6, p. 31.

hygienists and followers of fashion converged. Powder and cosmetics no longer enjoyed their former role. The faces of the nobility, of women in particular, lost their paint in favour of less striking colours. In 1785, the Duc de Lévis mocked a duchess glimpsed at the house of the Maréchal de Richelieu, whose face 'was covered with a thick layer of white, set off by two patches of brilliant red'.[19] Similarly, Mme de Genlis laughed at her grandmother, who had recourse to 'an enormous quantity of red and white'.[20] In the same way, a certain dancing-master, 'a fine man admirably coiffed and powdered with white',[21] became, by 1787, simply ridiculous. The Marquise de La Tour du Pin described him calculating every gesture to prevent his powder falling. She immediately detected hesitation in his manners and constraint in his expressions. She deemed his neck too stiff and his features too well-defined.[22] Crayon was more suited to the portraits of Vigée-Lebrun after 1780 than to those of Boucher or Nattier, with their greater contrasts, a few decades earlier.[23] The change shows most dramatically in children's clothes. The opposition between vigour and softness, simplicity and affectation, nature and artifice, applied here with especial force. A pedagogic dream, no doubt playing on the supposed plasticity of childhood, the standards were clearer.

One no longer sprinkles their heads with white as was hitherto the practice. They used to be quite disfigured with those pomaded rolls, those curls, and all that paraphernalia. Nothing was more ridiculous than these tiny creatures with a purse, a hat under the arm and a sword at their side. Since the revolution in hair, children have their hair styled in a round, well cut, very clean and powdered.[24]

The sentiment was common. Mercier used similar words to emphasise 'fair hair hanging naturally'.[25] Noble and bourgeois children were no longer the same after 1780.

The language of fashion explicitly exploited the word 'nature'. White powder 'hardened' and 'disfigured'.[26] It falsified features, rather than flattered them. For those who wanted to retain powdered

---

[19] Duc de Levis, *Souvenirs et Portraits* (1780–9) (Paris, 1815), p. 48.
[20] Mme S. F. de Genlis, *Mémoires* (Paris, 1825), vol. 1, p. 274.
[21] Marquise de La Tour du Pin, *Mémoires*, p. 75.   [22] *Ibid.*
[23] Cf. F. Boucher, 'La Marquise de Pompadour' (1759), London, Wallace Collection.
[24] Baronne d'Oberkirch, *Mémoires*, p. 295.
[25] Mercier, *Tableau de Paris*, vol. 5, p. 77.
[26] *Cabinet des modes* (Paris, 1785–6), p. 115.

hair at whatever cost, however, better to use a light-coloured cosmetic, lightly sprinkled. This respected the natural colouring, whilst giving 'greater softness to the face'.[27] The partial use of powder was thus itself coded. Similarly, the *Affiches et Annonces de Paris* cautiously refrained from recommending any but 'vegetable' whites and reds.[28] Fashionable man was incapable of condemning cosmetics outright. Such advice demonstrates the extent to which the argument between nature and artifice had, in the second half of the eighteenth century, transformed the criteria of distinction.

It was precisely this transformation which could change conceptions of cleanliness. It was the explicit attention paid to what was behind appearance which could call into question the long relationship between cleanliness and dress, imposing on clothes other criteria than simply those of show. Surfaces and perfumes could no longer stand alone. The scene had changed. Classical distinction, that of the seventeenth and early eighteenth centuries, was no longer achieved through profile but through structure. The assumptions underlying it began to collapse. The meaning of the word cleanliness changed in its turn. The *Encyclopédie* discovered this in 1765: 'Cleanliness should not be confused with the quest for luxury, affectation in dress, perfumes, scents; all these exquisite attentions of sensibility are not sufficiently refined to deceive the eye; too inconvenient for everyday life, they betray the motive which gave them birth.'[29] Cleanliness was no longer exclusively expressed in vestimentary signs. It had a more directly bodily manifestation – a significance obvious today, but which it took this lengthy attack on the dominance of appearance and profile to realise. Cleanliness was so much the less dependent on superficial appearance in that it could undo it. Just one example, in this series of displacements: the interpretation given by Mercier to the changing faces. 'It seems as if short hair intends to take over the empire: cleanliness, convenience, saving in time, perhaps even health, demand this fashion, because the head needs to breathe, which means it has to be perfectly clean.'[30] Wigs and powders, profiles and perfumes were no longer the foundation of cleanliness, they depended on it. In the same way, recourse to make-up required a prior condition. Mercier sang its praises when listing the whites and

27   *Cabinet des modes* (1786), p. 43.
28   *Affiches et Annonces de Paris* (Paris, 1773), pp. 132, 179; *ibid.* (1780), pp. 139, 208.
29   Article on 'Propreté' in the *Encyclopédie* (1765), vol. 13, p. 490.
30   Mercier, *Tableau de Paris*, vol. 11, p. 79.

the reds, their blending and their effect: 'What gives a woman real style: cleanliness, cleanliness, cleanliness.'[31]

With perfume there changed a major reference point whose significance is particularly revealing. An entirely surface effect, perfume could now only deceive. 'The smells belong less to cleanliness than to a certain depraved taste or a certain concept of fashion, of which the little masters are the arbiters.'[32] Criticisms multiplied of 'the smell of the essences and the powders perfumed with amber',[33] of the 'danger' of aromatics,[34] of the troubles and the 'vapours' provoked by musk,[35] all substances which enervated and enfeebled, all practices which went against nature. This extended even to innocent concoctions of rose petals, which 'could make you fall into a decline'.[36] Bomare, in his *Dictionnaire d'histoire naturelle* of 1764, seemed to delight in offering proofs of such affectations, comparing the limited sense of smell of man with that of the animals. Infirmity had only one source: 'the excess of strong odours with which men are constantly surrounded'.[37] This had already been affirmed by Buffon, referring, not without irritation, to that 'fury with which we try to destroy ourselves',[38] by recklessly seeking out smells. Heady perfume was effeminate. To which was added the suspicions about cleanliness which it might arouse; just as 'false beauty' produced 'an effect more repellant than the worst ugliness'.[39]

The artifice of perfume also seemed poles apart from the bourgeois spirit which was soon to triumph. Perfume vanished and evaporated, a symbol of waste and loss. It was not only superficial, it was evanescent. It was squandered. It dispersed with a fleeting and irreversible volatility; the antithesis of accumulation and saving.

---

[31] *Ibid.*, vol. 11, p. 72.   [32] Jacquin, *De la santé*, p. 290.
[33] Mercier, *Tableau de Paris*, vol. 1, p. 94.
[34] J.-C. Bomare, article on 'Aromate' in *Dictionnaire d'histoire naturelle* (Paris, 1764), vol. 1, p. 335.
[35] Pomme, *Traité des affections vaporeuses*, p. 423. Cf. also the article on 'Musc' in the *Encyclopédie*, vol. 10, p. 881.
[36] P. V. de Sèze, *Recherches physiologiques et philosophiques sur la sensibilité ou la vie animale* (Paris, 1786), p. 236.
[37] J.-C. Bomare, article on 'Homme', in *Dictionnaire d'histoire naturelle*, vol. 4, p. 436.
[38] G.-L. de Buffon, *Discours sur la nature des animaux* (1735) in 'Oeuvres philosophiques' (Paris, 1954), p. 331.
[39] Bernardin de Saint-Pierre, *Etudes sur la nature* (Paris, 1838, 1st ed. 1820), p. 203.

Perfume diffused and escaped. This instability was now a source of disappointment. These criticisms have been vividly commented on by Corbin. 'There is something intolerable for the bourgeois in experiencing the disappearance in this manner of the hoarded products of his labour. Perfume, accused of betraying softness, disorder and a taste for pleasure, is the antithesis of work.'[40] It thus doubled the negative effects of the values of appearance.

A similar disqualification inevitably applied to certain actions hitherto thought of as purifying. Before, perfume could correct body smells by modifying their intimate substance. It combatted unpleasant odours because it attacked their very substance. In a sense, it even washed. Its application alone cleansed and purified. It actually transformed the source of the unpleasant air. But it now 'lost all its value'[41] in acting against unwholesome air and noisome emanations. Another element in the toilet and even in hygienic practices disappeared. The effect of perfume was no longer to purify. It did not act on the very essence of the air. And, above all, it could not reach the source of the unpleasantness. 'All it does is substitute a pleasant smell for a fetid smell, it only masks the smell, it does not destroy putrid miasmas.'[42] At the very most its role was to disguise. The preferable response was to suppress the source of the evil smells and renew the surrounding atmosphere. It was better to open the window of a sickroom, mocked Tissot, than burn perfume there.[43] Scientific argument and sensibility converged. Perfume was even less efficacious in that it misled by its showy effects. It was doubly deceptive; it both enfeebled and gave an illusion of a real correction of unhealthiness. Frivolity and impotence converged. 'The pot-pourris so delightful in their refinement and the combination of their spices are often more inclined to harm the delicate, empty and exhausted brains of those idle deities than restore the freshness of the air.'[44]

THE INTERNAL VERSUS APPEARANCES

There remain certain exceptions to these denunciations, but they only confirm in their own way the appeal of nature. Mme Necker

---

[40] A. Corbin, *Le Miasme et la Jonquille* (Paris, 1982), p. 81.

[41] Article on 'Musc' in the *Encyclopédie*, p. 881.

[42] F. Vicq-d'Azir, *Instructions sur la manière de désinfecter une paroisse* (Paris, 1775), p. 8.   [43] Tissot, *Avis au peuple*, vol. 1, p. 100.

[44] Jacquin, *De la santé*, p. 290.

dreamed, in her memoirs, of essences 'simple' enough to imitate 'the smell of earth dampened by rain'.[45] Jaucourt, fulminating in the *Encyclopédie* against aromatics and cosmetics, excepted certain extracts of flowers and fruits 'such as, for example, strawberry water, lavender water, water distilled from beans'.[46] Jacquin, though exploiting the almost moral censure of perfume, also suggested several exceptions: 'We must not, however, proscribe all smells indiscriminately: some are sweet and agreeable and compatible with cleanliness: eau-de-vie of lavender is one.'[47] The pursuit of nature sometimes even imposed more complex artifices, such as the employment, in 1782, of tiny phials concealed in the hair, so that natural, fresh flowers could keep their stems in water.[48] The perfume was meant to espouse the energy of the sap. Cleanliness was associated with spring-like essences, with things brimming with life, with, most of all, a bodily strength. It meant dynamism and vigour.

A new autonomy was attributed to the body; it was desirable to separate it from its array of protectors and develop its innate qualities, accord a value to a vitality independent of dress and get-up. Freshness, cleanliness and even style, all now had organic connotations. Here lay the new worth. It stood in opposition to the old values of appearance, affirming a strength which was more internal. This is not to say, obviously, that this value was clearly defined, even less that it meant something close to the cleanliness of today. There is little washing, for example, in Rousseau, apart from a handful of references to cold baths in infancy. Water is not mentioned in connection with Julie's toilet. The transformation operating here was more a question of simplicity. 'She rediscovers the art of enhancing her natural graces without concealing them; when she emerged from her toilet, she was dazzling.'[49] Nor was much said about the socially sanitary role of cleanliness, even though cleanliness was being so obviously promoted. Tissot himself, listing in 1765 the causes of sickness amongst the people, mentioned drunkenness and excessive labour, but neither cleanliness nor dirt.[50]

But the opposition between nature and artifice, and between

---

[45] Mme S. C. Necker, *Mélanges extraits des manuscrits de Mme Necker* (Paris, year VI), vol. 1, p. 262.

[46] de Jaucourt, 'Cosmétique', p. 291.   [47] Jacquin, *De la santé*, p. 291.

[48] Baronne d'Oberkirch, *Mémoires*, p. 194.

[49] J.-J. Rousseau, *Julie ou la Nouvelle Héloïse*, (Paris, 1960, 1st ed. 1760), p. 530.

[50] Tissot, *Avis au peuple*, vol. 1, p. 101.

simplicity and affectation, important as early as 1760 but more pronounced after 1780, marked a change in sensibility with regard to cleanliness. It was a transformation all the more important in that it engendered new ways of thinking – attention to the body and displays of strength (albeit formal); cleanliness now belonged more to the sphere of medicine than of manners. It was less a matter of dress than a matter of health. It affected the regime of the humours, the control of the limbs, the actual physical condition of the body. It concerned the interior rather than the surface alone. The doctor, B. C. Faust, launched an appeal in 1792: 'Our clothes are like fetters, they are the invention of the barbarian and Gothic centuries. You must break these fetters if you wish to become free and happy.'[51] This appeal had its parallel in the 'life' of the skin: to attack body dirt was to give greater strength to the functions and greater liberty to the body. Cleanliness was no longer only a matter of the visible.

Treatises on hygiene once again rationalised the image of the pores. Keeping them in good order ensured that perspiration could escape, whilst assuring greater fluidity to the blood. In the face of the old visions of swellings and circulatory obstructions, arising from the discovery of Harvey,[52] in the seventeenth century, in the face of the diffuse risks of blockages and plethoras, cleanliness now acquired a stronger legitimacy. It facilitated the excretion of the humours and the movement of the blood. It was firmly functional. It protected the body by assisting its physiology. It fostered the circulation and internal movement, even helping to 'prevent sickness'.[53] It facilitated the 'insensible perspiration which is more important than all other evacuations'.[54] The emphasis on perspiration was not new, but it was now related to cleanliness in a more systematic fashion, and the justification of cleanliness itself became more functional; as a result of it, the organic evacuations would be more regular and better maintained. Care of the skin would guarantee this. The argument was similar to that for the cold bath. Just as a cold bath strengthened the fibres, cleanliness indirectly strengthened the functions. 'The foundation of health is the regularity with which perspiration takes place, to achieve this regularity it is necessary to strengthen the skin.'[55] Dirt

[51]   B.-C. Faust, *Sur le vêtement libre, unique et national à l'usage des enfants* (Paris, 1792). See also Perrot, *Le Travail des apparences*, who quotes Faust, p. 103.

[52]   W. Harvey, *De motu cordis et sanguinis in animalibus* (Frankfurt, 1628).

[53]   F. Frier, *Guide pour la conservation de l'homme* (Paris, 1789), p. 74.

[54]   *Ibid.*, p. 33.   [55]   Tissot, *Avis au peuple*, vol. 2, p. 62.

was dangerous because it blocked the surface exits. Strange tumours might result, swellings fed by the humours, or abcesses, the body swollen by internal pressures. To be clean, on the other hand, was to free the skin. 'It is necessary to keep the feet clean: the least dirt interrupts the perspiration and produces corns and painful and inconvenient swellings.'[56] Cleanliness, which in the seventeenth century was primarily aesthetic and a matter of manners, was clearly moving in the direction of functionalism.

The questioning of cosmetics and powders, in particular for the face, and also of appearance and get-up, the concern with body dirt, thus had their theoretical dimension: the liberation of the surfaces of the body the better to permit evacuation. It must be emphasised that this new thesis does not imply an immediate revolution in habits of washing. Scholarly treatises at the end of the 1770s remained evasive on the frequency of baths. 'Everyone has their own rule for baths: some take one every eight days, others every ten, others once a month, and many every year for eight or ten days in succession, when the weather is most suitable.'[57] Care of the skin could still to a large extent, and certainly for most people, be equated with care of linen. But the transformation of faces is a clear sign of a change in mentality. The reasoning based on health, though theoretical and preoccupied with often imaginary mechanisms, is another important indicator. There was born, after 1760, at least the possibility of an entirely new cleanliness.

[56] Jacquin, *De la santé*, p. 289.   [57] M. Dejean, *Traité des odeurs* (1777), p. 467.

10. *The stench of towns and people*

The foundation of *La Gazette de santé* in 1773 confirms a major shift in thinking in the last third of the eighteenth century. Produced 'for curés, seigneurs, charitable ladies and farmers',[1] it seemed intended to overthrow the traditional fatalism shown towards death and disease. It called on eminent people to heed the advice of doctors. By recommending new precautions in infancy, or arguing for healthier housing and towns, *La Gazette* encouraged concern. It propagated rules of hygiene and promoted sensibility to the theme of cleanliness. It discussed physical education for children and debated sources of contagion. The measures 'helping to maintain health'[2] masked social preoccupations. *La Gazette* was designed to inform and publicise. Its readers were to be relay stations; with its brief articles and simple formulas, it aimed to reach a wide audience. Local initiatives soon followed, such as the *Journal de santé* in Bordeaux in 1785,[3] and in Lyons in 1793.[4]

Such enterprises assumed an objective which was itself novel: to influence popular life-expectancy. The aim was to increase the population, to affect what Moheau had already called the 'lifespan'.[5] To record epidemics, attack uncontrolled disease and improve health was to exercise an indirect effect on the size of the population. To the old fight against suffering was added the more abstract fight against declining population. It was the population as a quantifiable entity which lay at the heart of these preoccupations. This supposes a new

---

[1] *La Gazette de santé* (Paris, 1773), 'Préface'.
[2] *Ibid.*, (1785), prospectus. [3] *Journal de santé* (Bordeaux, 1785).
[4] 'Création de la société de santé à Lyon en 1793', *Journal de santé* (Bordeaux, year I), p. 97.
[5] M. Moheau, *Recherches et Considérations sur la population de la France* (Paris, 1778), vol. 1, p. 191.

focus on the human mass. 'Men are the real wealth of States and it is this which is most neglected.'[6]

In this respect, the *Gazette* was only one amongst many consequences of this new demographic consciousness. The creation of the Royal Society of Medicine in 1776, the enquiries into epidemics which it was required to conduct and the fashion for medical topographies recording mortality in town and country are all evidence of this new awareness.[7] The population was seen as a specific resource. 'We must multiply subjects and beasts.'[8] Their lifespan must also be increased. This consciousness gradually took hold, especially after 1760, and is demonstrated by the first calculations of mortality and the first tables comparing births and deaths. The physiocrats obviously contributed to these perceptions by linking the wealth of the land and the profitability of people. 'The number of people who can wield a spade, drive a plough, work at a trade, bear arms, and, lastly, reproduce themselves: such is the basis of the power of nations.'[9] At a deeper level, it was the requirements of contemporary states which were emerging, requirements which treat the population as an anonymous force, whose potential is primarily to be measured in terms of its labour power.

The reasoning behind measures to organise collective sanitation was economic. It was aimed primarily at a transformation in the hygiene of groups and communities.[10] Prevention began to produce political policies in which administrators and doctors played key roles. Prevention gradually involved cleanliness to the point where it gained a new role in 'public health'.[11] It was a modest role as yet, certainly, because work on contagion and epidemics consisted primarily of work on climate. The old Hippocratic categories, taking account of weather and places, were far from being forgotten.

---

[6] Vandermonde, *Essai sur la manière de perfectionner l'espèce humaine*, vol. 1, p. 31.
[7] Cf. J.-P. Meyer, 'Une enquête de l'académie de Médecine sur les épidémies (1774–1794)', *Annales ESC* (Paris, 1966); J.-P. Peter, 'Enquête de la Société royale de Médecine (1774–1794)', *Annales ESC* (Paris, 1967).
[8] Turneau de La Morandière (1763), quoted by B. Barret Kriegel, 'L'hôpital comme équipement', *Les Machines à guérir* (Paris, Institut de l'environnement, 1976), p. 28.
[9] Moheau, *Recherches et Considérations sur la population*, vol. 1, p. 17.
[10] The approach to the theme of individual cleanliness through collective living conditions is deliberate. This approach is fundamental, even if only touched on here. Cf. M. Foucault, 'La politique de santé au xviiie siècle', *Les Machines à guérir*, p. 11.
[11] J.-J. Menuret, *Essais sur l'histoire médico-topographique de Paris* (Paris, 1786), p. 88.

Daignan, Razou and Lepecq[12] constructed their tables of mortality with reference to seasonal variations. It was the dampness or coldness of fogs, changing according to the month, which explained differential death rates, and the wind blowing from the marshes which explained the variable incidence of fevers. Research was concentrated on fluctuations of temperature and the fickleness of seasons; it was for ever measuring the dryness or humidity of soils, or bogged down in the instability of calms and gales.

But work on contagion, probably assisted by the investigations of chemists, also quickly became work on over-crowding, on smells, and on unwholesome exhalations. By a roundabout route, the way was prepared for an interest in cleanliness.

THE LOCALISATION OF UNHEALTHINESS

A story repeated hundreds of times after 1770, so often that its actual location became irrelevant, described a putrid emanation spreading death within a confined space. In the month of June 1774, some children were peacefully gathered in the church of Saulieu in Burgundy for their first communion. An 'evil exhalation' suddenly arose from a tomb dug that very day beneath the tiles of the church. The effluvium spread and its consequences, or so it appeared, were catastrophic. 'The curé, the vicar, forty children and two hundred parishioners who went inside, died.'[13] The story, almost mythical, was taken seriously, made an example of, and widely disseminated. The smell of decomposing flesh could be fatal. The dead physically threatened the living.

The hermetically sealed bells of Hales and Priestley,[14] in which experimental animals were doomed to die, poisoned by their own breath, sparked off a proliferation of corresponding images. Men died in confined spaces, of obscure bodily exhalations; their breath carried the poison of corrupt matter. Between this breath and the stink of corruption, whether of rubbish or of dead flesh, every

[12] J. Razou, *Tableau nosologique et météorologique* (Basel, 1767); L. Lepecq de la Clôture, *Collections d'observations sur les maladies et constitutions épidémiques* (Paris, 1778), 2 vols.; G. Daignan, *Tableau des variétés de la vie humaine* (Paris, 1786).

[13] J.-B. Banau and A.-F. Turben, *Mémoire sur les épidémies du Languedoc* (Paris, 1786), pp. 12–13.

[14] S. Hales, *Description of ventilators* (London, 1743); J. Priestley, *Experiments and observations on different kinds of air* (London, 1772).

possible analogy was drawn. Unwholesome emanations, decay, rotting objects, could all, in their turn, kill.[15] Cemeteries, like town drains containing faecal matter, rapidly spread 'their polluted air, dangerous in all weathers and all places'.[16] Recording the seasons was no longer enough. Corbin has convincingly shown the important role of what was already a detailed analysis of the atmosphere in this perception of disease. It was its decomposition, its stagnation, its fetidness, which caused death. The effluvium in itself was menacing, the smell gave concrete expression to the danger. Another frequently-repeated story illustrated death caused by cesspools or anything saturated by their contents. 'On 13 July, 1779, the gardener of the hospital at Béziers was struck dead by the noxious gas coming from water intended to water the garden; the water used for this purpose was carried in a drain into which also ran some of the water that ran through the streets.'[17] When, in 1780, the wall of a Parisian cellar finally collapsed under the weight of the neighbouring tombs, many witnesses told how the smell had asphyxiated the owner.[18] The danger, once again, came from an accumulation of dead bodies. Such fears continued to intensify.

What had been perceived as the almost inevitable accompaniment of the human environment, commonplace by reason of its constant proximity, passed over the threshold of tolerability: stinking towns, piles of rubbish, the stench of stagnant water. Death haunted filthy places. The stench was not only unpleasant, it was dangerous. Certain parts of towns became intolerable, such as the pavements where 'rubbish mixed with the water of the gutters, and especially with the greasy water from kitchens, forms that stinking mud which the considerable quantity of iron in it renders black and murky';[19] or the sites where animals were slaughtered, 'where animal matter lies about causing putrid fevers';[20] or the places where large numbers of bodies

[15] See, in particular, the article by Jacques Guillerme, 'Le malsain et l'économie de la nature', *Dix-Huitième Siècle* (Paris, 1977), vol. 9 (*Le Sain et le Malsain*). 'It is saying very little, in truth, to say that the inventions of pneumatic chemistry animated the picture of nature at the end of the century. We should speak rather of a dramatisation, involving visions which encompassed the orders and disorders of the phenomena of life' (p. 62).

[16] M. du Tennetar, *Mémoire sur l'état de l'atmosphère à Metz et ses effets* (Nancy, 1778), p. 23.

[17] P. Bertholon, *De la salubrité des villes* (Montpellier, 1786), p. 6.

[18] Quoted by P. Muray, *Le XIXᵉ siècle à travers les âges* (Paris, 1984), p. 33.

[19] J.-H. Ronesse, *Vue sur la propreté des rues* (Paris, 1782), p. 13.

[20] Londres, *Réflexions sur le projet de'éloigner du milieu de Paris les tueries de bestiaux et les fonderies* (Paris, 1788), p. 15.

accumulated, dead or alive, cemeteries, but also hospitals, whose effluvia released humid gangrenes which prevented sores from healing and ulcers from drying up. The accumulation of rubbish and bodies fostered an uncontrolled festering: 'beds impregnated with fetid substances, piles of linen or dressings left lying about, privies and fever-rooms inadequately isolated from the rooms of the injured'.[21]

Such places and their 'purulent fogs'[22] began to be listed, and the persistent connection between stench and dirt, of both places and bodies, noticed. But the places and bodies of the nobility and the bourgeoisie were excluded; the suspect places were where the poor gathered, and the suspect bodies those still not protected by linen. It was first and foremost the common people who were at issue. On the basis of these listings and the standards which informed them, there gradually emerged after 1780 the premisses of a 'public hygiene', the first intimations of what the nineteenth century would develop. To evoke cleanliness was to oppose the shortcomings of the people, urban stenches and promiscuous mixing. The critique, in the 1780s, was no longer confined to aristocratic artifice; the habits of the people were soon condemned in a quite new way.

The first targets were places. Cemeteries, prisons, hospitals and slaughter-houses so studded towns like sinister abcesses that a remodelling of urban space was undertaken. Measures were introduced at the end of the century to improve the circulation and the renewal of air and to remove the most obvious sources of fetidness. A stagnant atmosphere, above all, must be prevented, hence the removal of cemeteries whose stench provoked concern, the proliferation of reforms to change the architecture and location of hospitals, and stronger measures against depositing rubbish. On the night of 7 April 1786, heavy carts began to transfer the remains from the Cemetery of the Holy Innocents to the underground quarries of Paris. A strange convoy of hearses proceeded by torchlight to the sound of the rhythmic intoning of prayers. The few witnesses were astonished by what they saw; bones periodically fell off the overloaded carriers, the human remains were heaped up anyhow, and the smell was intolerable. But this removal of the Parisian dead was the first in a

---

[21] J.-L. Moreau de La Sarthe, *Essai sur la gangrène humide des hôpitaux* (Paris, 1796), p. 20.

[22] J.-J. Menuret, *Essai sur l'action de l'air dans les maladies contagieuses* (Paris, 1781), p. 85.

long line.[23] It was also the first act of a hygiene which transformed public space.

After 1790, bridges were cleared of the houses constructed upon them, and buildings made to align.[24] The town must be 'ventilated'. There were even schemes for machines designed to agitate the air, immense wings to be erected at street corners, like the sails of windmills but with the opposite purpose, intended to provoke rather than subdue the wind, to propel the air with large vanes driven by river-power. Such machines were never constructed, but that they were conceived of is revealing about contemporary preoccupations. The landscape of light changed at the end of the century, symbolised by the space that Paris won from the Seine by the clearing of its bridges. The town grew at its centre,[25] out of an urgent need to increase the volume and movement of air. It is this insistence on air which makes it possible to understand the concern about popular cleanliness, and which helps to explain its special character.

Medical topographies and enquiries occasionally penetrated the private space of the poor. They recorded at length the smell of beds and bodies; they hunted out the overcrowding and decay lying hidden from sight. Doctors vied with each other in their descriptions of overcrowding and stench. 'The people, under-nourished, badly housed, more crowded, more susceptible to fear and terror, are the first and the most numerous victims.'[26] Some doctors finished by describing their own feelings in the face of such confinement. They pondered a phenomenon which they seemed to be discovering, whereas in fact they were finding it harder to tolerate something they had always seen. They reverted once more to the contrast between enlightenment and ignorance. The stench, which they blamed for the existence of disease, provoked astonishment and exasperation. Their texts are permeated by the same images, so strong sometimes as to reveal hidden impotence and resignation.

When I pulled the arms of the sick from under the bedcovers, the air which came from the bed turned my stomach, and when I wanted to ascertain the

---

[23] Quoted by Muray, *Le xixe siècle à travers les âges*, p. 36.

[24] Cf. J.-L. Harouel, 'Les fonctions de l'alignement dans l'organisme urbain', *Dix Huitième Siècle*, vol. 9.

[25] Cf. G. de Bory, *Mémoire dans lequel on prouve la possibilité d'agrandir la ville de Paris sans en reculer les limites* (Paris, 1776); also the article by Bruno Fortier, 'La maîtrise de l'eau', *Dix-Huitième Siècle*, vol. 9.

[26] Menuret, *Essai sur l'action de l'air*, p. 75.

condition of the tongue, I had to bend right over a bed raised up on a bank which I had to climb; there emerged gusts of breath which would have felled a horse. I often came away covered in fleas, in other places ticks (*'les grelots de St. François'*) attacked me from all sides.[27]

The overcrowding increased the doctors' disquiet. By intensifying the emanations, the accumulation of bodies heightened the danger. This indiscriminate promiscuity was denounced by medical texts as never before. Disease was fostered by this accumulation of breath, things and people, mingling their jumbled smells. In Brittany, for example, the poor 'lie alongside the sick in the same beds, fail to change the straw of their beds when it is spoiled, and occupy the beds of those who had died of disease'.[28] The crowding and dirt of hospitals caused even greater disquiet. Beds, with their juxtapositions of bodies lying side by side or head to foot, long evoked in the deliberations of the Hôtel-Dieu,[29] became a common focus for criticism. In the absence of a chemical explanation, the vegetable metaphor drew on all the resources of dunghills and humus, of excrements and fermentation. It was within these narrow, confined and over-heated spaces that the worst exhalations were born. Disease worked there like leaven. The smells were concentrated so that evil fevers germinated. Contagions spread in the damp and mould of sweat, gangrenes fed off stifled effluvia, decomposition accelerated in contact with dead bodies.

Is it not well-known that scab is endemic there? Is it not the case that the warmth of four or six sick people renders the humours more acrid, and the itching more unbearable? Does this warmth not bring forth, nay, support vermin? Does it not promote even further the fetidness which is inevitable in these beds and which becomes more intolerable where the sick are lying head to foot?[30]

These were all practices of the common people, especially the poor. From 1780 in particular, the medical topographies drew an ever clearer distinction between popular dirtiness and bourgeois comfort, exemplified by their less crowded conditions. Menuret, for example,

[27] Jouanné, quoted by J.-P. Goubert, *Malades et Médecins en Bretagne (1770–1790)* (Paris, 1974), p. 192.
[28] Vigier, *Mémoire adressé au subdélégué de Landerneau (17 mars 1769)*, quoted by Goubert, *Malades et Médecins en Bretagne*.
[29] Brièle, *Document pour servir à l'histoire des hôpitaux*, vol. 1, p. 44.
[30] J.-S. Bailly, 'Examen d'un projet de translation de l'Hôtel-Dieu de Paris et d'une nouvelle construction d'hôpitaux pour les malades', *Histoire et Mémoires de l'Académie royale des Sciences* (Paris, 1785), p. 24.

described the 'well-off' of Paris as 'less exposed' to contagion because less crowded; in Lyons, Berthelot linked poverty, dirt and sickness. 'The workers of Lyons lead a very different life from those who are well-off; they are in general thin and emaciated, not well grown . . . The dirt and disease of these workers are such that one often sees sleeping in the same garret twelve or fifteen people whose linen is barely changed once a week.'[31] Books on health also noted these differences. When, in 1791, Ganne reviewed a number of different styles of life in order to determine the 'means of protection from various illnesses', he emphasised cleanliness, which had become an 'indispensable condition' for the people.[32] *La Gazette de santé* took up the same theme, and speculated about some of its consequences: decline, even depopulation. The first demographers began to conjure up the spectre of a quite specific, selective death. 'One of the principal causes which, in towns, constantly perpetuates disease is the general filth and the absence of those habits which tend to protect men: habits unknown, in particular, amongst the people, constantly infected by the contagious skin diseases so common in this town.'[33]

Certain practices changed at the end of the century. Elaborate mechanisms were proposed for separating hospital beds, cleaning their surroundings, and removing rubbish. Chirol even had the idea of sliding doors concealed behind each bed, which would make it possible, by whisking the beds away on runners, to clean the room more thoroughly and remove people's rubbish by a special corridor.[34] The master cabinet-maker, Garat, proposed, in 1779, a bed supporting the sick person by a system of movable levers, a contrivance which would make it easier to change basins, linen and sheets.[35] This was a technology often too complicated to be realised, but it shows how preoccupations had changed. Apart from the gradual individualisation of beds, the chief change concerned linen, in the number of shirts supplied to the sick poor, and the regularity with which they were changed. Standards long the norm amongst the elite began to be adopted in institutions designed for the masses. A cleanliness which was already old began to exist, as if practices

---

[31] Bertelet de Barbot, *Topographie médicale* (Lyons, 1783), quoted by R. Favre, 'Du médico-topographique à Lyon en 1723', *Dix-Huitième Siècle*, vol. 9, p. 154.

[32] Ganne, *L'Homme physique et moral*, p. 111.

[33] 'Dépérissement de l'espèce humaine à Paris', *La Gazette de santé* (Paris, 1777), p. 111.

[34] Chirol, *Idées neuves sur la construction des hôpitaux* (Paris, 1787), pp. 9–10.

[35] *Affiches et Annonces de Paris* (Paris, 1779), p. 183.

designed for the people must involve a time-lag and a fallow period. It was the totally traditional cleanliness, not that actually present amongst the nobility and the bourgeoisie, which served as chief reference.

The employment of linen found a new application within the hospital context. Children taken into the Paris Hospice received, in the year VII, 'four shirts and three handkerchiefs, two pairs of stockings for the winter and three pairs of socks',[36] whereas shirts and stockings had hardly been mentioned before.[37] Similarly, the *Cahier des charges pour les hospices de Paris* of the same date decreed that the 'sick and the poor had their linen changed every ten days and more often if necessary, except for those with scurvy and venereal diseases';[38] whereas changing on this scale seems not to have been provided for a few decades earlier, except, probably, for the hospice for incurables, where vests were changed every month in 1769.[39] Such concern was even greater in English hospitals. At Haslar, for example, near Gosport, the shirts of the sick were changed every four days, and caps, pants and stockings every week.[40] In certain military hospitals whose management was described and discussed by Daignan in 1785, an attendant was specially assigned to look after the linen of the sick, change it and sometimes even to wash them: he was

entirely occupied in washing the feet of the sick arrivals, as the doctors advised, in doing their hair, changing their linen and putting them to bed. You cannot imagine how necessary these precautions were to the success of the treatment of the major diseases which most often occur when evacuations of the skin do not take place, nothing presenting a greater obstacle to this than body dirt and filth.[41]

The argument had advanced. It was no longer only smell which was taken into account, but the functional role of the excretions. Cleanliness assisted the correct functioning of the organs. This had been noted by Pringle some years earlier. 'I noticed in the hospitals that when they brought in people with fever, nothing so provoked sweating as washing their feet in vinegar and hot water and giving

---

[36] J.-M. Audin-Rouvière, 'Règlement de l'Hospice des enfants à Paris, an VII', *Cahiers de charges pour les hospices de Paris* (Paris), p. 17.

[37] See note 50, chapter 5, p. 74.

[38] Audin-Rouvière, 'Règlement de l'Hospice des enfants à Paris', p. 24.

[39] Cf. P.-A. Alletz, *Tableau de l'humanité et de la bienfaisance* (Paris, 1769), p. 105.

[40] J. Howard, *Histoire des principaux lazarets et prisons* (Paris, 1790), vol. 2, p. 170.

[41] G. Daignan, *Ordre de service des hôpitaux militaires* (Paris, 1785), p. 173.

them white linen.'[42] Localised washing (often only washing the feet) facilitated the release of the humours, emphasising the importance of the preoccupation with the functions.

Washing was not, however, what was most important in these ideas and projects. It is true that Poyet, imagining, in 1786, the removal of the Hôtel-Dieu to the Isle des Cygnes, thought of constructing there 'any number of baths',[43] and that Tenon, listing the changes still needed at the Hôtel-Dieu, proposed the installation of mechanical armchairs or mobile hammocks, by means of which certain patients would be plunged into cold baths.[44] But what Poyet, amongst others, wanted most of all was to create draughts. He envisaged circular or open corridors, and rooms with different orientations, each exposed to a different wind, the disposition of walls and the angles of the windows being determined by the compass.

Hospital reform remained to a large extent dominated by the principles of ventilation and the removal of rubbish, the provision of individual beds and a cleanliness assured by linen. If the concept of bathing as necessary for the people existed by the end of the century, it was in a rather different context, that of projects aimed at reorganising the management and distribution of water. It was in inventing new networks for, amongst other things, more effective clearing and freshening of the streets, that baths for the populace were occasionally mentioned.

THE WATER THAT IMPROVED THE ATMOSPHERE

The alarmed descriptions of overcrowding and rubbish gave rise, in the last third of the eighteenth century, to a number of proposals designed to increase the supply and circulation of water within towns. There were schemes for water to wash steeply sloping pavements, for fountains to water market places, and for streams of water which, by carrying away the filth, would at last cure the smell. The pump of Notre-Dame, erected a century earlier, the supply via Arcueil and Rungis, and the old springs of Belleville and the Pré-Saint-Germain had never seemed so inadequate.[45] The consumption of water

[42] J. Pringle, *Observations sur les maladies des armées dans les camps et les garnisons* (Paris, 1763, 1st ed. London, 1752), p. 44.
[43] B. Poyet, *Mémoire sur la nécessité de transférer et reconstruire l'Hôtel-Dieu de Paris, suivi d'un projet de translation de cet hôpital* (Paris, 1785), p. 36.
[44] J.-R. Tenon, *Mémoire sur les hôpitaux de Paris* (Paris, 1788), p. 441.
[45] J. Bouchery, *L'Eau à Paris à la fin du XVIIIe siècle* (Paris, 1946).

became, in a novel way, a problem of collective strategy. It was now seen as essential for a town to have the facility for water to flow regularly through the streets. A network had to be created, which would consist not of a system of covered and articulated drains, or of main pipes leading into individual branches, but of more numerous and better placed points of distribution. The aim continued to be to disperse dirt by watering the streets and reach remote districts by multiplying the sources of supply. The town would be as if 'washed' by water sweeping away everything stagnant and foul. After 1780, most medical topographies accepted the connection between a new movement of water and the need to improve the atmosphere. The suppression of smells was primarily to be achieved through having more water flowing through the streets. 'May we not vow to see established in Lyons, and in all the principal towns, machines which would raise water from the rivers to distribute it in the town centres where it would circulate freely in every street; the healthiness of the atmosphere, the freshness in summer and at the same time the cleanliness of the streets would be the precious results which would ensue.'[46] Menuret proposed water-tanks, from which water would emerge at regular intervals, to stream through the streets.[47] In the debate, already extensively studied, between the 'passive' solution of water carried in aqueducts or canals, and the more 'active' solution of water pumped from rivers to supply towns, the goal remained always that of irrigating the streets. Watering them would prevent smell and sickness. 'In hot weather, it would be possible to wash the streets twice a day, and perhaps prevent much sickness.'[48]

It is in the context of this new provision of water that the idea of baths for the people occasionally occurred. Communal establishments could be installed near to the new points of supply. The presumed abundance of water would make this feasible. The references, though few, are clear enough. D'Auxiron, as early as 1765, included the establishment of such baths in his project for steam engines to pump water from the Seine over Paris. 'A splendid monument could be erected to enclose the machines and their works. It would be possible to embellish the principal water tower and the hot and cold public baths which I propose to construct, and which would be so useful to the people.'[49] Lavoisier chose a similar context

[46] Bertholon, *De la salubrité des villes*, p. 99.
[47] Menuret, *Essai sur l'histoire*, p. 84.
[48] C.-H. Piarron de Chamousset, *Oeuvres* (Paris, 1783), vol. 1, p. 333.
[49] Chevalier d'Auxiron, *Projet pour donner des eaux à Paris* (Paris, 1769), p. xiv.

to mention the idea of popular washing. 'There can be no doubt that such a shortage of water contributes to the dirtiness of the people and does much to render the atmosphere of the capital unhealthy.'[50] And Deparcieux, as part of his scheme for an aqueduct to bring water from the Yvette to the Estrapade to facilitate its distribution throughout the districts of Paris, included mention of the possibility of creating 'public baths and wash-houses'.[51] The idea existed, and was expressed; the common people should have 'their' baths. This requirement acquired status, at least in theory. Popular hygiene could be reformulated. Water for washing the people began to be considered, even if there was no question of private baths, or of water supplied to every household. This reformulation remained to a large extent theoretical. A handful of statements did not change practices.

In 1782, Chaillot's steam-pumps achieved a temporary solution for the better distribution of water in Paris at the end of the eighteenth century,[52] but no 'baths for the people' were constructed. They demanded an investment which other urgent needs made difficult. They also demanded a large amount of water. But if they failed to materialise, it was, at a deeper level, because they did not yet correspond to actual expectations of or ideas about collective cleanliness. Their utility was not universally accepted. Their failure to materialise reveals all the more clearly what it was that mattered in this new circulation of water. Clearly, it brought water closer to each house, though it was not intended, as would later be the case, to reach every household. 'The ordinary people and doubtless the majority of the inhabitants are not in a position to subscribe to private fountains.'[53] But above all, as far as health was concerned, it was the drainage of communal spaces which was desired. The atmosphere and the air had the highest priority, and water corrected them in proportion as it reached the streets. It absorbed smells by its movement alone; there was a vision of swirling water drowning impurities, a physical image of torrents destroying and dissolving dust. It was, in fact, the air itself which was washed. 'The running water exercises an attraction on the air, in consequence of which it

[50] A. L. Lavoisier, 'Lettre sur les moyens d'amener l'eau à Paris' (1786), *Oeuvres* (Paris, 1868), vol. 3, p. 255.

[51] A. Deparcieux, *Projet d'amener à Paris la rivière de l'Yvette* (Mémoire de 1767) (Paris, 1776), p. 136.

[52] *Prospectus de la fourniture et distribution des eaux de la Seine à Paris par la machine à feu* (Paris, 1781).

[53] Chevalier d'Auxiron, *Projet patriotique sur les eaux de Paris* (Paris, 1765), p. 26.

absorbs the putrid miasmas with which it is laden.'[54] This principle
was basic to the new arrangements for distribution. This is why water-
tanks were constructed in Paris, like the one in the Rue Vivienne,
regularly opened to water the streets.[55] They were also adopted by
provincial towns – Bordeaux, Caen, and even Aurillac.[56]

This insistence on water as intended primarily to improve the air is
important in that it emphasises what was the key element in the
relationship between healthiness and unhealthiness at the end of the
eighteenth century. Attention to the air took precedence over
washing the body. It was this which made the image of the peasant so
ambivalent; his existence embodied everything that was denounced
by the enquiries: promiscuous mixing and relative indifference to
linen. But the fresh air sufficed to make it a model of a healthy life. 'In
the country, the peasants who live in stables appear not to be
particularly affected by disease; but, by their way of life, they very
often breathe a different air.'[57] Even after 1780, the peasant
remained, almost contradictorily, a symbol of health, even salubrity.
It was the 'purified' atmosphere which was responsible. 'The physical
constitution of the inhabitants of Paris is amazingly less robust than
that of the inhabitants of the countryside, because the air of Paris is
neither so pure nor so bracing as that of the country.'[58] And the
difference could not be ignored when death-rates were calculated. It
was the atmosphere which primarily determined lifespan. Death
struck, in the same period, 'one inhabitant in forty in the countryside . . . and one in twenty-four to twenty-six in the towns',[59] according
to Tourtelle in 1797. According to Poyet, the proportion varied from
one in forty to one in twenty-eight.[60] A different calculation in
Daignan, in 1786, was even more eloquent: average lifespan fell from

---

[54] Banau and Turben, *Mémoire sur les épidémies*, p. 50.

[55] Menuret, *Essai sur l'histoire*, p. 86.

[56] Perrot, *Le Travail des apparences*, vol. 2, p. 658; J.-F. Capelle, *Tableau des améliorations sanitaires de Bordeaux* (Bordeaux, 1817), pp. 47–8; C. Grimmer, *Aurillac au XVIIIe siècle* (Paris, 1983), p. 96.

[57] H.-L. Duhamel de Monceau, *Moyen de conserver la santé des équipages des vaisseaux* (Paris, 1759), p. 38.

[58] J.-M. Audin-Rouvière, *Essai sur la topographie physique et médicale de Paris* (Paris, year VII), p. 17.

[59] E. Tourtelle, *Eléments d'hygiène* (Paris, 1815, text prepared in 1797), p. 128.

[60] Le Roy, 'Précis d'un ouvrage sur les hôpitaux dans lequel on expose les principaux résultats des observations de physique et de médecine, qu'on doit avoir en vue dans la construction de ces édifices, avec un projet d'hôpital disposé d'après ces principes', *Mémoires de l'Académie royale des Sciences* (Paris, 1787).

forty to twenty-two as one moved from a village in the hills to a mining town.[61] These calculations, never very explicit (it is difficult to discover on what evidence they were based), at the very least demonstrate the strength of the ideas behind them.

A politics of health, centred for the first time on the longevity of populations, and exploiting for the first time a strategy of water and a critique of popular housing, remained, apparently, the victim of its obsession with air.

---

[61] Daignan, *Tableau des variétés de la vie humaine*, pp. 284ff.

11. *All-over baths and local washing*

With theories about baths for the people which were rarely put into practice, and ideas about cold which had rather more, though still not much, application, the second half of the eighteenth century was essentially a period of changing conceptions. The new connection between cleanliness and vigour, though fundamental, failed for the most part to cross over the threshold of abstraction. And the theme of greater care for the skin did not always lead to a transformation in washing. A number of significant changes nevertheless resulted, from altered faces to the new circulation of water. And new strategies and standards of health also changed public and private space. But it was after 1780 that, for some people at least, the concrete conditions of hygiene began imperceptibly to change. The role of the bath, in particular, was not what it had been.

MORE BATHS

A demand now existed, though socially very restricted, which could be met. Certain habits developed and certain actions changed. The projects to increase the volume of water available may not have led to the establishment of baths for the people, but they did affect private bathing. The Périer brothers, offering to lay lead pipes to the residences of rich clients, employed the concept of the bath in their 1781 prospectus. It is significant that they assumed this would attract the very rich at least. 'The immense advantage of this undertaking would be to have . . . an uninterrupted supply of wholesome water in whatever quantity is desired; to be able to take baths in one's own home, conveniently and at no cost.'[1] D'Auxiron used similar arguments in support of his project of 1769. 'There will be in addition abundant water for the kitchens, baths, sinks, stables and gardens of every lord [*seigneur*] who so desires.'[2] The term *seigneur* indicates the

[1] *Prospectus de la fourniture et distribution des eaux*, p. 6.
[2] Chevalier d'Auxiron, *Projet patriotique* (1769), p. 7.

156

intended audience. The volume of water shifted by Chaillot's pumps in 1782 was less than expected,[3] and it did not really transform the individual availability of water for most people. But bathrooms were more often installed in the final years of the century.

The evidence for this increase is sometimes vague, as with the very brief and certainly exaggerated statement in the *La Gazette de santé* to the effect that 'baths are infinitely multiplied in Paris'.[4] It is sometimes more precise, as with the assertion formulated by Ronesse in 1782 and based on the evidence of buildings:

The volume of water entering houses is infinitely greater than it was a dozen or more years ago; this is the result of the very frequent baths which doctors advise today for many more illnesses than formerly, and from the taste which the public has developed for this practice; to the point where there are baths in every new house, and that when a rich man wants to rent an apartment, he regards a bathroom as one of the rooms which is most essential.[5]

Such assertions must be treated with caution. The appointments of the large private mansions suggest a less pronounced transformation. When, in 1801, Kraft recorded the plans of sixty-six luxurious mansions built between 1770 and 1800 (and mostly after 1775), he noted twenty bathrooms.[6] At 30 per cent, this percentage is well above the 6 per cent obtained from an identical count in 1750.[7] It nevertheless emphasises that only one out of three large, prestigious residences possessed a bath in 1800. The increase was real, but was obviously far from applying to all rich houses. It is the change within a period of a few years which is significant. It was sufficient to give contemporaries the impression of an increase, and sufficient, most of all, for the concept to gain a tangible presence in the preoccupations of the rich.

A number of public baths, often luxurious, were established, also after 1780. These were for the rich rather than for the people. The model remained the Poitevin establishment,[8] of which five copies were constructed in Paris between 1780 and 1800.[9] All made use of the river by means of boats pumping up water and distributing it to

---

[3] Bouchery, *L'Eau à Paris*, p. 140.   [4] *La Gazette de santé* (1776), p. 107.
[5] Ronesse, *Vue sur la propreté des rues*, p. 91.
[6] J.-C. Kraft, *Plans, coupes, élévations des plus belles maisons et des hôtels construits à Paris et dans les environs depuis, environ, 25 à 30 ans* (Paris, 1801).
[7] See chapter 7.   [8] *Ibid.*
[9] L. Prudhomme, *Miroir de l'ancien et du nouveaux Paris* (1804), vol. 2 'Bains publics', p. 231.

cabins fitted with baths. These establishments, like that of Poitevin, offered a hydropathic as well as an ordinary bath. The Albert baths, in particular, constructed in 1783, provided ascending and descending showers to combat 'rheumatic pains, paralysis, wrenches, sprains, swellings, back pains, gout, sciatica . . .'.[10] But the purpose of these installations was more clearly cleanliness. This was the case with the Chinese baths built at the same date by Turquin,[11] and with the Vigier baths, which comprised three boats, after 1790,[12] all 'to be recommended for the order and the cleanliness found there'.[13] The price ensured a well-off clientele: two livres eight sous at the Albert baths, and three livres twelve sous at Gaignard's establishment in 1787,[14] which corresponded to about three to five times the daily wage of a day-labourer. The cheapest were the Chinese baths, which provided a bath for twenty-four sols, which still represented almost twice the daily pay of a day-labourer.[15] Establishments of this kind were not confined to Paris. At the same period, the Bourassier baths were installed on the Ouche at Dijon,[16] the Dusaussay baths on the Orne at Caen[17] and several establishments on the Rhone and the Garonne.[18]

With altogether about 150 baths in Paris in 1790, a number which was doubled by 1800,[19] these institutions signalled a transformation. Saint-Ursins was thinking of them when, in 1804, he spoke of 'the practice of bathing recently introduced in France'.[20] They appear from time to time in novels and memoirs; Mme de Genlis tells how she was followed to the Poitevin baths by an anonymous admirer, and a character in Rétif drowned in one of Vigier's bathtubs at the

---

[10] *Décret de la Faculté de médecine sur les nouveaux bains établis à Paris* (Paris, 1785), p. 7.   [11] *La Gazette de santé* (1782), p. 87.

[12] *Vie publique et privée des Français à la ville, à la cour et dans les provinces, par une société de gens de lettres* (Paris, 1826), vol. 2, p. 206.

[13] J.-A. Dulaure, *Nouvelle Description des curiosités de Paris* (Paris, 1787, 1st ed. 1785), p. 61.

[14] *Ibid.*, pp. 61, 62. Cf. also *Le Guide de Thiery*. Gaignard was the successor to Poitevin. His establishment was bought by Vigier at the Revolution.

[15] For the cost of the Chinese baths, cf. *La Gazette de santé* (1782), p. 87. For the wages of a labourer, cf. J.-C. Perrot, *Genèse d'une ville*, vol. 2, p. 790, n. 76.

[16] Garnier, *Les Etuves dijonnaises*, p. 35.

[17] Perrot, *Genèse d'une ville*, vol. 2, p. 912.

[18] Capelle, *Tableau des améliorations*, p. 147.

[19] The establishments usually comprised between fifteen and thirty baths. Vigier, in 1799, had a new building constructed containing 140 baths, one of his boats having been damaged by ice in the Seine (cf. Prudhomme, *Miroir de l'ancien et du nouveau Paris*).

[20] P.-J. Marie de Saint-Ursins, *L'Ami des femmes* (Paris, 1804), p. 70.

end of the century.[21] It is clear that they were patronised by a limited public. Mercier, in 1789, mentions their novelty at the same time as emphasising their numerical and social limitations. These institutions designed for people to wash in were still too little used. Mercier was indignant. 'There are on the river hot baths for twenty-four sous, but without linen. We have there the means to cleanse the people of Paris. Alas, half the town never washes and never enters a bath in the whole of its life.'[22] The judgement is more severe in Rétif a few years later; the small number of these establishments betrayed 'the dirtiness of the largest town in the world'.[23] Regrets and 'established facts' – the legitimacy of the argument seems obvious; it confirmed a reality to the extent of counting it. But the reality was itself new. Baths, of whatever type, had now been established, and the assertion that there were too few is in itself a sign of change. Establishments had been created, with hopes that their appeal would increase. It was only because baths had begun to exist that these expectations, comparisons, even recriminations, could in their turn be formulated. Their significance can even be turned on its head; the establishments of the end of the century, with the accusations and the praise that they excited, reveal primarily that the practice existed. They also reveal the enhanced significance of washing; in the last decade of the eighteenth century, the Vigier baths, like the Chinese baths, were primarily for washing the body.

So bathing was slowly established in the habits of the elite at the very end of the eighteenth century. Its presence was limited but real. It had become more utilitarian, and the role of water more functional, more neutral even. A certain familiarity seemed to have been established. It was impossible, however, to escape all the complications of the past. The action of Corvisart in 1810, when he forbade the Empress Marie-Louise, in order to preserve her fertility, from abusing hot baths,[24] reveals continued anxieties about enfeeblement and languor. The physical action of the liquid mass enveloping and pressing on the bather retained its grip on the imagination. The impact of water was not always confined to washing. And Pissis was

---

[21] Mme de Genlis, *Mémoires*, vol. 2, p. 221; and cf. Rétif, *Monsieur Nicolas*, vol. 4, p. 136.   [22] Mercier, *Tableau de Paris*, (ed. of 1789), vol. 2, p. 164.

[23] N. Rétif de La Bretonne, *Les Nuits de Paris* (about 1790), in *Oeuvres* (Paris, 1930), vol. 1, p. 106.

[24] Cf. Constant, *Mémoires intimes de Napoléon* (Paris, 1967, 1st ed. 1830), p. 764.

still patiently explaining in 1802, that 'the bath always relaxes the already weak fibre and augments the volume of the humours'.[25]

Nevertheless, Pissis himself could imagine no other recourse than 'water and linen' to remedy 'disgusting and fetid dirtiness'.[26] And texts on hygiene in the early nineteenth century are less confident about the intrinsic virtues of cold. They do not so much explicitly reject them, as accord warm water a larger role. They calculated the correct temperature for cleanliness. Hufeland, for example, a great amateur of cold baths, and a theoretician of the internal reactions of the body and of the dynamisation of the fibres, developed in his *Art de prolonger la vie humaine* (published in France in 1810) parallel considerations on the subject of warm baths for cleanliness.[27] Willich, too, very concerned about toughening young children, pondered, in 1802, the possible limitations of cold, which risked 'exposure to all the vicissitudes of the weather and the seasons'.[28] Protat, giving free play to the natural reference, recommended, in 1802, water previously warmed by the rays of the sun, at least in summer.[29] All in all, hygienic texts now more often associated bathing and cleanliness, water and skin. A narrow and privileged social fringe put this into practice. Linking such baths with the image of the rich Parisian lady, Rétif dreamed of nymphs and sylphs: 'Frequent baths maintain her health in warm weather, even in winter she spends a few minutes three times a week in the warm water.'[30] It was this practice which constituted the real novelty.

LOCAL WASHING

This practice has to be understood in all its diverse and varied forms. Bathing amongst the elite easily accommodated intermediate formulas. Between changing linen and immersion there developed acts of 'local'[31] cleanliness, with the use of foot-baths and hip-baths, and

---

[25] J. Pissis, *Manuel d'hygiène* (Le Puy, 1802), p. 250.   [26] *Ibid.*, p. 104.

[27] A. J. L. Hufeland, *L'Art de prolonger la vie humaine* (Paris, 1810, 1st ed. Iéna, 1796), p. 285.

[28] A. F. Willich, *Hygiène domestique* (Paris 1802, 1st ed. in English, 1798), vol. 1, p. 41.

[29] E. Protat, *Eléments d'éducation physique et médecine des enfants* (Paris, 1803), p. 68.

[30] N. Rétif de La Bretonne, *Les Contemporaines* (ed. Paris, undated reprint, 1st ed. 1780), vol. 3, 'Les Parisiennes', p. 45.

[31] The adjectives used today to describe this sort of washing (local, limited, partial) are, to say the least, ambiguous. They may suggest that the cleanliness achieved is clearly seen as 'local' by those concerned. However, when Turben and Banau

an emphasis on friction to supplement washing to treat the skin, 'principally the joints and the places least likely to be in contact with the air'.[32] It was amongst the elite that these 'limited' practices were established at the end of the eighteenth century. They sustained cleanliness in the periods between baths, or they acted as substitutes, or equivalents for them. Mlle Avrillon was playing the *faux naif* when she described Josephine 'seized by the head and the feet', when the new empress washed her legs while having her hair done.[33] It takes the angry act of Napoleon smashing against a wall the earthenware bowl used for washing his feet, to reveal the existence of the practice. Equally, it needs the occasional survival of 'public', aristocratic toilets, similar to those of the Ancien Régime, for Rémusat to describe the daily washing of the deformed legs of Talleyrand at the beginning of the nineteenth century; before interested eyes, the minister removed his woollen stockings and his flannel bandages, before plunging his legs into a little pail of water of Barrèges.[34] In this case, washing and hydrotherapy are clearly closely connected.

These partial practices reveal how the frequency of baths, still rarely specified, implies an inverse importance of local washing. One indication, but telling; when, in a treatise on the toilet, in 1806, Caron attempted a definition of cleanliness, it was inevitable that he would include 'the meticulous care of the body', and mention 'frequent washing',[35] even though this washing was very far from always involving immersion. Cleanliness could not now be defined, for the elite at least, without going beyond the barrier of clothing.

But the real importance of the theme lay elsewhere. It was the social terrain of cleanliness which was defined by partial washing. It was its best indication, once the use of water had become more functional. It defined its sphere and its boundaries at the end of the eighteenth century. The objects employed were additional indicators. The batteries of earthenware, the intimate furniture, and their spatial distribution reveal that, with the end of the Ancien Régime, a radical transformation was under way. Far from the texts, irrespective of

advised country-dwellers in 1786 to wash their feet in times of epidemic, and rub their bodies, they were, in their own eyes, advising a 'complete' cleanliness. The words 'local', 'partial' and 'limited', as used in this chapter, are used only to distinguish between a bath and other washing.

[32] Marie de Saint-Ursins, *L'Ami des femmes*, pp. 55–6.
[33] Mlle M. P. J. Avrillon, *Mémoire*, p. 156.
[34] C. de Rémusat, *Mémoires de ma vie* (Paris, 1958), vol. 1, p. 270.
[35] Constant, *Mémoires intimes de Napoléon*, p. 730.

bathtubs and baths, cleanliness was no longer limited to linen or to the visible parts of the body.

The bidet, for example, still exceptional in the bourgeois world in 1770, became more common after 1780, whilst remaining completely unknown amongst artisans and workers. It even penetrated the houses of certain intermediate groups in contact with elite examples, such as clerks, domestic servants, and wage-earners not employed in manual labour. Jacques-Auguste Cerfvol, sub-manager in the department of public works, whose son became inspector of posts, possessed a bidet in 1797.[36] So, also in 1797, did Adrien Gobeau, a nurse at Les Invalides.[37] This item of furniture penetrated the houses of some clergy: that of canon Afforty, for example, at Senlis, in 1786.[38] Where it was present, the bidet was found in interiors which already possessed many well-furnished rooms (that is, for example, marquetry, vases and pictures). Space, in bourgeois houses, was just beginning to be differentiated; bed alcoves were sometimes flanked with wash-rooms or bedrooms had small rooms off. A good example is the furnished house taken for the Rochezeuil couple, in the well-off district of the Madeleine; all the bedrooms had adjoining offices, there was a wide range of furniture, some of it valuable (such as secretaires, bureaus, armchairs and gaming tables), and, finally, courtyards with several coach-houses, one of which housed a cabriolet. The inventory drawn up on the death of Charles-Nicolas Rochezeuil in 1800 records a bidet in one in every two of the apartments.[39]

More widespread were tubes and syringes intended for intimate washing or therapeutic injections. They generally accompanied a bidet and its earthenware bowl, but they were more common than the bidet itself. Many artisan and some peasant homes began to have them after 1780. A farmer of Aubercourt, in Picardy, for example, had in his kitchen in 1787 'one syringe and two tin tubes'.[40] Paul Durand, lacemaker, had 'one tin syringe' in 1788,[41] and the widow of a Parisian currier, Duval, had 'one large and one small tin syringe' in 1797.[42] Intimate acts, rarely discussed, the practices requiring these

---

[36] AN, Minutier central, LXV, 604.   [37] *Ibid.*

[38] A. Margry, 'Inventaire du chanoine C. F. Afforty, doyen de Saint-Rieul', *Revue du Comité archéologique de Senlis* (1879), p. 63.

[39] AN, Minutier central, LXV, 604.

[40] A. Ledieu, 'Mobilier de quelques paysans picards', *La Picardie* (1884), p. 508.

[41] AN, Minutier central, LXV, 602.   [42] *Ibid.*, LXV, 604.

instruments are difficult to uncover. Regular washing or therapeutic acts – it is not clear which. The categorisation of the items themselves is unclear; are they archaic instruments of digestive therapies, or more delicate tools of private toilets? The fact that the inventory of Victoire Coilly, wife of a volunteer gunner in the revolutionary wars, listed, in 1795, 'one syringe and one female syringe with its tube' indicates the range of uses.[43] All the same, this 'preoccupation with genital health'[44] did not extend to the populace, but affected, in general, only its margins.

The most common instruments of cleanliness at the end of the eighteenth century were clearly basins. Made of pewter or porcelain for the very rich (sometimes taps surmounting a fixed basin), stoneware or earthenware for the rest, they were often counted as part of the household crockery. They grew in number at the end of the eighteenth century, especially amongst the common people. Washing the hands and face became common again, along with care of the clothes and changing linen: traditional cleanliness, in fact, essentially expressed in decent and clean clothing, and measured by numbers of shirts, handkerchiefs and stockings. Basins do not invariably appear in lists relating to the world of workers, whether as a result of their relative absence or their negligible value. And shirts rarely numbered more than half a dozen; Charles Guyot, journeyman mason, had four in 1782;[45] the wig-maker Du Crest had three in 1792;[46] Jean-Baptiste Coignard, launderer, had seven in 1783.[47]

Local washing reflected a twofold regime of cleanliness at the end of the eighteenth century: one playing on sensibility and health by breaking through the clothes to reach the skin, the other deriving from the respectability and appearance of the covering of clothes. The former, though clearly not comparable to either the concepts or practices of today, signals a trend which the nineteenth century would develop.

[43] *Ibid.*, LXV, 602.
[44] D. Roche, *Le Peuple de Paris* (Paris, 1981), p. 158. This work is fundamental. Its evaluation of the hygienic tools in common use is both detailed and statistical. See especially pp. 157–9.   [45] AN, Minutier central, LXV, 602.
[46] *Ibid.*, LXV, 603.   [47] *Ibid.*, LXV, 602.

Part 4 *The water that protected*

12. *The functions of the skin*

Having secretly sought refuge in 1837 with his friends, the Guidoboni-Visconti, Balzac went to ground in their apartment in the Champs-Elysées. Under pressure from his creditors, he wanted to produce within a few weeks *La Femme supérieure*, a novel bought and paid for long ago by *La Presse*, as well as several short stories for which he had also contracted. He worked at night. He wore himself out, ate little, worked into the small hours and drank cup after cup of coffee, but he completed his project; the novel was written within a month. Balzac had meanwhile neither shaved nor washed, reluctant to spare a moment from the table where he was so unsociably entrenched. The episode would hardly merit our attention but for Balzac himself describing his return to 'normal' life: a 'toilet' again, some physical attentions, and relaxation. He revealed both his need for and his ambivalence towards washing after his month of total isolation. For example, he bathed, but was aware of a risk. The potentially enfeebling effects worried such a ferocious worker; the water might have a debilitating effect. 'After writing you this letter, I will take my first bath, not without anxiety, as I fear the loosening of fibres stretched to the utmost, and I must recommence to complete *César Birotteau* which is ridiculously delayed.'[1] Balzac was accustomed to wash; when he lived in the Rue Cassini in 1828, he had a bathroom with white stuccoed walls constructed adjacent to his bedroom.[2] The example is significant; the bath had gradually gained ground in the first half of the nineteenth century. But the hesitation of the exhausted and nervous Balzac shows how the practice was still not without its problems.

Theories, too, were changing; warm water was again respectable, the physiology of the skin was better understood and the frame of reference was increasingly functional. Attitudes had changed significantly, practices much less so.

[1] H. de Balzac, *Lettres à l'étrangère* (Paris, 1899), vol. 1 (1833–42), p. 407.
[2] Cf. E. Werdet, *Souvenirs de la vie littéraire (portraits intimes)* (Paris, 1879), p. 326.

THE NEW USE OF THE WORD 'HYGIENE'

The word 'hygiene' occupied a new position at the beginning of the nineteenth century. Manuals dealing with health changed their titles. Hitherto they had been concentrated on the maintenance or conservation of health.[3] They now became treatises or manuals of hygiene.[4] They defined their subject matter by this previously little-used term.[5] Hygiene was no longer an adjective qualifying health (*hygeinos* in Greek means 'that which is healthy'), but the collection of practices and knowledge which helped to preserve it. It was a specific discipline within medicine. It was a body of knowledge and no longer a physical qualification. With this term, a specialised field was rapidly established. Its 'links with physiology, chemistry, natural history',[6] were emphasised by insisting on its scholarly appurtenances. It was impossible to evoke such a discipline without reference to some rigorous requirement; impossible to conceive of it without making it a special branch of medical knowledge.

Its status also changed. Medicine, at the end of the eighteenth century, had entered politics. It had played a role in the planning of towns and other public places. It had promoted communal measures (from watering the streets to opening up certain districts). This influence on daily life could not but have its consequences. The medicine of the beginning of the nineteenth century claimed in this regard more rigour and more system: not new knowledge of the laws of health, but a greater determination to assert a total knowledge, an insistent emphasis on a 'scientific' competence.

The change in the status of this knowledge is demonstrated by the appearance of new institutions, for example the commissions of health established under the Empire with responsibility for local inspection of factories, workshops and establishments which emitted noxious emanations.[7] It is also revealed by the rapid discovery made

---

[3] Cf. the works already quoted: Mackenzie, *Histoire de la santé et de l'art de la conserver*; de Préville, *Méthode aisée pour conserver la santé*; Le Bègue de Presle, *Le Conservateur de la santé*.

[4] Pissis, *Manuel d'hygiène*, or P. F. Vidalin, *Traité d'hygiène domestique* (Paris, 1825), or J. Briand, *Manuel complet d'hygiène* (Paris, 1826).

[5] The word was not really in current use, even though it merited an article in the *Encyclopédie*, no negligible matter. However, no book employed the term in its title during the eighteenth century.   [6] Briand, *Manuel complet d'hygiène*, p. 7.

[7] The Council of Health for the Seine published an annual report from 1802, the date of its foundation. The first reports were in manuscript. A copy, also in manuscript, exists in the Archives de Police.

by the review *la Dominicale* of a Christianity which had always attached importance to scientific standards of cleanliness. These are the first texts of hygiene in a Christian periodical. 'Today above all it behoves us to draw the proofs of religion from the scientific order which has for so long been its enemy.'[8] The scholar had discovered what the priest had long known – a nice way for *La Dominicale* to emphasise, in spite of itself, the new status of this knowledge. More important, finally, was the chair of hygiene created in the year II in the Faculty of Medicine in Paris, occupied by Hallé till 1822 and by Royer-Collard from 1838 to 1850.[9] There was recognition, therefore, in very diverse milieus.

The texts on hygiene themselves, at the beginning of the nineteenth century, emphasised several changes in practices, for example the use of soap. Soap removed and dissolved body dirt. It 'purified'. Washing involved the application of elementary chemistry. 'The cosmetic *par excellence, the* instrument of cleanliness, is soap.'[10] It was no longer an aid to elegance, but a tool of health: 'soap cleanses the cutaneous surface of greasy substances'.[11] It was helpful to the physiology. It was 'one of the most important elements in cosmetics'.[12] The explanation did not go unchallenged. The artifice of soap excited some reservations. The thesis of hygienic bathing still made shift with some fragile tools in the first half of the nineteenth century; pure water, for example, with its secret virtues, was the sole 'material' of cleanliness for Londe in 1847,[13] whereas Bouchez and Trélat pointed to the obscure dangers of emulsive substances. 'Anointing with soap diminishes the disposition to sweat; it is also a mild irritant.'[14] The bath accessories soon seen as traditional were slow to gain acceptance.

The heavy emphasis on body dirt also affected attitudes to temperature, and hot water gained in importance. The prime role of the hygienic bath was to cleanse, a precondition for facilitating the action of the bodily functions.

[8] 'Considérations religieuses sur l'hygiène', *La Dominicale, journal des paroisses* (Paris, 1883), p. 271.

[9] See the thesis of J. Léonard, *Les Médecins del'Ouest au XIXe siècle* (Université Paris IV, Paris, 1976), vol. 3, p. 1141.

[10] M. Lévy, *Traité d'hygiène publique et privée* (Paris, 1857, 1st ed. 1845), vol. 2, p. 246.

[11] *Ibid.*, vol. 2, p. 247.   [12] L. Fleury, *Cours d'hygiène* (Paris, 1852), p. 552.

[13] C. Londe, *Nouveaux Eléments d'hygiène* (2nd ed. corrected, Paris, 1847), vol. 2, p. 631.

[14] P.-J. Buchez and U. Trélat, *Précis élémentaire d'hygiène* (Paris, 1825), p. 101.

This thesis, already apparent in the last years of the eighteenth century, settled for a long time to come the form of the hygienic bath. 'The warm bath is the hygienic bath *par excellence*: it produces a pleasant sensation; it cleans the surface of the body of the deposits left by perspiration and sweat.'[15] Warm water was preferred over all others. It was essential to the cleansing bath. Cold baths did not go out of favour, but they increasingly served a specific purpose, that of dynamising. The goals diverged; it was not cold which washed, but warmth. And it was the latter which allowed 'the functions of the skin to operate, not with more energy, but with more ease'.[16] Cleansing with warm water, stimulation with cold, the two practices had different purposes.

THE SKIN AND THE ENERGETIC BALANCE

One particular idea gained in importance, especially after 1830 – that of the purifying function of warm water and the respiratory role attributed to the skin. Obstruction of the pores affected gaseous exchanges. The idea was all the more important in that it introduced a new theory of energy. It concerned the conception of the body as much as cleanliness. The mechanism was simple; dirt could prevent the expulsion of carbon dioxide by the skin. Edwards' experiment on frogs, half strangled and enclosed in a hermetically sealed sack, were the basis for such assertions; the sack which had held their bodies, with their heads alone emerging, contained carbon dioxide after only a few hours.[17] Edwards in 1824, and several hygienists after him, did not hesitate to transpose from frogs to man. In 1816, Magendie himself had pronounced on the respiration of the skin. 'The skin exhales an oily substance and carbonic acid.'[18] The old experiments of Abernethy, who had plunged his arm into bell-jars sealed with mercury, and then analysed for traces of gas, now acquired a new topicality; the English surgeon had discovered some detectable indications of carbon dioxide in the bell-jars into which he had put his arm.[19]

But the theory was slow to gain acceptance. It needed the

[15] E.-A. Ancelon, *Manuel d'hygiène*, (Nancy, 1852), p. 53.
[16] Briand, *Manuel complet d'hygiène*, p. 147.
[17] W. Edwards, *De l'influence des agents physiques sur la vie* (Paris, 1824), p. 12.
[18] F. Magendie, *Précis élémentaire de physiologie* (Paris, 1816), vol. 2, p. 356.
[19] J. Abernethy, *Surgical and physiological essay* (London, 1793).

conceptualisation of thermodynamics by S. Carnot in 1824[20] for this concept of energy linked with that of an organism which burned to be defined: the volume of work done and the volume of heat consumed by the body were equivalent. A new horizon opened for ideas about organic dynamisms and even, indeed, about health. Every trace of possible combustion would arouse interest.

It was above all the effect of artificial coatings applied to the skin of mammals by physiologists, increasingly conscious of the possibilities of experimentation, which seduced the hygienists. Bouley, when he coated the shaved hide of horses with tar, observed in 1850 'all the effects of a slow asphyxiation'.[21] Death appeared even quicker (within a few hours) when a strong glue was mixed with the tar. Fourcault had already described the death throes of numerous animals coated with varnish.[22] The conclusion seemed obvious. 'If one considers that the skin is a respiratory organ, that it absorbs oxygen and exhales carbonic acid, one understands just how useful it is for it to be maintained in a clean and supple condition.'[23] The concept of an organism which burned, with calorific consumption and specific energy, began to gain ground over the old models of simple machines. Steam engines became far more attractive models than levers. The calorific energy of the body took precedence over the simple hardening of the fibres. The forces became more 'profound', supposing exchanges and flux. The role of cleanliness was enhanced as the picture of energetic combustion was defined. New arguments were adduced for the dynamising of the functions, and more generally, for hygiene. 'The skin which is well cleaned is suppler, it functions and breathes better – because the skin breathes like the lungs – and sleep taken in these conditions produces an infinitely more restorative rest, which gives the whole body new vigour and new energy.'[24]

[20] S. Carnot, *Réflexions sur la puissance motrice du feu* (Paris, 1824). It was Hirn above all, with his *Esquisse élémentaire de la théorie mécanique de la chaleur et de ses conséquences philosophiques* (Strasbourg, 1864), who systematised the application of thermodynamics to physiology.

[21] H. Bouley, *Recueil de médecine vétérinaire* (Paris, 1850).

[22] A. Fourcault, 'Expérience démonstrant l'influence de la suppression mécanique de la transpiration cutanée sur l'altération du sang', *Compte rendu de l'académie des Sciences de Paris*, vol. 4. It is now known that such occurrences are much more due to some disturbance of thermal control than to any respiratory phenomenon.

[23] C. Labouverie, *Notions de physiologie et d'hygiène à l'usage de la jeunesse et des maisons d'éducation* (Paris, 1868), p. 308.

[24] T. Gallard, *Notions d'hygiène à l'usage des instituteurs primaires* (Paris, 1868), p. 28.

It was a long time before the importance of respiration through the skin was diminished. Too much still appeared to confirm it; pigeons enclosed except for their heads in containers filled with toxic gases died, even though they could breathe through their beaks; certain chemical precipitates obtained from the skin indicated the presence of carbon dioxide. As early as 1849, applying the sacks of Edwards to hens and ducks, Regnault found only minute quantities of carbon dioxide after several hours.[25] But the time was not yet ripe for questioning this belief in respiration and even less the ability of body dirt to obstruct.

In their insistence, on the contrary, on gaseous exchanges, and in the fervency of their belief, numerous hygienists fostered alarm about dirt. They also indirectly emphasised the strength of one particular idea: the body's energy derived from the consumption of calories. From reference to thermodynamic theories to the less obvious image of dirt disrupting respiration, the hygiene of cleanliness thus came to participate in the vast energetic mechanisms of the body – an indication of the forces and resources of the body whose image had to a large extent been overturned since the eighteenth century. These no longer came *a priori* from some very material solidity of parts joined one to the other; they came from calories consumed and exchanged, from their management, and from their measured and calculated use.[26] The engine, with its consumption and its output, was more important than the purely mechanical rigidity of the parts. These changes, too, played a role in the transition from the cold to the hot bath.

These major modifications in conceptions of the body need to be emphasised. It was steam engines which now provided analogies. It was on their model, more or less consciously, that the code of bodily efficiency was based; health supposed plenty of combustion energy. The skin, in this connection, was simply an additional tool. The transition from the cold to the hot bath was part of a reconstruction of ideas about energy.

---

[25]   V. Régnault and J. Reiset, *Recherches chimiques sur la respiration des animaux des diverses classes* (Paris, 1849), p. 211.

[26]   The steam engine, and above all theories of thermodynamics, led to a completely new view of the body in the nineteenth century. Cf. on this point Georges Vigarello, *Le Corps redressé* (Paris, 1978), 'The energetic analysis', p. 199.

THE RESISTANCE OF PRUDERY

A series of obstacles, however, opposed this norm of efficiency. They limited its diffusion and probably explain the disparity between the proliferation of hygienic texts in the first half of the nineteenth century, and the rarity of their application. Large numbers of people, clearly, remained immune to these concerns. It was no doubt partly a question of tradition, but also of the intuitive power of certain feelings, which were assured by the care of linen and, more generally, by the values of appearance. Georges Sand, paying a visit during the Restoration to her old schoolmistress, was struck by the cleanliness of this elderly nun, now retired to a provincial convent. Sand scrutinised the old woman's face, noted the freshness of her clothes and rediscovered forgotten perfumes. It was an absolutely classical cleanliness which she evoked in her description of this unexpected visit to people from her youth. 'I was agreeably surprised to find her of an exquisite cleanliness, all perfumed with the scent of jasmine wafting through her window from the cloister. The poor sister was also clean: she wore her robe of new purple serge; her few toilet articles neatly arranged on a table testified to the care she took of her person.'[27]

The disparity between hygienic practice and theory in the first half of the nineteenth century was, however, more complex than simply the persistence of the appeal of the visual. Hot water, in particular, still left a lingering unease. Anxiety about it and criticism of it persisted. Insistence on the need to take baths and the danger of taking too many often existed side by side in the same text. Balzac demonstrated this by the cautiousness of his immersions when staying with the Guidoboni-Visconti.[28] The image of enervation persisted; water was not yet completely liberated from its tendency to dissolve. It retained its disquieting capacities, muted, certainly, but nevertheless real. The theme was still prevalent in the decade 1830–40. 'When people take baths for no other reason than whim, it relaxes the parts which should not be relaxed, and causes them to lose their tone.'[29] Moistness and weakness still went hand in hand. They were a source of unease, even though it was the frequency, rather than the principle,

---

[27] G. Sand, *Mémoires* (Paris, 1970), vol. 1, p. 969. [28] Cf. above, p. 167.
[29] M. Morin, *Manuel théorique et pratique d'hygiène* (Paris, 1827), p. 190.

of washing which was at issue. 'Too many baths enervate, especially when the baths are rather hot.'[30]

There were other fears – the head should be excepted. Washing the hair was always a source of anxiety, and aeration preferred to washing. Little explanation was offered beyond descriptions of old troubles. 'Washing the head often causes headaches or persistent toothache.'[31] The comb and drying powders remained the essential tools in the first half of the nineteenth century. Tessereau mentioned only these as late as 1855. 'All that is needed to look after the hair and care for it is to grease it a little or to cleanse it with bran or starch powder.'[32] Shampooing was a practice of the Second Empire. The theoretical insistence on the functional role of water thus had both its blind spots and its obstacles. The image of water, like that of the bodily envelope, was transformed, but retained its ancient fixations.

At an even deeper level, throughout the nineteenth century, prudery presented an insidious resistence. There were fears of 'the awakening of sexual desire'[33] brought on by hot water, and fears of the solitude licensed by the bathtub. Some doctors, still in 1850 employing almost unchanged the theme of dynamisms and organic strengths, were prey to doubts: baths were dangerous because they provoked evil thoughts. They might pervert. 'Bathing is an immoral practice. Unhappy experience has taught us of the moral dangers of spending an hour naked in the bathtub.'[34] The risks were particularly great amongst boarders; too long in the bath could lead their submerged bodies astray. Warmth and solitude were conducive to an evil which texts hesitated to name. 'In solitary bathtubs, every pupil cannot be watched . . . They think evil thoughts in solitude. They are encouraged by the influence of the hot water. In colleges, hot baths are desirable only for the sick who are not left alone for a single moment.'[35] Instead, summertime swimming fulfilled the function of all-over washing. The sight of college boys being taken to the Seine in June and July became quite familiar in the middle of the century. And

[30] F. Foix, *Manuel d'hygiène* (Paris, 1844), p. 526.
[31] Briand, *Manuel complet d'hygiène*, p. 158.
[32] A. Tessereau, *Cours d'hygiène* (Paris, 1855), p. 265.
[33] Lévy, *Traité d'hygiène publique et privée*, vol. 2, p. 178.
[34] Meeting of the Central Council of Health of Nantes in 1852, recorded in Léonard, *Les Médecins de l'Ouest*, vol. 3, p. 1142.
[35] C. Pavet de Courteille, *Hygiène des collèges et des maisons d'éducation* (Paris, 1827), p. 84.

the *Journal des enfants* could turn this into an edifying theme. 'Every Thursday, when it is warm, the master takes us to the cold baths.'[36]

Prudery was more directly at issue when it came to the undressing, and above all the touching, required when washing was for cleanliness. Both what had to be done and what was seen were suspect. Drying the genital organs, for example, was problematic. 'Shut your eyes', suggested Mme de Celmart, 'until you have finished.'[37] In a very earnest text, Foix exploited allusion to the full. Dangers and discretion were evoked, but nothing was named. 'This daily washing of certain parts of the body should be carried out once only, in the morning on rising; some people, however, especially women, repeat this several times a day. We do not advise this. We wish to respect the mystery of cleanliness. We will content ourselves with observing that everything which goes beyond the boundaries of a healthy and necessary hygiene leads imperceptibly to unfortunate results.'[38] Hence the habit of washing in a shirt, of which nineteenth century convents provide the most extreme example. 'Many former inmates of convents testify that they could only bathe enveloped in a shirt until the middle of the nineteenth century.'[39] Hence, also, the resistence to immersion found in certain rich families right up to the end of the nineteenth century. 'No-one in my family took a bath! We washed in a tub with five centimetres of water, or we sponged ourselves down in large basins, but the idea of plunging into water up to our necks seemed pagan, even sinful.'[40] When, in 1900, a doctor prescribed a bath to check the fever of the little Pauline de Broglie, her entourage were appalled; there was no bathtub in the house, albeit extremely rich. One was, accordingly, hired and placed 'near a large fire even though it was the month of June'.[41] A fresh problem arose; should the little girl undress? This was out of the question; Pauline was bathed in her nightshirt.

For the habit of bathing to spread, people had to be convinced that it did not offend against modesty. This idea retained its force right through the nineteenth century. Mme Staffe, in 1892, was still

[36] F. de Courcy, 'La partie de natation', *Le Journal des enfants* (Paris, 1842), p. 55.

[37] Mme E. de Celmart, *Manuel des dames ou l'Art de l'élégance* (Paris, 1833), p. 100; quoted by Corbin, *Le Miasme et la Jonquille*, p. 210.

[38] Foix, *Manuel d'hygiene*, p. 526.

[39] O. Arnold, *Le Corps et l'Ame, la vie dans les couvents au XIXe siècle* (Paris, 1984), p. 81.

[40] Comtesse J. de Pange, *Comment j'ai vu 1900* (Paris, 1975), p. 86.   [41] *Ibid.*

endeavouring to render undressing and immersion familiar. She emphasised a physical purity which resembled that of the 'angels of light',[42] and, in particular, a misinterpretation of religion; impiety lay not in entrusting oneself naked to water, but 'on the contrary, in not taking care of one's body'.[43] The reticence evoked by Mme Staffe, and against which she struggled, was not, however, directly religious. It was the reticence of tradition hesitating in the face of the emollient effects of water, the reticence which connected warmth and lascivity to the extent of detecting in them the beginnings of vice – it was against them, amongst others, that nineteenth-century hygiene battled.

Other, more immediately apparent, obstacles sprang from the relative lack of water circulating in towns, and also from the disparity between bourgeois and popular cleanliness. These two themes merit particular attention.

[42] Baronne Staffe, *Le Cabinet de toilette* (Paris, 1892), p. 55.   [43] *Ibid.*, p. 51.

13. *Water's itineraries*

When the first victims of cholera in Paris died in the Rue Mazarine in March 1832, some people resorted to traditional remedies; the Comte Apponyi, for example, offered his friends 'little cassolettes containing a scented lozenge made of mint and camomile'[1] for protection against unwholesome air; Rémusat determined to avoid 'fatigue and cold';[2] the archbishop of Paris stepped up the number of pastoral letters, offertories and *Te Deum*s in an attempt to limit the plague.[3] It was even widely believed that some mysterious poison had been thrown into the fountains.[4] The disease revived forgotten fears of great communal disasters. Its advance was unpredictable, uncontrolled and sudden, breaking through quarantine and *cordons sanitaires*. It destroyed the systems it afflicted within hours. It provoked general stupor by attacking seemingly at random and causing terrible agonies.

The sick man was a corpse even before he lost his life. His face grew haggard with amazing speed. You could distinguish his muscles beneath skin which had suddenly gone bluish-black, his eyes were hollow, dry, shrunk to half their size, and sunk deep, as if pulled by a thread towards the nape of his neck and the inside of his skull.[5]

WATER AND PROTECTION AGAINST EPIDEMICS

But Apponyi's cassolettes were merely archaic survivals. The sanitary reactions in April and May 1832 showed how the models of the late eighteenth century had gained acceptance – more street fountains (for example, four at Passy within a few weeks),[6] watering of the streets,

---

[1] R. Apponyi, *Vingt-Cinq Ans à Paris* (Paris, 1913), vol. 2, p. 162.
[2] de Rémusat, *Mémoires de ma vie*, vol. 2, p. 560.
[3] Archevêque de Paris, *Mandement à l'occasion de choléra morbus* (Paris, 30 March 1832).
[4] L. Blanc, *Histoire de dix ans, 1830–1840* (Lausanne, 1850), vol. 3, p. 185.
[5] *Ibid.*, pp. 174–5.
[6] Anon., *Projet d'amélioration et d'embellissement pour Auteuil et Passy* (Paris, 1832), p. 13.

whose residents sometimes clubbed together to have the frequency increased,[7] closure of excessively narrow alleys, chlorine put into cesspools,[8] and promulgation of measures aimed at increasing the circulation of air and water. The fears remained those of the eighteenth century; the danger lay in uncontrolled emanations. Buckets of chlorine were even placed here and there to 'attack' smells.[9] Criticism and denunciations abounded of a town mired with cesspools, choked with faecal matter, and crammed into confined and restricted spaces – the Paris, in fact, of *La Fille aux yeux d'or*, exactly contemporary with the cholera. 'Half Paris sleeps in the putrid exhalations of courts, streets and privies.'[10] The attempts, immediately the cholera was known, to flood the drains of the Ile Louviers, in order to evacuate its receptacles and refuse, simply confirmed the enhanced role of water.[11]

Water had so gained in importance that new measures were now proposed; baths, for example, were encouraged as an additional defence against contagion, and, most important of all, the circuits for the supply and evacuation of water were reconstructed. A hundred millions were voted in 1832 for public works which included the construction of canals to carry water (and for shipping).[12]

The 'warm bath' was treated as a potential means of protection in general directives offered by the town;[13] any 'dubious' build-up of matter on the skin would thus be avoided. The recommendation was regularly repeated in Paris and the provinces, echoing the successive waves of the disease. 'The skin should be kept as clean as possible, by regular changes of linen and by taking an occasional warm bath.'[14] The enquiries undertaken at this period into communal installations regularly recorded public baths amongst the instruments of defence, counted along with spouting fountains, street fountains and the circuits for watering the streets, all temporarily assimilated amongst

[7] *Ibid.*, p. 14.
[8] L. Chevalier, *Le Choléra, la première épidémie du XIXᵉ siècle, étude collective présentée par L. Chevalier* (La Roche-sur-Yon, 1958), p. 17; cf. also P. Trolliet, *Rapport sur le choléra morbus de Paris* (Paris, 1832).
[9] de Rémusat, *Mémoires de ma vie*, vol. 2.
[10] H. de Balzac, *La Fille aux yeux d'or*, in *Oeuvres complètes* (Paris, 1867), vol. 1, p. 63.
[11] Blanc, *Histoire de dix ans*, vol. 3, p. 176.
[12] de Rémusat, *Mémoires de ma vie*, vol. 3, p. 45.
[13] Blanc, *Histoire de dix ans*, vol. 3, p. 177.
[14] Anon., *Conseils pour se préserver du choléra morbus, adressés par la société médicale de Dijon aux habitants de la ville et des campagnes* (Dijon, 1849), p. 7.

protective measures.[15] A derisory defence, obviously, in an over-crowded and sick Paris, traversed by vehicles 'piled high with dead bodies, stacked one on top of the other like casks',[16] but a defence which emphasised how the role of bathing had been definitively reversed since the terrors of the plague. Water now seemed to play a protective role, even though the concept of miasma was still dominant. It remained scarce, carried, pail by pail, from the Fontaine Saint-Michel by the Raphael of *La Peau de chagrin*, still too poor to pay the porter,[17] or fiercely hoarded by the Mayeux of Eugène Sue, so as not to use more than four buckets a week.[18] Water was even scarcer when some natural gradient presented an obstacle; at Montfermeil, the inhabitants of the plateau had to cross the village before they could draw water from the lakes bordering the wood.[19] Awareness of this scarcity informed the enquiries into mortality from cholera after 1832. Death had struck hardest in poor districts, ill-provided with light and water. Poumiès, reporting on medical visits required by the town, described 'lodgings deprived of air and light, refuse everywhere . . . everywhere dirt . . .'[20] The *Répertoire des connaissances utiles* put it bluntly in 1850: 'The most exposed are those who pay least attention to the rules of hygiene and cleanliness.'[21]

This was a seemingly modern conception, in which care of the skin activated obscure forces, as well as removing smells and deposits. Water no longer weakened the bodily openings, but protected them. It preserved them from still ill-defined dangers and dynamised the organic functions by increasing both perspiration and energy. It had completely changed its meaning by comparison with the old practices in times of plague. It was now a defence; it no longer exposed to, but protected from, risk. The authorities, aware that a warm bath was not always feasible, insisted in their advice on at least some washing: 'The feet, for example, should be frequently washed in warm water.'[22]

But water circuits also changed, to the point of transforming the

---

[15] Anon., *Projet d'amélioration et d'embellissement*, p. 15.

[16] A. Bazin, *L'Epoque sans nom, esquisses de Paris (1830–3)* (Paris, 1833), vol. 2, pp. 269–70.

[17] H. de Balzac, *La peau de chagrin*, in *Oeuvres*, vol. 2, p. 20.

[18] E. Sue, *Le Juif errant* (Brussels, 1845, 1st ed. 1844), p. 119.

[19] V. Hugo, *Les Misérables* (Paris, 1980, 1st ed. 1862), vol. 1, p. 407.

[20] F.-L. Poumiès de La Siboulie, *Souvenirs d'un médecin de Paris (1789–1863)* (Paris, 1910), pp. 234–5.

[21] I. Bourdin, 'Le choléra', *Le Répertoire des connaissances utiles* (Paris, 1850), vol. 5, p. 526.

[22] Anon., *Conseils pour se préserver du choléra morbus*, p. 21.

urban image. The central concern was no longer only distribution, but now also evacuation. And the bath, despite its obvious social limitations, was an integral part of this network.

THE CIRCULATION OF WATER AND PUBLIC HYGIENE

Cholera greatly encouraged measures which transformed the conception of the town: a place no longer drained on the surface, but underneath, by a system of buried pipes. The transformation was not immediate. In 1832, for example, there was still hesitation over whether to invest in monumental architecture or in invisible machinery – a wealth of impressive facades, or a more secret, and sometimes more costly, wealth of hidden conduits. England was in general ahead of France. The various missions sent to London noted, as early as 1832, that at least a third of the houses had water laid on, and evacuated by concealed pipes.[23] English travellers, on the other hand, were astonished by what they saw in Paris. 'Whatever one's admiration for the church of the Madeleine, I think it would have been more useful, for the town of Paris, to have saved the sums it cost to build for the construction and laying of pipes to distribute water to private houses.'[24] The American, Colman, some years later, was surprised that cesspools were still regularly emptied in the streets of Paris. 'In London, this ordure passes into the drains, and from there to mix with the water of the Thames . . . In Paris, faecal matter is generally removed by what is called the atmospheric process. The cart is stationed at the door, in the street; a long leather pipe is laid from the cesspool to the cart, and air being pumped, the semi-fluid faecal matter passes straight into the cart.'[25] There is a double image here, of English water irrigating houses, then flowing away through subterreanean channels. The great originality of these installations lay in the association of a new actor with a new manifestation; it was the engineer, not the architect, who undertook the articulation of the network of pipes. The doctors engaged in a new dialogue. And it was with the linking of the underground flows into an integrated system

[23] C.-F. Mallet, *Notice historique sur le projet d'une distribution générale d'eau à domicile dans Paris* (Paris, 1830), p. 28.
[24] Mme F. M. Trollope, *Paris et les Parisiens en 1835* (Paris, 1836), p. 303.
[25] H. Colman, *European agriculture and small economy* (Boston, 1848), quoted by G. de Bertier de Sauvigny in his recent work, *La France et les Français vus par les voyageurs américains, 1814–1848* (Paris, 1982), p. 136.

that there developed a new vision of a town whose farthest points were connected by means of invisible conduits. All the principles for the distribution of water, like the methods for evacuating the waste, were revised. The modern town was based on a concealed infrastructure. Everything turned on the calculation of levels, the speed of flow through pipes, and the flexibility of the network; attention was concentrated on the diameters, gradient, and numerous intersections of pipes, in fact, on matters of engineering technique. As Beguin has recently emphasised with great clarity: 'The originality of the conceptions of health which were developed in the first half of the nineteenth century lies not in those principles (water, air, light) which, for the most part, remained as they emerged from the reflections of eighteenth century doctors, but in their investment in vast systems which obeyed a new logic of health.'[26] With them, the town underwent a rationalisation of these physical flows, which were now channelled, buried, and apportioned. It seemed as if housing was only possible if constructed over hidden hydraulic machinery.

Such solutions were still tentative in France. The argument, widely debated, was not really settled before the middle of the century. The Chief Water Engineer for Paris thought it would be too expensive and too dangerous to extend the pipes right into houses; ineradicable damp would result.[27] But other projects proliferated: for conduits under the pavements to receive 'rain water and domestic water from houses',[28] and, in particular, for conduits to carry water directly to upper storeys. 'It is a question here of changing our habits, of exchanging the niggardly manner with which we now use water in favour of a generous use of this element essential to life and domestic health, and in favour of the habits of washing which are so beneficial to health, and which will eventually be introduced into France as has for long been the case with our neighbours across the sea.'[29] Such projects were often only actually realised as a result of the activities of Haussman two decades later.

But some significant changes were, nevertheless, made to the Parisian water system in the 1830s. The principle was one of

---

[26] F. Beguin, 'Machineries anglaises du confort', *L'Haleine des faubourgs* in the review *Recherche* (Fontenay-sous-Bois, 1977), p. 161.

[27] P.-A. Girard, *Simple Exposé de l'état actuel des eaux publiques de Paris* (Paris, 1831), p. 24.

[28] H. Horeau, *Nouveaux Egouts* (Paris, 1831), p. 6.

[29] Mallet, *Notice historique sur le projet d'une distribution générale d'eau*, p. 23.

absorption, as opposed to the permanent and expensive labour of pumping. The project, in fact, was old, conceived under the Directoire, and was based on supply by means of canals. The works slowly got under way after 1817, speeded up after 1832, and were completed in 1837. The conception was very different from that of the eighteenth century. The water was no longer pumped, but collected; the aim was a gain in cost and quantity. A considerable financial investment was necessary to create the system for carrying the water, but distribution by simple inertia would result: natural flow as opposed to unreliable manipulation by pumps, physical gravity as opposed to the expensive power of machines. The length of drains, firstly, was tripled between 1830 and 1837,[30] even though they did not always receive household waste water. And the very principle of the water supply was transformed. With the Ourcq canal, in particular, dug over more than fifteen years, Paris became, in part, a centre supplied passively; the height of the point of arrival (twenty-five metres above the Seine)[31] made it possible for water to flow into many districts. This construction tripled in quantity the water pumped into the Seine, though it remained, obviously, well below the demands of today. The total output was calculated on a consumption of 7.5 litres per inhabitant per day.[32] The number of subscriptions did not increase: eighteen out of 178 houses and mansions in the suburbs of Roule and Saint-Honoré were supplied by water from the Seine in 1831, and 380 in all the districts supplied by the Ourcq canal, which, in 1831, reached a seventh of Paris.[33] The essence, however, lay in the project for a new town totally unified by its subterranean fluxes. The project gradually took shape, though its realisation remained tentative under the July Monarchy. But the supply of water, at least, began to change, which had consequences for the growth of public baths.

Firstly, the bath-houses changed location; thanks to the new conduits, they were sited in the middle of Paris, no longer only on the banks of the Seine. Next, their number increased, revealing the imperceptible growth of healthy habits. The outbreak of cholera constituted a significant date in this regard. The number of these

---

[30] A. Chevalier, 'Mémoire sur les égouts de Paris, de Londres, de Montpellier', *Les Annales d'hygiène publique* (Paris, January, 1838). p. 368.

[31] H. C. Emmery, 'Statistiques des eaux de la ville de Paris', *Annales des Ponts-et-Chaussées* (Paris, 1839), p. 67.

[32] Girard, *Simple exposé*, p. 39.   [33] *Ibid.*, pp. 26–7.

establishments grew from fifteen in 1816 to seventy-eight in 1831, most of them supplied with the less expensive water from the Ourcq. And their number grew by a further 25 per cent between 1831 and 1839.[34] This attracted flattering remarks in certain guides to Paris; Abel Hugo, for example, commented as early as 1835 on 'the fact that every district of Paris has its bath-houses';[35] and equally admiring remarks were made by certain foreigners who described some very luxurious establishments. 'You are received in beautiful rooms opening onto a garden in the centre of the building, ornamented with statues and fountains. The bathrooms are tastefully furnished; the bathtubs are of marble and lined with spotless linen.'[36] Even the writers of vaudevilles made a point of portraying some of these new locations.[37] It is hardly surprising that these establishments were seen as 'progress'. This was a perennial assertion of contemporaries, for whom each increase in their numbers marked a new peak. Such praise does not prove novelty. It was repeated from one decade to the next from the end of the eighteenth century, adapted to the changing figures, obviously echoing their growth, but not the cause of it.

There were, however, two new perspectives in the second third of the nineteenth century; baths began to be considered in relation to the issue of the evacuation of water, and their number to be submitted to comparative statistics, also concerned with the problem of flow.

When Valette, in 1820, had the novel idea of an enterprise providing baths in people's homes, he was aware that, apart from the reception by the public, his problems were the manoeuvrability of the materials and the evacuation of the dirty water. Valette used a pump to empty the bath 'which, in a minute and a half, removes the water and pours it away by means of waterproof pipes, supported on stands, to issue onto the pavement'.[38] The mechanism, apparently so simple, was not without its drawbacks. It disrupted the pavements, it was clumsy, and it was visible. A more discreet method was gradually

---

[34] P.-S. Girard, 'Recherches sur les établissements de bains publics à Paris depuis le xvᵉ siècle jusqu'à présent', *Annales d'hygiène publique* (Paris, 1831), p. 51; Emmery, 'Statistiques des eaux', p. 184.

[35] A. Hugo, *La France pittoresque* (Paris, 1835), p. 120.

[36] N. P. Willis, *Pencillings by the way, written during some years of residence and travel in Europe* (New York, 1852, 3rd ed.), p. 150.

[37] Cf. 'L'Hôtel des bains' (Paris, 1820), AN F18 635; 'Les bains à la papa' (Paris, 1819), P18 632.

[38] Cf. F. P. N. Gillet de Laumont, *Rapport fait à la Société d'encouragement pour l'industrie nationale sur les bains tempérés portés à domicile . . . entrepris par M. Valette* (Paris, 1819), p. 3.

preferred in the 1830s: evacuation of the water into cesspools, the underground constructions in which the faecal matter of Parisian houses accumulated. But, by increasing the amount of water flowing into these restricted containers, baths brought to the home filled them more frequently, necessitating more frequent emptying. All the more so as the majority of establishments started to provide portable baths. In 1836, Parent Duchatelet held this practice (among others) 're-sponsible' for the malfunctioning of the cesspools. 'Their nuisance has increased for some years now to a significant degree.'[39] He saw only one solution to the problem: the separation, in the cesspool itself, of solid and liquid matter, indirect proof that branch-pipes leading into a main drain were not clearly envisaged. But his recommendations reveal, on the other hand, how the bath and emptying it had begun to be associated. The bath was now being integrated into a circuit, a sign of greater frequency of use, and also of greater interest in the itineraries of water.

Even more significant were the statistical calculations about baths which began to be made, especially after 1832, such as the estimates of the total number of baths provided by these establishments, with allowance for seasonal or locational differences. The exercise was economic – calculating numbers so as to be able to improve regulation of supply and channels, establishing that consumption fluctuated according to month or that demand varied from one district to another, determining what changes were needed in the network of pipes, and also, obviously, in the estimates of output. The *Annales des Ponts-et-Chaussées* provided, between 1830 and 1840, the best examples of such careful and accurate calculations. 'It is a sort of budget of water consumption and cash revenue, it needs to be understood in all its aspects, its significance appreciated to the full, and its movements regulated.'[40] The bath-houses thus became an integral part of the computations of the engineer. It remained, however, an interim period, when all deficiencies were explained by the still very real geographical heterogeneousness of the bath-houses and, above all, by the parsimony, equally real, which still dominated the provision of water.

The fact remains, however, that the bath was included in a unified calculation of urban water flow, and that this implies a new conception of water measured in bulk to wash the urban population,

[39] A. J. B. Parent-Duchatelet, *Hygiène publique* (Paris, 1836), vol. 2, p. 253.
[40] Emmery, 'Statistiques des eaux', pp. 177–8.

a conception which, for the first time, gauged, like a wave apportioning its strength and differentiating its impact, the water destined for washing bodies. This wave was both centralised and unevenly distributed; its flow was controlled and regulated by engineers.

Doctors, too, were involved in these calculations. The *Annales d'hygiène publique*, first published in 1829, in this respect echoed the *Annales des Ponts*. Public baths, the distribution of water, and calculations of quantities were added to a group of measures which had, in their turn, found the term which embraced them: public hygiene.[41] The sanitary protection of populations gained coherence with the acquisition of this title. The measurement of water for washing, the counting of communal emplacements and the vision of a quantified 'wave' washing bodies, did not systematically overthrow the wisdom of the eighteenth century. But they emphasise how the terminology and the evaluatory projects were in themselves significant; they show how far the need and status of hygienic knowledge had been accepted. And, finally, the figures help the contemporary reader to appreciate a gradual change in the social distribution of bathing. Both the bathing public, and the practices themselves, imperceptibly changed.

BATHING AND SOCIAL HIERARCHY

The global calculations give us some idea of scale. For example, 600,000 baths were provided by Parisian establishments in one year, 1819, for a population of 700,000 inhabitants,[42] two million were provided in 1850 for a population which had not quite doubled:[43] that is, just under one bath per year per inhabitant under the monarchy of Louis XVIII, and just over two under the Republic of the Prince-President. Put like this, the figures are not particularly revealing. The same is true of the budget calculated by Abel Hugo in 1835: a Parisian spent on average three francs fifty on his annual baths, which meant he took between three and five a year.[44]

The sociological interest of these figures lies elsewhere. The

---

[41]   The term began to appear in titles of books or chapter headings at the beginning of the nineteenth century. Chairs of public hygiene were created in Faculties of Medicine.

[42]   Cf. Gillet de Laumont, *Rapport fait à la Société*, p. 4.

[43]   Cf. *Le Moniteur* (Paris, 1850), p. 1951.

[44]   Hugo, *La France pittoresque*, p. 122.

establishments, it is clear, were not uniformly distributed throughout the social tissue. They could not, for obvious reasons, reach the whole population. Their location, very specific, is in itself significant. Most of them (eighty-three out of 101 in 1839)[45] were situated on the right bank of the Seine, where the wealthiest districts (with the exception of the suburb of Saint-Germain) were found. And many of them were established, after 1830, to the west of the Rue Saint-Denis, the area of the newest bourgeois districts. Of the eighty-one on the right bank, for example, fifty were west of the Rue Saint-Denis (Chaussée-d'Antin, Boulevard des Italiens, Rue Richelieu)'[46] It is difficult on the basis of these very general figures to indicate a precise frequency for baths, even if some communal rules cast a glimmer of light: one bath per month, for example, in the Collège Stanislas, a very bourgeois establishment, after mid-century.[47] The geographical distribution does, however, make clear the social disparity, as well as revealing new attitudes amongst the bourgeoisie: recourse to public establishments in the absence of private installations in the new districts, while popular practice apparently remained unchanged.

Apartment houses, for example, however luxurious, did not have bathrooms in mid-century. The plans of houses of several storeys in the *Paris moderne* of Normand in 1837,[48] and those of the *Revue d'architecture* of Daly, beginning in 1840 and for long after,[49] both tell the same story: no bathrooms, though washrooms leading off bedrooms were beginning to appear. Internal space was becoming more elaborate and more specialised. Even the facades of bourgeois houses were being enlivened, with sculptures and entablatures proliferating. But bathrooms did not follow washrooms. When, in 1846, Emile Souvestre tried to imagine, with heavy humour, the interior of the house of the future, he did not include a bathroom. The apartment in the *Monde tel qu'il sera* possessed the most ingenious technology, the best, at any rate, that the mid-nineteenth century could imagine: drawing rooms and bedrooms stuffed full of pulleys and wires, rails and racks, springs and bell-pulls, even steam engines. The washroom had running water, its shelves had every type of soap,

---

[45] Emmery, 'Statistiques des eaux', p. 184.   [46] *Ibid.*

[47] Cf. H. Lynch, quoted by E. Weber in *La Fin des terroirs* (Paris, 1983, 1st ed. 1976), p. 223.

[48] L. Normand, *Paris moderne* (Paris, 1837–47), 2 vols.

[49] C. Daly edited the *Revue de l'architecture et des travaux publics* published in Paris from 1840 to 1873.

its walls concealed mirrors, but no space was set aside for a bath.[50] It remained very much the case, then, in 1846, that baths were taken in a public establishment, or were 'delivered' at home, and were therefore rare. The inventory on the death of Berlioz, drawn up at the end of the Second Empire, records two washrooms attached to bedrooms, but the apartment had no bath.[51] Bourgeois space in the middle of the century had acquired what the very great residences had acquired in the first half of the eighteenth century: private places where the toilet and local washing had their private space.

Not much space, it must be said; these 'cabinets' were still minuscule annexes to bedrooms in the *Pot-Bouille* of the Second Empire, the wealthy house minutely described by Zola. 'Near the alcove a washroom was contrived, just space to wash the hands.'[52] They were often 'blind', although it was frequently recommended that they should not be closed, or the air would become stale. Such places slowly became the norm in the bourgeois world after 1830–40. And a new item of furniture appeared: a tall wooden frame supporting a basin to make it easier to wash the hands and face. This is the contraption used by Daumier's young man in *Le Vocabulaire des enfants* (1839); he wets his hands with a sponge whilst, on the threshold, a servant shrugs his shoulders. The latter, in his apron, duster in hand, mocks such washing, for him, obviously, a sign of excessive refinement and cleanliness.[53] Nevertheless, the basin now had its special support. The piece of furniture sometimes included a jug placed underneath, in the space left free: a tripod of flexible shape, jug and basin one above the other.[54]

In contrast, the very large private mansions were almost all equipped with bathrooms from the 1830s, as is shown by the plans of Normand in 1837, and, even more, those of Daly in 1864, whose examples date from 1820 to 1860.[55] The ways that bathing would develop in the second third of the nineteenth century were becoming

[50] E. Souvestre, *Le Monde tel qu'il sera* (Paris, 1846), p. 65.
[51] B. Gérard, 'L'inventaire après décès de L. H. Berlioz', *Bulletin de la société de l'histoire de Paris* (Paris, 1979), p. 186.
[52] E. Zola, *Pot-Bouille* (Paris, 1979, 1st ed. 1882), p. 33. The novel is supposed to be set in the late 1860s.
[53] *Le Vocabulaire des enfants* (Paris, 1839), p. 249.
[54] A few examples of this type of furniture appeared in great residences at the very end of the eighteenth century. See Dumonthier, *Mobilier national*.
[55] Normand, *Paris moderne*; also C. Daly, *Architecture privée aux XIXe siècle* (Paris, 1864), 3 vols.

clear: a wide range of practices in which it was the bath itself which was elaborated by distinctive actions and places. The different ways of bathing would demonstrate, more than ever, social distinctions.

The first type of practice was that of the great private houses. It no longer surprised contemporaries. There had to be some special circumstances for it to be described or referred to. Apponyi, for example, expressed surprise at the ingenious machinery possessed by the Duke of Devonshire. 'A large basin of white marble: steps of the same material descending to the bottom, water as transparent and clear as crystal rises and falls at will; it is always hot, because the fire which heats it is kept going day and night so that a bath can be taken at any hour.'[56] Similarly, Alexander Dumas was surprised at the precautions taken by Mlle George. 'She carried out a preliminary toilet before getting into her bath, so as not to dirty the water in which she was going to spend an hour.'[57] Eugène Sue went out of his way to emphasise the ostentatious behaviour of Adrienne de Cardoville, who needed the assistance of three female attendants before plunging into a bathtub made of chased silver with 'natural coral and azure shells'.[58] The bath was a normal element in the luxury of these great mansions. It was no longer mentioned, so normal had it become; the inevitable fate of all norms. Only some excess of luxury or attentions seemed worthy of remark. Another example is provided by the importance accorded to the prolonged bath of his courtesan by Balzac. He added, in this case, a very specific emphasis on feminine washing and a renewed parallel between warmth and languorousness. Beneath the values of energising and health there thus continued a current of a more obscure, even more lasting, connection – present at least since the new baths of the nobility – between warmth, rich women, and cleanliness. Warmth and cleanliness, at a subterranean level, conserved a feminine value, from which the bath seemed incapable of escaping. 'She bathed, and proceeded to that meticulous toilet, unknown to most Parisian women, because it takes up so much time and is hardly practised except amongst courtesans, easy women, and great ladies who have all day to themselves.'[59]

Another type of practice was that of the luxurious establishments

---

[56] Apponyi, *Vingt-Cinq Ans*, vol. 2, p. 292.
[57] A. Dumas, *Mémoires* in *Oeuvres complètes* (Paris, undated, about 1900, 1st ed. 1857), vol. 2, p. 119.   [58] Sue, *Le Juif errant*, p. 146.
[59] H. de Balzac, *Splendeurs et Misères des courtisanes*, in *Oeuvres complètes*, vol. 1, p. 15.

of which the best example is provided by the Chinese baths on the Boulevards. There were many servants, and freely available accessories, even bath-robes, long linen garments, previously warmed by a fire; also rest rooms, reading rooms and private boudoirs. The price varied from five to twenty francs, when the daily wage of a worker had risen, in mid century, to two francs fifty centimes.[60] Such establishments were few, and their clientele consisted in particular of rich travellers or a few new rich capable of creating fashionable places.

In most other establishments, yet a different type of practice was found: bath cubicles furnished with linen and seats, differing according to the richness of the chairs, the wall-hangings, or the amount of space. The real disparity, however, no longer lay in the establishment itself, but in the possibility of having the bath transported to private houses. The extent to which this signified an additional degree of comfort is clearly indicated by the statistics of Emmery from 1839. One establishment in the Boulevard Montmartre, for example, and another in the very heart of Saint-Germain, provided in 1838 an approximately equivalent annual number of baths, 40,960 in the case of the former, 37,720 in the latter. But whilst in the case of the Faubourg Saint-Germain more than a third of these baths were transported to homes, less than a sixth were transported from the Boulevard Montmartre.[61] The difference was social. The wealth of the two districts was reflected in the practices adopted. In the better-off districts, private spaces were found for baths, without going so far as actually constructing or furnishing places for them. It was an intermediate choice between the public baths and the baths of the great mansions. The social fringe concerned, once again, is hinted at rather than precisely defined; Gavarni's ladies of easy virtue, sitting gossiping on the edge of a bathtub mounted on wheels, wedged up against the fireplace of a very bourgeois salon,[62] or a certain Parisian landlord, in Kock's vaudeville, receiving a series of baths, whose porters drench his carpets and overturn his ornaments.[63]

---

[60] For the Chinese baths in the middle of the nineteenth century see Bertier de Sauvigny, *La France et les Français*, p. 137. For the wages of workers, see G. Duveau, *La Vie ouvrière sous le second Empire* (Paris, 1946), p. 320.

[61] Emmery, 'Statistiques des eaux', p. 185.

[62] S. P. Chevalier (called Gavarni), *Les Lorettes*, in *Oeuvres choisies* (Paris, 1845), vol. 1. [63] P. de Kock, *Les Bains à domicile* (Paris, 1845).

So practices differed according to a gradation of distinctions. The disparities were no longer between baths and partial washing, but between many different types of bath.

Finally, there was the practice of the people: baths in the Seine in summer. There were several establishments in close proximity in Paris, installed actually in the water, roughly enclosed with wooden fencing, the *bains à quatre sous*. They were sufficiently common under the July Monarchy for Daumier to have often recorded them.[64] A particular type of public, many bodies, jumbled and crammed together, a mixture of actions and practices, places seeming indiscriminately designed for people to swim, wash, relax or look on. A place where people congregated in hot weather, the 'penny bath' reveals stealthy and seasonal washing, an immersion still hesitant, bearing little resemblance to baths taken in bathtubs.

The humblest baths of all were taken hurriedly in the river, outside any establishment – informal baths, taken wherever the water permitted, fairly rare, and confined to summer. The lithographs of Daumier reveal, here too, a possible way of washing: 'Le Charivari' of 13 August 1842 shows two lanky individuals paddling, partly clothed, in the grey water of the Seine. They mop their backs and heads with large, extravagant gestures. They 'wash', while several elegant apparitions, apparently indifferent, stroll along the bank. But a problem lay in this 'indifference', which, at this very period, was no longer in evidence. A new wave of prudery, firstly, was now less tolerant of the spectacle of such half-naked people, huddled in the river at two paces from the bank. Daumier's bathers are aware of this: 'Take care, Gargouset, there's the bourgeois walking past with his wife.'[65] An old law, dating back to the Ancien Régime, already prohibited sportive bathing in summer outside carefully defined places.[66] The regulation was strengthened in the nineteenth century, repeated year after year by the prefecture of police. 'No-one must bathe in the river, except in the covered baths.'[67] But why the indifference of the passers-by in the lithograph is only apparent, is

[64] H. Daumier, *Les Bains à quatre sous*, in *Le Charivari* (Paris, 26 June, 1839). See also E. Briffault, *Paris dans l'eau* (Paris, 1844), p. 78.

[65] H. Daumier, *Attention Gargouset*, in *Le Charivari* (Paris, 13 August, 1842).

[66] *Ordonnance de par les prévôts des marchands et échevins de la ville de Paris, concernant les bains dans la rivière* (Paris, 12 June 1742), manuscript BN, reg. 21.629, Fo. 170.

[67] *Ordonnance concernant les bains de rivière*, advertisement of 30 April 1840. Cf. for this question, the archives of the préfecture de police, côte DB. 227.

that it was contemporary with quite new projects to manage and maintain the cleanliness of the poor; a cleanliness imposed, as it were, from outside, and mixed up with strategies attempting to arrest the growth of poverty.

But before considering these strategies, we must look again at the social spectrum of the various practices. The differences were not only a matter of the luxury or the frequency of washing. They lay also in the different types of water used, and in the variety of motives revealed. Amongst the well-off, bathing assumed increasingly diverse forms in the first half of the nineteenth century; warm water helped to energise the organs, hot water favoured intimate relaxation, whilst cold water was an element in hydrotherapy. The sea bath, in particular, deriving from the arguments of eighteenth century hygienists, took a very specific form, especially after 1820–30. With it, water was simply an ordeal, a milieu of shock and toughening. It must be confronted; bodies were thrown into the waves to receive strengthening shocks, or had buckets of salt water poured over them. An army of attendants was appointed and trained to be able to grasp the bodies of those taking the cure, throw them by brute force into the sea, then take hold of them once again before repeating the process. The whole effect depended on repeated shocks and on cold.[68] The baths of which Dieppe long remained the geographical centre were not yet meant for swimming. Nor had they any connection with cleanliness. Hydrotherapy went its own way, after having come close to hygiene, to the point of ambiguity, during the eighteenth century. The functions of water were definitively separated, without the virtues of cold being totally obliterated. It was the very rich who could take advantage of these various qualities. Their practices were diversified and specialised. The very poor, on the other hand, were those whose hygiene was soon to be seen to by others. A new set of norms, from 1840, was explicitly intended for the needy. Daumier's bathers were about to face a veritable pastoral; special establishments were about to be invented, just for them.

---

[68] We cannot deal fully with sea-baths here, even though evidence for them is plentiful before 1850. Cf. for example *Mémoires de la comtesse de Boigne, de Louis XVI à 1848* (Paris, 1971, 1st ed. 1907–9), vol. 1, p. 167. They are also often mentioned in the *Mémoires* of Apponyi and of de Rémusat. For the 'theory' of sea bathing, cf. one of the first French works on the theme, A. Assegond, *Manuel des bains de mer* (Paris, 1825). Cf. also G. Vigarello, 'Pratiques de natation au xixe siècle, Représentation de l'eau et différenciations sociales', in the collective work *Sport et Société* (Saint-Etienne, 1982).

14. *The pastoral of poverty*

What really changed, in fact, was the image of the poor and, above all, of poverty, which became more disquieting and more threatening with the advent of the new industrial towns. The education designed for the poor and the significance attached to clean habits also changed. There was widespread acceptance of a new connection; the cleanliness of the poor was a token of their morality, and a guarantee of order. Such ideas gained ground especially after 1840.

MAKING CLEANLINESS MORAL

The aim was both complex and comprehensive; from clean streets to clean houses, and from clean rooms to clean bodies, the intention was no less than to transform the habits of the most deprived sector of the population, to banish their supposed vices, concealed or visible, by changing their bodily habits. A veritable pastoral of poverty was established, in which cleanliness had almost the force of exorcism. Urban technology and morality became confused in a quite new way, without any change, it must be emphasised, in the basic assumptions about the dangers of miasma.

When, in 1843,[1] Clerget described a cart designed to sweep rubbish from the streets with the aid of mechanical brooms, he demonstrated the increasing role played by machinery in the nineteenth-century imagination. A complicated contraption, consisting of toothed wheels and continuous chains, would make it possible to clear the ground, according to a principle of circular and alternating friction. Horse-power alone set the mechanism in motion. The human hand had only to drive the cart. The old bucket-chains found a new role; containers disposed to form a moving chain scraped along the ground and, one after another, tipped their rubbish into the cart. It was an ambitious machine, and still utopian, so heavy was the apparatus of

[1] C. E. Clerget, 'Du nettoyage mécanique des voies publiques', *La Revue de l'architecture* (Paris, 1843), p. 267.

chains and wheels which propelled it, not to speak of the inadequacy of the machine's adjustment to the uneven ground of Paris.

The interest of Clerget's project lies less in the complex and ambitious machinery than in the author's comments on it. It was not just that this machine of the future was proposed as a tool of health, it was proposed as a tool of morality, of a cleanliness which approached ever closer till it reached the intimate habits of the very poor, an all-conquering cleanliness, which brought with it, gradually and by obscure means, order and virtue. The stages are significant in themselves: from the street to the house, and from the house to the person. 'Cleanliness calls to cleanliness, clean houses demand clean clothes, clean bodies, and, in consequence, clean morals.'² It was not, as in the eighteenth century, simply a question of energy, it was a question of the unsuspected resources of order, and the ethic of 'purity'. 'Dirt is only the livery of vice.'³ And the public concerned, far from being the bourgeoisie, was obviously the urban poor, the people condemned by the cities of the early nineteenth century to overcrowded lodging houses, even dark cellars, the people of whom the enquiries of Villermé painted such a sombre picture. 'In Nîmes, for example, in the houses of the very poor, I would say in the case of the majority of third class weavers, there is only one bed, without a mattress, on which the whole family sleeps; I always saw sheets, only their material sometimes resembled dirty sacking.'⁴ No purpose would be served by elaborating on these pictures of the poor, crammed into windowless, verminous rooms, the sexes indiscriminately mixed, or on the palliasses alive with vermin of the stonemason's family in *Les Mystères de Paris*.⁵ There had to be exceptional circumstances for the young Turquin, a workman from Rheims hitherto in only casual employment, to be washed, in 1840, by his future employers, *demi-mondaines* who saw in him a docile helper. This practice, new to him, astonished him to the extent of leaving an indelible memory. 'They heated the water in a large cauldron, cut my hair, undressed me and washed me, rubbing me till my skin glowed, since I was pretty lousy.'⁶ The young lad continued to be astonished

---

² *Ibid.*   ³ *Ibid.*
⁴ L. R. Villermé, *Tableau de l'état physique et moral des ouvriers* (Paris, 1840), vol. 1, p. 408.
⁵ E. Sue, *Les Mystères de Paris* (1844), vol. 1, second part, p. 63.
⁶ N. Turquin, *Mémoires et Aventures d'un prolétaire à travers la Révolution* (Paris, 1977), p. 28.

by the amount of water consumed by these courtesans, and which he had to manhandle. The garrets he had known, overcrowded and evil-smelling, were certainly less hospitable. Such accumulations of bodies grew with the towns of the first phase of industrialisation. They also aroused fears of their political, sanitary and social dangers. Paris nourished in its bosom a new type of savage,[7] who must be contained and mastered.

It is impossible to evoke these descriptions without stressing their insistent emphasis on the dirtiness of the poor. 'And his skin? Though his skin was filthy, you could recognise it on his face, but on his body, it was coated, hidden, if you like, by the gradual deposits of diverse exudations, there is nothing more disgustingly dirty than these disgraceful poor.'[8] Smells and sweat came, then, to amalgamate with doubtful morals. 'They show you a room already inhabited sometimes by a dozen individuals raised like Tartars in their disdain for shirts, and who do not know what it is to wash.'[9] The imagination was firmly wedded to the concept of a dirtiness which purveyed vice, of a disquieting poverty, whose rags and vermin were signs of an ever-present potential lawlessness and an at least latent delinquency. 'If a man becomes accustomed to rags, he inevitably loses his sense of dignity, and, when this is lost, the door is open to every vice'.[10]

EDUCATION

The response to these rather obscure fears was a policy of dispersal, as is well known.[11] In the sphere of hygiene, the response was primarily pedagogic.

After 1845, in particular, there was a burgeoning of the *Hygiènes des familles* and the *Hygiène populaires*, philanthropic literature which dispensed precepts, suggestions and advice. Massé, one of the first, relied on materials pared down to essentials, and adapted, in theory, to ordinary homes. He described a series of basic actions, employing utensils in general use which, in the absence of baths, would popularise all-over washing. Massé, like a good teacher,

[7] L. Chevalier, *Classes laborieuses et Classes dangereuses* (Paris, 1958), pp. 162–3.
[8] *Rapport sur les travaux du Conseil central de salubrité du département du Nord* (1843), pp. 28–9.
[9] P. de Kock, *La Grande Ville, Nouveau tableau de Paris* (Paris, 1842), vol. 1, p. 170.
[10] Clerget, 'Du nettoyage mécanique des voies publiques', p. 267.
[11] Cf. the number of the review *Recherche* already quoted, *L'Haleine des faubourgs* (Paris, 1977).

wanted to explain everything, the simplest actions, the humblest objects, their material, form and number. He laid down how much water should be used, its temperature, and how long washing should take. He listed utensils, places and times, not afraid to repeat himself, specifying every last detail, persuaded that the public he was addressing was completely ignorant. His language was painstaking and serious, wordy but solemn, struggling constantly to achieve simplicity. Massé, a passionate believer in popular education,[12] convinced that everything had to be described down to the last detail, well-meaningly spelled things out.

First of all you need a small, empty tub; a dish half full of cold water; a kettle of hot water; two fairly large sponges, what grocers call household sponges because they are used to clean floors; a large piece of flannel; towels or cloths. You take the woollen cloth and rub the body all over with it. You rub in particular the chest, under the arms, wherever the warmth of the bed might have produced perspiration . . . Needless to say, before starting, you tip into the dish holding the cold water enough hot water to produce a temperature of at least twenty degrees. Obviously, you put this dish on the corner of a table in such a way that it is accessible for the operation. Then grasping the two sponges, one in each hand, and plunging them into the dish, you begin the task of washing . . . Do not leave off for a moment, use your water in such a way that you have enough to operate for at least one minute; and as soon as you have finished, step out of the tub and quickly take a towel to dry yourself.[13]

Everything in this text is geared to economy, of materials and water, obviously, but also of time and space – not much space, but an all-over wash. Such washing should be possible as long as the basic instructions, right down to the most insignificant, were observed. The treatise of popular hygiene is here essentially militant, with a special, persuasive militancy. Conceived for the 'workers of town and country', the advice of the Rouennais Guillaume provides another example, also denouncing dirt as being 'almost always the result of laziness'.[14]

The primary school was another, even more important, arena for the diffusion of the norms created for the poor. After 1830, manuals

---

[12] For J. Massé, see the long passage devoted to him by F. Mayeur in *L'Education des filles au XIXe siècle* (Paris, 1977).
[13] J. Massé, *Encyclopédie de la santé, cours d'hygiène populaire* (Paris, 1855), vol. 1, p. 157.
[14] A. Guillaume, *Catéchisme hygiénique* (Paris, 1850), p. 237.

for schoolteachers frequently repeated the basic principles of contemporary treatises of hygiene. Some manuals aimed at scholars did
the same. In 1836, the *Règlement de l'instruction primaire de Paris*
recommended that they should be read regularly, and even learned by
heart, by the 'pupils of the six first classes'.[15] The manual of hygiene
became part of schoolwork. It is hardly surprising that this sort of
teaching was linked 'essentially to moral and religious instruction'.[16]
It was, indeed, a catechism. Hygiene had confirmed its status as
official, taught, knowledge. In practice, the observance of some of the
recommendations prescribed in these texts, in particular those
suggesting 'one warm bath a month in winter', was hardly possible
for poor children in the towns or in the country;[17] a practice hardly
practicable, it would appear, from a reading of Villermé's descriptions of housing conditions. But it was, after all, primarily a matter of
pastoral.

Schools did, on the other hand, influence external appearance.
Mme Sauvan, for example, insisted on the patient modification of the
parts which were visible. There was nothing here which went against
tradition. 'Do not show yourselves either discouraged or disgusted by
your new connections, be good girls, if I may use the expression; do
not allow coarseness of manners or dirtiness of clothes to put you off.
Fight them, destroy them in your pupils.'[18] Overberg's advice, long
become an incantation by 1845, was similar. 'They should wash their
hands and faces properly.'[19]

These pedagogic sermons are completed by the regular recommendations which the various councils of health caused to be
promulgated. These organisations had spread throughout the provinces, extending even to the *arrondissements*, since the law of 1848.
Their recommendations proliferated, unchanging and repetitive;
thus the Council of Health of the Seine insisted in 1821 on the
creation of free public baths in the river for the use of the poor,
'because people acquainted with cleanliness, are soon acquainted
with order and discipline'.[20] Only the impermanence of these
bathing-placing and, in particular, the expectations of their disci-

[15] M.-J. Orfila, *Préceptes d'hygiène à l'usage des enfants qui fréquentent les écoles primaires* (Paris, 1836).   [16] *Ibid.*   [17] *Ibid.*, p. 8.
[18] Mme J. L. Sauvan, *Cours normal des instituteurs primaires* (Paris, 2nd ed. 1840), p. 17.
[19] B. Overberg, *Manuel de pédagogie* (Liège, 1845, 1st ed. in German, 1825), p. 84.
[20] *Travaux du Conseil de salubrité de la Seine* (Paris, 1821), p. 16.

plinary consequences (order, no longer simply vigour) make the appeal particularly significant. The councils were echoing a moralising hygiene. They spread to the four points of the compass a uniform teaching, specifically destined for the poor.

But the evidence they reported from their respective provinces emphasised the relative conservatism of local practice. The complaints of the Council of Aube, for example, in 1835, included that 'the inhabitants of Villemaur are wrong to neglect bathing. Many of them are sufficiently well-off to procure a bathtub, at least of wood. Further, the local administration ought to establish public baths in the Vanne.'[21] The complaints of the council of Nantes, in 1825, also regretted the absence of baths for the very poor in the Loire.[22]

Where, however, these statements strike a completely new note, is in their harsh criticism of peasant life. This severity merits attention. The doctors of the late eighteenth century, passionate believers in fresh air and country life, had always shown themselves ambivalent on this subject. The farms and stables seemed to them confined and smelly, but the fresh air of the open country was more important. Now, however, the hygiene of the countryman began to be condemned in a quite new way. 'Having, with bare feet, cleaned out their animals, or been out with the muck-cart, they do not hesitate, just as they are, to go to bed or put back on their clothes.'[23] The resistance of these sons of the soil to accepting the new norms was now also recorded. The Councils made this resistance explicit for the first time. They even attempted to understand it; the criteria of the peasantry possessed their own coherence, which responded, amongst other things, to the specific expectations of country life, which were very remote from the hygiene of towns. 'They refuse to change their linen when they are wet or even running with sweat, or they even then take no precautions against catching cold, because they are afraid of becoming soft.'[24] This was the resistance of tradition. A disturbing power was attributed to animal smells; rubbish and its effluvia exercised an obscure seduction. Urban hygiene encountered a totally alien sensibility, occasionally visible in certain scholarly texts. Such allusions were not, as a rule, made explicit, derived from the most buried sensations, attributing the power of a stimulant to the smell of sweat or even of dirt. The masculine significance of sweat, amongst

---

[21] *Rapport sur les travaux du Conseil de salubrité de l'Aube* (Troyes, 1835), p. 62.
[22] *Rapport sur les travaux du Conseil de salubrité de Nantes* (Nantes, 1817–25), p. 10.
[23] *Conseil de salubrité de l'Aube*, p. 30.   [24] *Ibid.*

other things, was mentioned by Bordeu in a medical text dating from the very beginning of the nineteenth century. 'The hairy, scaly state of the skin, the smell coming off it, are proofs of vigour, the product of a disposition inclined to procreation and of the phenomena of seminal cachexia.'[25] Complicity with seductions of this type was clearly no longer possible.

It was the conception of relationships between town and country which changed. It was not that urban accumulation was suddenly seen as less dangerous. It had never, perhaps, seemed so threatening. But those who thought about public hygiene and preached against poverty abandoned all reference to the virtues of peasant life. The city concentrated on the need for internal, autonomous and specific transformations.

REGENERATING MEASURES

Talk and education could not, obviously, remain the only responses to the threat presented by poverty. Nor could the social order expected to accompany hygiene remain simply a matter of incantation. Very concrete measures aimed at correcting the dirty practices of the poor were devised from the middle of the nineteenth century. They made it possible to expect real, and regenerative, transformation.

The establishment of free or cheap public baths and wash-houses towards the middle of the century is the most significant and the most obvious illustration of these sanitary and moral measures. In 1852, the Emperor publicly announced his personal participation in these enterprises. He produced 'from his own pocket'[26] the necessary funds for the foundation of three establishments in poor districts of Paris. He also contributed to the setting-up of a model establishment at Romorantin. The concept excited the politicians. In 1850, the Assembly debated opening an 'extraordinary fund of 600,000 francs to promote the creation of model public baths and wash-houses for the benefit of the working classes'.[27] Some projects were completed: the baths and wash-houses in the Rue de la Rotonde,[28] for example, to which was added a lunatic asylum whose social importance is well

[25]   T. de Bordeu, *Oeuvres* (Paris, 1818), vol. 2, p. 959.
[26]   A. Bourgeois d'Orvanne, *Lavoirs et Bains publics à prix réduits* (Paris, 1854), p. 9.
[27]   Cf. *Le Moniteur* (Paris, 1850), p. 1951.
[28]   Cf. *Le Moniteur* (Paris, 1852), p. 144.

known. The plan of this ensemble was publicised as a model: separate entries for men and women, a courtyard planted with trees placed between the baths and the wash-house, and fountains in the courtyard, demonstrating the abundance of water and emphasising the symbolic value the place held. In all, there were a hundred places for washing clothes and a hundred baths. Adoption of this policy would provide the people with the chance to use apparently accessible water. Linen and skin were clearly associated in the mind of its proponents, a desire to spread the habit of bathing along with that of changing linen, and make it unnecessary to dry at home clothes which had been washed, which only aggravated damp and unhealthy conditions.

Most of these foundations remained for a long time simply model establishments,[29] and the heavy investment in them was rarely compensated by the income received (the baths were free or cost ten centimes). But these institutions posed, in the clearest terms, in mid century, the problems of a hygiene totally conceived for subject people. In the first place, strict utility was insisted on for both places and objects. 'Excessively prolonged baths produce in working girls and the women of the people a troublesome susceptibility.'[30] So the length of a bath was restricted, the period of occupation of the cubicles being limited to thirty minutes. The control of the consumption of water also involved surveillance; the taps shut automatically, once a certain amount of water had been provided. The warmth, finally, must be neither too great nor too expensive; its temperature was controlled and limited. Education was thus continued in the standards imposed on utensils and space. This hygiene for the poor could not, it appears, be their own.

But the concept was central, in mid century, when it combined all the official legitimation given to the hygiene of the poor. The debate in 1850 became a veritable theoretical digest. It was a question of morals, certainly, which the reporter stressed with excessive ponderousness. 'All those who have lived a little with the working class know very well the difference which exists between two families possessed of the same resources but of which one, accustomed to

---

[29] Cf. Lévy, *Traité d'hygiène publique et privée*, vol. 2, p. 726: 'Unhappily, the liberal views of the government have not yet borne full fruit: a small number of towns have sought the allocations which the law accords them to establish baths and wash-houses.'

[30] Bourgeois d'Orvanne, *Lavoirs et Bains publics à prix réduits*, p. 72.

cleanliness, brings health and order into the home, whilst the other, in contrast, given over to filth, if you will excuse the expression, accompanies this habit with vice and disorder.'[31] It was a question of cholera, too, a new outbreak having left over 20,000 dead in Paris in 1849. 'The idea of the project, gentlemen, is not far to seek. You have all still present in your minds the misery which struck France in 1849, the way in which cholera raged through the country . . .'[32] It was essential to increase 'the hygienic means that the country possesses to defend itself against invasion by such a plague'.[33] The baths, once again, were to protect and avert. There was, lastly, a more general argument, in part new, in which biology and morality gave support to proposals aimed at regeneration. The spectre of uncontrollable poverty nourished the spectre of a possible physical and social regression. The masses, perpetually rebellious, chaotic, ever more numerous, swelling and disturbing the towns, brutalised by the labour required by the first industrialisation, gave credence to the idea of a possible 'regression'; nothing less, in fact, than an enfeeblement of the race. There were anxious investigations into the workers, tables were compiled of the height of conscripts, sicknesses were recorded by the army medical boards. A rhetoric fed by hasty statistics, bound to a rigid concept of progress and exploiting through metaphor the new reflections on the animal species,[34] elaborated the risk of degeneration. It also pondered the need for regenerating measures, combining philanthropy and social control. Baths for the poor, ensuring the actual removal of body dirt, seemed entirely appropriate for such projects. Dumas, a minister seeking funds, expressed it bluntly in the course of the 1850 debate.

When the conditions of health of a part of the population are improved, it is not done solely for their own benefit; the children who result, when they are in due course conscripted for service in the army, when they become citizens of the State, are, as far as the relation between health and strength for work is concerned, in an infinitely preferable condition than if they had been left to themselves.[35]

---

[31] *Projet de loi tendant à obtenir l'ouverture d'un crédit extraordinaire de 600,000 francs*, p. 3336; for enquiries into the working world around 1850 and after, cf. the studies of Frédéric Le Play, presented by B. Kalavra and A. Savoye, *Ouvriers des deux mondes* (Paris, 1983).

[32] Intervention of J.-B. Dumas, 'Débat sur le projet de loi . . .', p. 3335.

[33] *Ibid.*

[34] The theories of Lamarck were here put to the service of anxiety about the biological 'regression' of the race.

[35] Intervention of J.-B. Dumas, 'Débat sur le projet de loi . . .', p. 3335.

The wheel had turned full circle. The water which washed also dispensed energy and accelerated organic interchanges and functions, and thus strengthened and protected. And in the case of the very poor, it added to clean skins the apparently reassuring guarantee of moral order.

15. *The children of Pasteur*

When, at the end of the nineteenth century, Remlinger carried out a day by day enumeration of the microbes in his bath water, he revealed the extent to which post-Pasteurian microbiology had, since the 1870s, been able to transform perceptions of cleanliness. Remlinger accumulated 'verifications': average number of microbes after a bath by a healthy person, average number of microbes after baths by soldiers who had gone unwashed for a long time, even average number of microbes emanating from different parts of the body.[1] Washing, not surprisingly, limited the skin's flora. The calculation remained imprecise. The very principle of the average number failed to distinguish between germs of different noxiousness. And the sterile gases which were passed from one place to another, from armpit to throat, or from sphincters to the most exposed parts of the skin, still offered, when compressed, only approximate indications. It was not, however, the figures that mattered. At a more fundamental level, it was a perception which was important; the bacteriological world, which Pasteur had begun to explain, transformed the concept of washing. Water obliterated microbes. The bath had a new purpose, to get rid of minute bodies. There was a world of difference between this concern and that of the doctors of the late eighteenth century, immersed in their bathtubs to measure the rhythm of their pulse or to see how long they could hold their breath.[2] But also significant was the difference between this new objective and the attention which had, for decades, been paid to choking body dirt. A danger existed quite independently of such dirt. The skin bore hidden germs, it could support invisible agents. Consequently, from then on, cleansing had a very precise role: scouring every nook and cranny to remove a presence at once infinitesimal and dangerous.

It was the theory of miasma itself which had, at the end of the eighteenth century, initiated these transformations. By attacking the

[1] P. Remlinger, 'Les microbes de la peau', *Médecine moderne* (Paris, 1896), p. 157.
[2] See chapter 8.

smell of dirt, water touched the very principle of fevers and contagions. It addressed the presumed sources of infection, even without their mode of transmission being clearly defined. It at least limited the pathological consequences of unpleasant smells and effluvia. But it was entirely concerned with breath and fetidity. The microbe, however, became a more precise cause, which could be both located and logged. It was independent of smell and could be seen. Pasteur's colouring matters made it possible to describe its shapes and sizes. It had its own locale, life and timespan. With a good instrument, the eye could follow its movements and its penetrations. The microbe thus materialised the risk and identified it. Hence the new role for cleanliness – fighting against enemies now quantifiable. 'Cleanliness is the basis of hygiene, because it consists of removing from us all dirt, and, in consequence, all microbes.'[3] However, this multiform being, pullulating on coloured plates, totally escaped the naked eye. The consequences were inevitable: to wash was, as never before, to operate on the invisible.

THE 'INVISIBLE MONSTERS'

This new cleanliness destroyed the primacy of sight; it removed something neither seen nor smelt. Neither the visible dirt on, nor the smell of, the skin, nor physical discomfort, were any longer the sole manifestations which made it necessary to wash. The clearest water might contain innumerable bacilli, the whitest skin might sustain every sort of bacteria. It was no longer possible to see what was dirty. Old assumptions disintegrated whilst requirements increased. There was far more to worry about. Public objects were the first to become suspect. Attempts to disinfect library books with Pictet gas,[4] to identify every deposit of microbes on the spouts of public fountains,[5] and to record the microbes stagnating in church stoups,[6] all sprang from the same design: to disclose, on the microscopic scale, dangerous contacts. The proposals to protect the pipes of fountains

[3] Cf. F. David, *Les Monstres invisibles* (Paris, 1897).
[4] E. Arnould, 'Désinfection des livres de bibliothèque', *Revue d'hygiène* (Paris, 1897), p. 555.
[5] Chavigny, 'Contagion indirecte par voie buccale aux fontaines publiques', *Revue d'hygiène* (Paris, 1899), p. 894.
[6] Cf. F. Abba, 'Sur les conditions bactériologiques déplorables de l'eau bénite dans les églises', *Revue d'hygiène* (Paris, 1899), p. 929.

from the hands of visitors[7] and to leave a trickle of water running through stoups[8] were very different in scale and importance, but they reveal the same concerns, and they reveal how broad was the spectrum covered by this new consciousness. The most innocent objects might prove to be threatening. 'The mouth of a sick person leaves its germs on the objects it touches . . . Children's toys, postage stamps, banknotes, penholders.'[9]

Nor could bodies escape microbes entirely. Even Remlinger's daily baths were incapable of eliminating their ubiquitous presence. There was a threshold of resistance; a bath could not remove them all. For the first time, hygienists pointed to a perfection perpetually beyond reach. Some, at the end of the century, even imputed to damp bathtubs 'the development of microbes thanks to the humidity and favourable temperature'.[10] In other words, according to this pessimistic line of argument, even a bath for the purpose of washing could encourage microbes. Others suspected that dirty bath water clung to the skin, so that floating germs reinsinuated themselves into the folds of the bathed body. Only vigorous washing and rubbing after immersion would be effective. Taking a bath, consequently, became ever more complicated. 'Frequent baths, with resultant washing, constitute one of the best disinfectants.'[11] In the terminology itself, washing slipped into asepsis.

This emphasis, at its height between 1880 and 1900, was at first limited to hygienists. Its technical nature by the end of the century inevitably distanced them increasingly from popular consciousness. They studied a microbe invisible to the naked eye. The enumeration of viruses, the classification of microbe forms, and the culture of germs went on unseen. A new knowledge, which counted and threatened, took over cleanliness. 'Bathing diminishes to a very marked degree the number of microbes on the skin.'[12] This knowledge also caught the imagination.

These tiny creatures became so many 'invisible monsters' capable of breaking down all bodily barriers. They were even capable of reviving forgotten perceptions of systems traversed by fluids and old

[7] Chavigny, 'Contagion indirecte', p. 894.
[8] Abba, 'Sur les conditions bactériologiques déplorables', p. 929.
[9] Chavigny, 'Contagion indirecte', p. 894.
[10] S. Broïdo, 'Souillure de la peau par des microbes', *Revue d'hygiène* (Paris, 1894), p. 717.   [11] *Ibid.*, p. 718.
[12] A. Vigoura, 'Sur la quantité et la variété d'espèces microbiennes sur la peau des sujets sains', *Revue d'hygiene* (Paris, 1895), p. 930.

images of infiltration and impregnation. 'They penetrate our bodies in their thousands.'[13] The fragility of surfaces and the vulnerability of orifices loomed large, with obscure visions of invasions by invisible objects gradually spreading to every organ. 'Nothing escapes their attack: they exist in their myriads, in the air, in water, in the ground, they are ceaselessly active about their business.'[14] There were, lastly, fears of the danger arising from such minute creatures. The body was all the more vulnerable in that its attackers were so tiny. It was an invasion by the infinitely microscopic, a case of the invisible undermining the strong. Hence the constant possibility of attack and the repeated exhortations. 'If an opening appears on the outside, these microbes penetrate the structure and it takes only a few hours, in some cases, to destroy for ever the strongest system.'[15]

There was no real connection, however, with the porous body that had once been a source of anxiety. The bodily covering had long seemed almost hermetically sealed. The skin could not be passively open to liquid or the surrounding atmosphere. Entry might, to be sure, be effected by minute bodies. But the real danger remained indirect, in deposits on the hands and clothes, or in contaminated food and air. Hygienists described the familiar journey from clothes to mouth by way of the hands. The skin, obviously, was involved, but it was the hands in particular which did the transmitting. The bodily zones traditionally the concern of treatises of manners (hands and face, mouth and teeth) were rapidly adopted by treatises of hygiene at the end of the century. It was on finger tips, under fingernails or in the grooves of the parts of the skin that touched that microbes were counted. The hands of workers were particularly suspect. 'With coachmen and workmen, there have been found, in about fifty per cent of cases, golden and white staphylococcus, the microcoque pyogene of the saliva, and the liquid pyogene staphylococcus.'[16] A social discrimination was emerging, more discreet but very palpable. Dirt became something which could deceive the eye. This social distance, differently expressed, remained on occasion extreme. 'There are fifty times as many microbes in the houses of the poor than in the foulest air from drains.'[17]

[13] L. Marchand, *Les Microbes* (Paris, 1887), p. 15.
[14] R. Blanchard, *Les Ennemis de l'espèce humaine* (Paris, 1888), pp. 2–3.
[15] Dujardin-Baumetz, *L'Hygiène prophylactique* (Paris, 1889), p. 4.
[16] Vigoura, 'Sur la quantité et la variété d'espèces microbiennes', p. 930.
[17] Marié-Davy, *De l'évacuation des vidanges* (Paris, 1882).

The texts stepped up the frequency of local washing. 'The hands, which touch everything, should be the object of constant care . . . They must be washed with soap several times a day.'[18] How often was no longer specified, so frequently must the washing be repeated. This intensification replaced what had previously been a clearly established routine. It could no longer be restricted to rising or to mealtimes. 'The hands should be washed whenever it is necessary. But above all whenever one comes home or goes out.'[19] Hands were also the prime concern of David, formerly a primary inspector, who, in retirement, in 1897, wrote an impassioned text destined for schoolchildren. His thesis insistently reconstructs what the child could not see. In fact, by metamorphosing microbes into so many wolves or lions, he gave them a visible presence. Science collaborated with the bestiary of childhood. 'Do you know where your hands have been all day? Who knows what you have touched and in what breeding grounds of infection they have dabbled? And you put them in your mouth, or touch your food without thinking or any curiosity, because you would be appalled if someone showed you what is crawling all over them.'[20] Precautionary measures concentrated on contamination. Cleanliness engaged in a battle with contact. School hygiene, in particular, promoted new habits; pages were turned without fingers being licked, and touching a graze was medically forbidden. 'Dirtiness seems to favour the development of warts – inkspots should be removed with the aid of pumice-stone. The child should not introduce his fingers into his nostrils – should not lick his finger to turn the pages of a book – should not scratch his spots.'[21] And, lastly, the danger increased when decayed teeth seemed to provide a means of penetration – breeding grounds for bacilli and internal fissures.

Your teeth decay, you are prey to all these countless nothings . . . which will happily heal on their own, until one day, with your dirty hands, you introduce a fine bacillus of typhoid fever, a pneumococcus of pneumonia, an "odium" of thrush, or a streptococcus of influenza, from which you die. Dirty surgeon, you have poisoned your own wound, you will succumb to your own infection.[22]

[18]   P. Degrave, *Manuel d'hygiène élémentaire* (Paris, 1902), p. 8.
[19]   E. Monin, *La Propreté de l'individu et de la maison* (Paris, 1884), p. 17.
[20]   David, *Les Monstres invisibles*, p. 82.
[21]   Breucq, *La Propreté de l'écolier* (Bayonne, 1909), pp. 8–9.
[22]   David, *Les Monstres invisibles*, pp. 82–3.

On such matters, the treatises on manners came to be definitively outmoded. Care of the teeth had a direct relation to microbes. To look after the mouth consisted first and foremost in preventing it from being burgled. Washing, once again, signified asepsis. 'In the case of children and even grown-ups whose teeth decay easily and quickly, oral antisepsis is essential: morning and night, after every meal, cleaning of gums and teeth with a brush, a little sponge, and rinsing the mouth with one or two gulps of an antiseptic solution.'[23] New places were mentioned by name, gums, and the space between the teeth; new areas had been appropriated, which, tiny though they were, expressed much larger changes.

The premisses of contemporary hygiene seem to be present in these texts, but with a doom-laden dimension probably to be explained by the emotional power of the discoveries of Pasteur, and with an explicitly pedagogic and medical flavour. The nascent norm needed support. Educators and therapeutists were still insistently emphasising what popular knowledge would eventually find almost commonplace, or, put another way, would no longer reckon to be disquieting. They adopted a serious, almost solemn tone; their threats had never been so erudite or so awesome. Infection, with its abrupt appearance and its dramatic consequences, provided the perennial bogey-man. 'The folds of the oral mucous, the interstices between the teeth, and decayed teeth attract in passing organic particles floating in the atmosphere, the remains of food, gobs of spit, all the dirtiness which infects our mouths.'[24]

Cleanliness, in fact, changed its meaning. The microbe became its negative pole, asepsis its ideal. To be clean meant primarily to be free of bacteria, protozoa and viruses.[25] To cleanse was to operate on these invisible agents. 'Dirty people carry with them everywhere the germs of every disease, to the detriment of themselves and everyone they come into contact with.'[26] It was impossible to mention oral cleanliness without constantly bringing in aesthetic and pathological considerations. 'Children should early on acquire the habit of practising this scrupulous hygiene, not only to preserve healthy and

[23] F. David, *Les Microbes de la bouche* (Paris, 1890), pp. 278–9.
[24] Degrave, *Manuel d'hygiène élémentaire*, pp. 9–10.
[25] See R. Bouisson, *Histoire de la médecine* (Paris, 1967), in the chapter on Pasteur: 'Microbes are divided into *bacteria*, vegetable organisms, *protozoa*, unicellular animal organisms, and *ultravirus*, also called virus filtrables, organisms so tiny that they pass through all known filters' (p. 308).
[26] Breucq, *La Propreté de l'écolier*, p. 3.

attractive teeth, but also to prevent the entry of numerous infections included amongst the most dangerous known to medicine.'[27] And it was similarly impossible to mention the cleanliness of physical surroundings without alluding to those denizens that Pasteur's microscope and colourants had succeeded in identifying. In describing the town of the future, Jules Verne created an anti-microbe defense based on a massive amount of washing, extending even to the walls. To make something clean was to protect it. 'The walls are washed . . . Not a single morbid germ can lie in ambush there.'[28] It was a major theme; the cleanliness of *Franceville* dictated physical surroundings and determined the expenditure of time. 'Clean, clean without ceasing . . .'[29] It was also a pedagogic theme, which could only reinforce the link between medicine and morals; every child learned to regard as shameful every stain on his clothes. With the utensils and frequencies of the nineteenth century, *Franceville* was the first Utopia dominated by the 'war against the microbe'.[30]

Other novels predicting the future exploited this same theme, more or less directly, at the end of the nineteenth century. No decay, for example, entered Flammarion's *Uranie*, where fermentation was excluded, the atmosphere unvarying, and the physiologies self-sufficient. These creatures did not even eat. The imagination of Flammarion preserved them from all threat; infection was impossible. 'The women of Mars, living off our spring air and the perfume of our flowers, are so very voluptuous in the simple fluttering of their wings and the ideal kiss of lips which never touch food!'[31] *Uranie* was above all an image of totally sanitised beings, bodies protected to the point of becoming diaphanous.

More concretely, it was in caring establishments that cleanliness and asepsis were unambiguously all-important at the end of the nineteenth century. It was with disinfection in mind that Martin insisted on the necessity of a weekly bath for the hospitalised sick. 'We have for long been preoccupied with disinfecting surroundings, instruments and dressings, without paying sufficient attention to the fact that people, too, carry germs.'[32] The same aim can also be seen in a

[27] E. Monin, *Le Trésor médical de la femme* (Paris, no date, about 1905), p. 266.
[28] J. Verne, *Les Cinq Cents Millions de la bégum* (Paris, 1879).   [29] *Ibid.*
[30] Cf. Grellety, *La Guerre aux microbes* (Mâcon, 1900).
[31] C. Flammarion, *Uranie* (Paris, 1889), pp. 200–1.
[32] L. Martin, 'Hygiène hospitalière', in P. Bouardel and E. Mosny, *Traité d'hygiène* (Paris, 1907), vol. 8, p. 236.

circular of 1899 which for the first time imposed a 'full weekly bath' on the hospital staff themselves.[33] It was the fabric of the hospital, disinfecting rooms or operating theatres, which systematically stimulated this 'scientific' definition of cleanliness. In 1896, Lutaud emphasised 'the cleanliness, the order, the good administration which reigns in American hospitals'.[34] He revealed in passing how the model came now from New York and no longer from London, as he associated such cleanliness primarily 'with the refinements unknown in Europe to assure in particular aseptic operating conditions'.[35]

Thus cleanliness was no longer the same after the discovery of microbes. The theme of protection had rapidly increased in importance. It was no longer a matter of what was visible. Aims had been established and casualties till then unknown accepted. An invisible, minute creature, the microbe, had transformed thinking, extending beyond even body dirt itself. And this transformation was all the more important in that it was effective; the incidence of postoperative infections was much reduced when, at the end of the nineteenth century, surgeons operated with sterile gloves rather than with their bare hands.[36] Similarly, the number of cases of diphtheria diminished once the modes of communication by contacts carrying the disease were better understood.[37] Proofs were publicised and confidence abounded. 'The epidemic illnesses are the consequence of ignorance and a punishment for the negligence of peoples and individuals.'[38] The objectification of the microbe reinforced positivist discourse at the end of the nineteenth century. Cleanliness was, after all, for the first time, the subject of real experimental work, with statistical proofs, calculations and measurements of the microbe.

The theme was not, however, limited to a simple matter of establishing proofs. Scientific cleanliness had implications for the imagination.

WHAT COULD NOT BE SEEN

Why meticulously exclude every microbe when the healthy subject often demonstrated imperviousness in practice? In 1895, Remlinger

[33] *Hôpitaux et Hospices, Règlements intérieurs* (Paris, 1910), p. 86.
[34] A. Lutaud, *Les Etats-Unis en 1900* (Paris, 1896), p. 94.   [35] *Ibid.*
[36] Martin, 'Hygiène hospitalière', p. 237.
[37] 'Diphtérie – mesures prophylactiques', *Médecine et Chirurgie* (Paris, 1893), p. 917.
[38] E. Duchaux, *Le Microbe et la maladie* (Paris, 1886), p. 259.

detected the typhoid bacillus in the faeces of many soldiers, although there was no epidemic, and the diphtheria bacillus was identified by Roux in the mouths of many schoolchildren, when there was no infection.[39] There were 'germs which do not operate because the terrain is unfavourable'.[40] Pasteur himself, as early as 1880, relativised the harmfulness of microbes when he examined induced or acquired immunity. The organic system possessed its own resources, its innate defences and internal barriers. Inoculated hens varied in their resistance to the cholera bacillus;[41] not all were affected alike. It was even possible to accustom them, safely and progressively, to doses of the most virulent cholera. And the bacillus changed over time. The microbe was not omnipotent. It was affected by each subject's past life and their own individual defences. The presence of microbes became less threatening as the importance of immunisation grew. The justification for cleanliness was affected and its implications diminished. Washing was by no means the only protection. The elimination of microbes counted less, in some cases, than a gradual habituation to their noxiousness.

It was in the last years of the nineteenth century in particular that this argument was in a position to transform the fight against infection. The hygienists were aware of these theoretical developments. They knew that very personal organic resistance could withstand the invasion of microbes. They also knew that this resistance varied according to each person's past life or the structure of their tissues. They, in their turn, described the 'struggle between the leucocytes and the bacteria',[42] which opposed the cells of the body against cells which destroyed it. They, too, knew that the debate now revolved round the 'preparation' of the tissue rather than the systematic elimination of microbes. Immunisation ruled. Did the preventive role of clean skin become less crucial?

Such a conclusion was still unacceptable to hygienists. But, in the last years of the nineteenth century, they gradually shifted their ground; cleanliness served not only to eliminate invisible agents, it served to kill infection by strengthening the organs. By accelerating

---

[39] Cf. E. Vallin, 'De la présence du bacille d'Eberth dans l'eau, le sol et les matières fécales d'individus sains', *Revue d'hygiène* (Paris, 1896).   [40] *Ibid.*, p. 816.

[41] L. Pasteur, 'Sur le choléra des poules', *Comptes rendus de l'académie des Sciences* (Paris, 1880). On this 'second' Pasteurianism, cf. F. Dagognet, *Méthodes et Doctrine dans l'oeuvre de Pasteur* (Paris, 1967): 'Microbiology renounces its initial dogmatism', p. 211.

[42] L. Gautié, *Notions d'hygiène* (Philippeville, 1892), p. 53.

oxygenation, it assisted the destruction of microbes. The respiration of the skin was once again quoted. Energising measures discovered a new legitimacy; facilitating combustion promoted immunity. The fight against bacteria continued according to a new concept: protection by calorific accumulation. An invisible fire, which cleanliness helped to stoke, made it easier to resist disease. 'The microbe is only harmful if we let it be. We must invigorate the body . . . We must make the muscles work, the blood circulate, the skin breathe and perspire.'[43] The hygienists intensified these colourful arguments. Cleanliness protected as never before, because it carried the fight into the heart of the chemistry of the tissues, by activating its energies. If body dirt, in contrast, rendered the body vulnerable, it was primarily by limiting the activity of the calories. It both smothered and exhausted. 'We should avoid any cause of weakness, one of the most common being dirtiness.'[44]

The illusion of a skin that breathed had thus not been destroyed. On the contrary, the energetic model worked out in the middle of the nineteenth century[45] was elaborated to serve organic immunisations. Cleanliness secured a double role; it eliminated microbes and strengthened resistance to them. It had a truly hygienic function. 'Cleanliness is one of the conditions essential to the preservation of health.'[46] It participated in the chemical defence of the cells.

This hygienic cleanliness acquired, at the end of the nineteenth century, a legitimacy which was never surpassed. This was associated with the conquest of science, certainly, but it was also an affirmation of energy accelerating combustion, oxygenation as a sign of strength, and calorific consumption as an index of health. The frequent employment of the metaphor became, in this connection, transparent. 'Every machine needs its wheels to be frequently cleaned and the cinders or unused parts of the coal to be as frequently cleared out. The human body being a particularly delicate machine, it is necessary to see to its cleanliness and the regular expulsion of its waste matter.'[47] Cleanliness and the image of the body were once more interdependent.

[43] A. Lutaud, 'Le microbe et la nature', *La Médecine anecdotique, historique et littéraire* (Paris, 1901), p. 230.
[44] Gautié, *Notions d'hygiène*, p. 54. For the theory of oxygenation by the skin as held by hygienists, cf. also E. Pécaut, *Cours d'hygiène* (Paris, 1882): 'The skin breathes, exhales carbonic acid and water vapour and absorbs oxygen' (p. 97).
[45] See chapter 12.   [46] Breucq, *La Propreté de l'écolier*, p. 3.
[47] Degrave, *Manuel d'hygiène élémentaire*, p. 7.

But this last example reveals a point of difficulty for the thesis of the hygienists. An implicit logic led it, at the end of the nineteenth century, to search for ever more emphatic justifications; hygienists spread alarm so as to convince, and dramatised so as to shock. The discoveries in the field of microbes assured it, clearly, legitimacy and verisimilitude. But they demonstrated, on the other hand, how hygienic assertions exaggerated in order to emphasise the danger. The hygiene of the end of the nineteenth century to a degree fabricated its justifications, that is, the oxygenating role of the skin and the anti-infectious virtues of energy. It invented reasons; it asserted more than it justified. It is clear, as Rist stated in 1934, that 'the specific resistance, natural or acquired, that a living body opposes to an infectious illness has absolutely nothing in common with the resistance that a boxer opposes to the blows of his opponent, or an athlete opposes to fatigue'.[48] It was not physical strength which *a priori* guaranteed immunity. In this, hygiene made exaggerated claims; it went too far.

This excess, certainly, was primarily rhetorical; it was essential to convince. But it had other causes. Why did cleanliness so easily acquire a new role (that of supporting an immunising energy), once the immediate danger of microbes was relativised? Why was there a tendency to search for good scientific reasons, as if it was necessary at all costs to prove, when proof was sometimes lacking, and persuasion prevailed over demonstration?

This cleanliness was based, in fact, on a need which was altogether internal, intimate and initially difficult to formulate, so gratuitous could it appear: the need for systematic washing of what was not seen, in the absence of any smell or dirt. Its roots lay in the social code, not in science. But when it appeared in its social version, at the very end of the nineteenth century, the difficulty of putting it into words was clear. How was something totally invisible to be expressed? One of Célestine's mistresses, in Mirbeau's *Le Journal d'une femme de chambre* (1900), explained it in terms of an obsession. She emphasised without explanation. 'The care of the body . . . I value it more than anything . . . In this regard I am demanding, demanding . . . to the point of mania . . . You will have a bath tomorrow . . . I will show you.'[49] Mme d'Alq, too, suggested that these actions with hidden

---

[48] E. Rist, *La Tuberculose* (Paris, 1934), p. 336.
[49] O. Mirbeau, *Le Journal d'une femme de chambre* (Paris, 1900), p. 389.

results were a matter 'of caring firstly for her person'.[50] Mme Staffe employed the metaphor of purification, and evoked compulsion resulting from an internal summons. Baths and washing obeyed 'an internal voice'.

It was science which at first relayed these injunctions, whose reasons were felt more than explained. It reflected and gave them authority; it helped to objectify and transmit them as norms. It was necessary for these norms to be firmly established, and their existence confirmed or widely accepted, for such needs to at last be made explicit, or, at any rate, sufficiently recognised for them to no longer need the justification of a directly utilitarian role. It was in the middle of the twentieth century that these precepts, long accepted, became less strident and revealed their more hidden aspects.

It is possible to provide proof that a person who rarely washes can remain perfectly healthy or reveal only a few trivial local problems. But it seems that one can allow:

1 there is a social necessity to be clean, if only because of the disagreeable smell and appearance presented by dirty people.
2 in addition, the psyche is influenced by bodily cleanliness
3 lastly, the daily constraint of caring for the body is amongst the disciplines favourable to an education of the will, which promotes a good equilibrium.[51]

The hygienist of 1950 used psychological and social arguments (not all of which, however, escape 'utilitarianism'!) to explain behaviour which dated back to the end of the century, and which purported to serve, first and foremost, physiological ends. He said what could once not be formulated so much did these practices seem to derive from intangible criteria.[52]

This was clearly a cleanliness of the elite, whose actions had increasingly less relationship to utility and the visible. It was self-love of the body which was primarily concerned, an internal approbation, serving an ever more elaborated sensuality. It was a matter of creating, even projecting, the assured conviction of cleanliness, an assurance which could be demonstrated, but whose source remained hidden. It was as if the bourgeoisie no longer needed to signal their immediately obvious powers, but needed to explore largely inter-

[50] L. d'Alq, *Les Secrets du cabinet de toilette* (Paris, 1882), p. 1.
[51] Baronne Staffe, *Le Cabinet de toilette*, p. 4.
[52] P. Sédaillon and R. Sohier, *Précis d'hygiène et d'épidémiologie* (Paris, 1949), p. 155.

nalised resources; it was a work on oneself for oneself, and an affirmation of secret powers.

With this cleansing, established at the end of the nineteenth century, and whose results were less and less visible, the final stage of bodily cleanliness had begun. The microbe had played a dual role; it had made it possible to evoke objective menaces and it had supported the altogether internal conviction of an invisible cleanliness. It gave a radical new form to cleanliness, which, having once concerned the most external parts of the body, now concerned the most secret.

16. *Installations and privacy*

In 1888, in one of Feydeau's farces, a bathtub appears on stage.[1] A young woman is on the point of taking a bath, but changes her mind. The bathtub remains in full view. There follows a series of rather banal misunderstandings. The interest of the text lies elsewhere, in the suggestion of nudity, highly audacious in 1888. The scene was also audacious in that all the works of this period which discuss how bourgeois bathrooms should be organised are absolutely insistent on the question of privacy. The author confirms the taboo in his own fashion. He played on it by rendering the scene disturbing, with undressing half-begun and privacy obscurely violated. But he also played on it by evoking the norm; Laurence complains bitterly that she does not possess a bathroom. The bathtub full of warm water standing in a bourgeois antechamber was an incongruity essential to the plot.

The taboo was strong. The early projects, especially from 1880 on, for transforming the little washrooms attached to bedrooms into proper bathrooms were quite clear on this point; when a woman entered her bathroom, it became 'a sanctuary into which no-one, not even a loved husband, in particular a loved husband, should penetrate'.[2] It was above all a private space, which each person entered alone. A range of increasingly functional accessories, from towel-racks to skirt-hangers, made it possible to dispense with all external aid. Indiscreet contacts were distanced; certain drawers were put out of bounds to servants.[3] No-one was to look. 'One does not enter in company.'[4] The door must be locked. This is, perhaps, not particularly surprising, since such a dynamic had begun long ago. But the dominant image was no longer that of Mme de Cardoville's

---

[1] G. Feydeau, *Un bain de ménage* (Paris, 1888), act 1, scene 1.
[2] Baronne Staffe, *Le Cabinet de toilette*, p. 4. See, on the same theme, Perrot, *Le Travail des apparences*, p. 134, quoting the Comtesse de Tramar, *A la conquête du bonheur* (Paris, 1912): 'All is carried on in the greatest privacy with *the absolute certainty of not being interrupted.*'
[3] D'Alq, *Les Secrets du cabinet de toilette*, p. 4.   [4] *Ibid.*, p. 1.

attendants assisting and supporting their mistress in her bath; it was of the employment of appliances and utensils. In this context, a more demanding relationship of oneself to oneself was established.

The insistence on privacy had probably never been so clearly demonstrated, and the history of cleanliness never associated to such a degree with that of a space; an ever more private place was created, where one attended to oneself without witnesses, and the specificity of this place and its furnishings increased. Célestine, as interpreted by Mirbeau in *le Journal d'une femme de chambre*, experienced this prohibition as an exclusion. 'Madame dresses herself and does her own hair. She locks herself into her washroom and it is as if I hardly have the right to enter.'[5] The exclusion of others became an obligatory element in the cleanliness of the elite at the end of the nineteenth century. The employment of new devices made it possible to dispense with the traditional servants.

EXTENDING THE BEDROOM

In 1908, the establissements Porcher offered services which minimised handling and made external intervention redundant. 'A match is all that is needed for, when it is time to undress, the shower or the bath to be ready.'[6] From the beginning, the new circulation of water played an essential role. As far as supply was concerned, from the 1870s, aqueducts carried the waters of the Dhuis and the Vanne over the Seine, the pipes which collected the Marne above Paris were extended, and reservoirs were constructed at Montsouris and Ménilmontant, Haussmann completing projects which had been conceived in mid century.[7] The service could be individualised. The available volume was transformed, once the network of Belgrand was completed after 1870 (114 litres per head per day in 1873).[8] The evacuation of water, too, was improved; the branch pipes carrying domestic discharge into the underground sewers, in particular, caught the imagination. There was an almost biological perception of a town traversed by the flow of supply and evacuation. 'The underground galleries, the organs of the big city, function like those

[5] Mirbeau, *Le Journal d'une femme de chambre*, p. 51.
[6] Catalogue of the Etablissements Porcher (Paris, 1908), p. 101.
[7] See chapter 13.
[8] L. Figuier, *Les Merveilles de l'industrie* (Paris, 1875), vol. 4, 'L'industrie de l'eau', p. 351.

of the human body, without being seen; pure, fresh water, light, and warmth circulate there like the various fluids whose movement and maintenance support life.'[9] The identical metaphor was employed for bourgeois houses where, gradually, especially after 1870, water was pumped to every storey. There were calculations of output, pressure, and resistance, focusssed on the circulation of water. 'Just as with the animal machine, the functioning of water in the home can, if everything is not anticipated, lead to extremely unpleasant accidents, such as nocturnal leaks and inundations, obstruction of the evacuant organs, etc.'[10] The thickness and diameter of pipes were standardised, and directions and routes were settled. Water climbed service staircases, fed kitchens, and supplied washrooms and water-closets.

Heating, in its turn, encouraged standardisation in the employment of space. The 'geyser' was integrated into the circuit and reduced in size. It changed position, leaving the place specifically reserved for its installation in the great private mansions[11] to be brought conveniently closer to the bathtub. Between 1880 and 1890, the *Semaine des constructeurs* illustrated a series of experiments in which this device occupied every conceivable position. It even became portable, a nomadic heater plugged in to wall pipes, before, towards 1900, being stabilised above the bathtub;[12] town gas facilitated its integration.

Bathroom furniture was the subject of numerous experiments in form, such as the folding bath, the bed-bath and the table-bath,[13] before becoming increasingly functional after 1890. What was crucial, however, was the mechanisation of the transport of water and fuel, as also were the fixed holders which systematically assembled the various accessories, such as soap, sponge and towel. Every detail was greeted as a new discovery, down to prosaic descriptions of linen

---

[9] A. Mayer, 'La canalisation souterraine de Paris', *Paris guide* (Paris, 1867), vol. 2, p. 1614.

[10] 'Etudes d'intérieur, L'eau à domicile', *La Semaine des constructeurs* (Paris, 1833), p. 245.

[11] The work of J.-P. Darcet, *Description d'une salle de bains* (Paris, 1828) is a good example of these old constructions often needing several rooms, including one for the heating system.

[12] For the portable bath-heater, see *La Semaine des constucteurs*, Paris, 1885, p. 437.

[13] Cf. S. Giedon, *La Mécanisation au pouvoir* (Paris, Pompidou Centre, 1980, 1st ed. New York, 1948), p. 557. Giedon traces in a few pages a most stimulating evolution of the mechanisation of sanitary places. A. Moll Weiss, in *Le Livre du foyer* (Paris, 1924), gives further examples of folding baths and bed-baths, which assume independence of pipes.

baskets, or of niches set into tiled walls.[14] Objects were joined together, put in pairs and related to each other, new aids which economised on movement within a totally private space.

The bathroom finally won space for itself, and appeared in some apartment houses after 1880. It extended the apartment, occupying different locations according to the imagination of the architect, the constraints of the surroundings or the distribution of water. Gradually, however, the great bourgeois houses made it an annexe to the bedroom. The model was that of the American hotel which, at the end of the century, seduced every European visitor. 'Travellers are given not only a good sized room, four or five metres high, but also a large bathroom and a closet . . . You find in these delightful places, not only the essential conveniences, but a series of marvellously fitted basins.'[15]

The *Nautilus* of Captain Némo, in 1870, suffered the constraints of a submarine as well as the normal constraints of contemporary apartment houses, but included, significantly, a bathroom. Its lavish use of electricity, its water circuits, and its numerous sources of power did not necessarily mean that the bathroom was next to the bedroom. The apartment of the *Nautilus* retained a spatial arrangement which did not survive, that is with the bathroom adjoining the kitchen. In this regard, buildings still conformed to the norm, though very rare, of the rich.[16] But in 1885, *La Semaine des constructeurs* showed a private mansion built that year at 30, Avenue du Bois, in Boulogne, as a remarkable phenomenon; its numerous bathrooms were on the second floor, all attached to bedrooms.[17] The pleasure of water laid on 'at will',[18] and of the bath as an explicitly private place, was made manifest. It marked an extension of the private sphere within the bourgeois way of life.

Within two decades, bathrooms had become much more common. Rented apartments containing them were still rare in 1880, though

[14] D'Alq, *Les Secrets du cabinet de toilette*, pp. 34ff.; cf. also H. de Noussanne, *le Goût dans l'ameublement* (Paris, 1896), pp. 179ff.; cf., lastly, *Le Catalogue des établissements L. Grumberg* (Paris, 1912).

[15] Lutaud, *Les Etats-Unis en 1900*, p. 61.

[16] J. Verne, *Vingt Mille Lieux sous les mers* (Paris, 1870), p. 87.

[17] 'Hôtel particulier à Paris', *La Semaine des constructeurs* (Paris, 1885), p. 463.

[18] The expression crops up in many texts. The bathroom of the *Nautilus* already had running water 'at will' (p. 87). *La Semaine des constructeurs* devoted several articles to it (in 1881 and 1883 especially). This 'running' water was a major theme in the new arrangements.

some existed, especially in Paris. Significantly, in the Préfecture in Oran at that date, the Préfet's apartment included a bathroom, but that of the Secretary General did not.[19] In the early twentieth century, however, such installations became standard. All the 'remarkable' houses listed by Bonnier between 1905 and 1914[20] had adopted these new arrangements. The Etablissements Porcher claimed to have sold 82,000 geysers in 1907.[21] This bourgeois practice, resembling that of today, was becoming established.

References to washing and its literary presentation also changed. Zola, in several novels of the end of the century, was able to suggest the rosiness of skin lengthily bathed, or the billowing steam of overheated bathrooms. He lingered over the suffocating perfumes of bathtubs, and over drops of water beading limbs. He captured gestures, dwelled on contacts, recalled colours and noises, even echoed the gentle movement and lapping of water. His bourgeois ladies had their skins perpetually a little damp under their shirts and wrappers – Nana, for example, barely dressed, receiving Philippe after her bath, or 'going over and washing' her body, before endlessly scrutinising it in front of a mirror.[22] Equally realist is the picture of Sténo, the Countess in Bourget's *Cosmopolis* (1893), regularly stimulating her blood with a vigorous morning wash,[23] or the picture of Silvert, in Rachilde's *Le Venus* (1884),[24] revealing to Raoule a body still moist, barely emerged from the water. The bathing scene lost in academism but gained in spontaneity. It offered an image already familiar, certainly more 'natural', despite its perennial power to disturb. It offered the chance to portray intimacy by the unexpected detail, water running over or drying on the skin, soap mingling its moist smell with the perfumes of creams and potions. It was an art of direct sensation and furtive glances and a way of emphasising curiosity about washing, about simple, but still hidden

[19] 'La préfecture d'Oran', *La Semaine des constructeurs* (Paris, 1880), p. 451.
[20] L. Bonnier, *Maisons les plus remarquables construites à Paris de 1850 à 1914* (Paris, 1920). Cf. also T. Bourgeois, *La Villa moderne* (Paris, 1910).
[21] Etablissements Porcher, *Catalogue*, p. 101.
[22] E. Zola, *Nana* (Paris, 1977, 1st ed. 1880), pp. 416, 326. Zola, as Corbin has convincingly shown, in *Le Miasme et la Jonquille*, dwells on dubious toilets, perfumes mixed with unpleasant smells, and reveals, less directly, a taste for the 'dirty'. See certain descriptions of places in *Nana*: 'In the corridor, it was even more suffocating; the sharpness of toilet water, the perfumes of soap drifting down from the boxes, cut across the poisoned breath' (p. 151).
[23] P. Bourget, *Cosmopolis* (Paris, 1893), p. 152.
[24] Rachilde, *Le Venus* (Brussels, 1884), p. 45.

acts, an intimacy familiar yet nevertheless concealed. With this profusion of secret attentions, the literary excitement, if nothing else, confirms that the practice was widespread amongst the privileged at the very end of the nineteenth century.

CELLS

In other milieus, things were very different. There, the norm took authoritarian paths – not the growth of private space, where the internal demands of cleanliness combined assurance and pleasure, but a very pedagogic insistence on a particular public adopting habits acquired elsewhere. The principle of transmission was not new; the 'pastoral of poverty'[25] was the mid-nineteenth-century illustration. But the strict precautions in the wake of Pasteur, the transformation of the water supply and the diversification of installations together changed the conditions for such a transmission. Nor were the results expected of popular cleanliness, order and health, new. For 'the poor people, that is the vast majority of workers who do not take baths... that is so much strength and vitality lost'.[26] But the exaggeration too, was greater; transmitting the norm was essentially fighting against the 'appalling foulness'[27] of workers, soldiers and scholars, the whole public for whom the popular baths of 1850 had been intended, but had never really reached.

One increasingly clearly formulated constraint added a further pressure: to wash the largest possible number of bodies with the least expenditure of time and consumption of water. Cleanliness for the common people was still unable to escape meticulous supervision of the flow of water. In this context, the bath itself constituted a problem. 'The bath in a bathtub, by the old procedure, takes too long and is too dear for the mass of workers. Loss of time and money . . .'[28] Reaching large numbers, avoiding excessively heavy investment, and limiting washing strictly to cleansing became the established aims. In these circumstances, popular cleanliness was doomed to the public establishment designed for large numbers, with surroundings and utensils specific to them. A model was worked out in

[25] See chapter 14.
[26] J. Arnould, *Sur l'installation de bains à peu de frais pour les ouvriers* (Lille, 1879), pp. 1–2.   [27] *Ibid.*, p. 2.
[28] J. Arnould, 'Sur la vulgarisation de l'usage du bain', *Annales d'hygiène publique* (Paris, 1880), 3rd series, vol. 3, p. 403.

the second half of the nineteenth century which used a jet of water rather than a bath, and kept the subject upright rather than prone. This invention emerged from specific groups, the army and the prisons.

The army was the first, around 1860, to adapt the hydropathic shower to spray, 'like rain', a carefully measured amount of water.[29] This system was all the more attractive in that it could involve lining up, discipline, and collective and regulated movements. An external hand controlled the jet, each soldier presenting himself according to a set pattern. Dunal organised a first attempt in 1857, for the 33rd Regiment of the Line at Marseilles. The soldiers passed in groups under one same vertical jet. 'The men undress in the first room, and equipped with a piece of soap, proceed to stand, three at a time, under the water-pipe: three minutes is enough for them to clean themselves from head to foot. As soon as the first group has emerged, it is replaced by three others, already prepared, and so on.'[30] The formula was taking shape. Dunal had installed a wood hut in the courtyard of the Corderie of the 33rd Line. It was there that the jet sprayed the men with water: the first sanitary shower. But the arrangements were still tentative. There was too much milling about and too much excitement. The men passed under the common jet in a little group; they bumped into each other and got in each other's way. There was room for improvement.

In 1876, in the 69th Infantry, showers, always the same for all, were now controlled. The process was individualised. 'An attendant directs the jet from above onto each man, standing in a zinc basin, with his feet in water. It is possible by this means to bath the whole regiment (1,300 men) in a fortnight, at a cost of one centime per head.'[31] A man perched on a ladder delivered the water, controlled the timing and directed the shower.

The system soon changed once again. For a more rapid operation, there had to be a line of appliances for every line of men. Experiments were tried out in the prison at Rouen some months later, involving

---

[29] This process was clearly differentiated both from the bath and from the hydropathic shower, the latter based on the principle, amongst others, of the force of the jet. Emancipation from the latter was essential. G. Heller sees this as a reason for the late appearance of the 'rain shower'. Cf. his *Propre en ordre* (Lausanne, 1979), p. 61. This work contains an extremely valuable iconography.

[30] Dunal, 'Bains par effusion froide', *Recueil de mémoires de médecine militaire* (Paris, 1861), 3rd series, vol. 5, p. 380.

[31] Haro, 'Bains-douches de propreté', *Recueil de mémoires de médecine militaire* (Paris, 1878), 3rd series, vol. 34, p. 502.

fixed jets, adjacent cabins, external control of the water, and bathers passing through in 'waves'. The flow of men and the flow of the jets corresponded. 'With eight compartments . . . , in the space of an hour, ninety-six to 120 prisoners can be washed, with an expenditure of about 1,500 to 1,800 litres of water, corresponding to the contents of six to eight bathtubs.'[32]

The system of a disciplined employment of space in the drilling of squads found, in this a context, a belated response. The army had been familiar with such group control since the eighteenth century: thin lines, parades, successional movements.[33] It needed the very slow growth of hygiene, and also, no doubt, the difficulty of transposing this discipline to other spheres, like the difficulty of conceiving an orchestration of pipes and jets, for this organisation to be reinvented with the apparatus of cleanliness. However that may be, the cellular shower became the model after 1880. It became common in many prisons and routines were established: once a month in winter and twice in summer.[34] In regiments at the end of the century, the rules were fairly standardised: 'A rain bath every fortnight and a foot bath every week'.[35] The formula gradually extended to school boarders: sixty-nine *lycées* out of 109 were equipped with shower-baths in 1910, and all forty-seven *lycées* for girls.[36]

The arrangement became, to all intents and purposes, that of the popular shower-baths, with narrow cabins, adjacent jets, and measured water and time. The structures were insubstantial; only curtains separated bathers in the night shelter in the Rue Saint-Jacques in Paris in 1879,[37] while thin partitions, extending from knee to shoulder, served the same purpose in the establishment constructed by Depeaux for the dockers of Rouen in 1900.[38] They were strictly functional places, consisting solely of pipes and individual cabins. 'To respond to their definition, to fulfill their aim of true social and popular hygiene, such establishments should be installed in conditions of simplicity which, without excluding elegance, reject useless architectural refinements.'[39]

---

[32] M. Merry-Delabost, *Sur les bains-douches de propreté* (Paris, 1889), p. 5.
[33] Cf. M. Foucault, *Surveiller et Punir* (Paris, 1975).
[34] Merry-Delabost, *Sur les bains-douches de propreté*, p. 5.
[35] Cf. the discussion in the *Revue d'hygiène* (Paris, 1876), p. 1124, of the book by Lincoln Chase, *Baths and bathing for soldiers* (Boston, 1895).
[36] Cf. M. Pain, *Bains-douches populaires à bon marché* (Paris, 1909), p. 13.
[37] Cf. Arnould, *Sur la vulgarisation*, p. 406.
[38] Cf. Pain, *Bains-douches populaires*, p. 8.   [39] *Ibid.*

So a private 'popular' space emerged, but it was only a matter of geometry, an abstract and interchangeable unit, anonymous and bare. It was simply the delimitation of a calculated volume of space.

The bathrooms of bourgeois apartments and the shower cabins of establishments for the masses reveal two distinct regimes of cleanliness. Water, as instrument, was common to both. In the latter, however, water continued to be imposed from the outside, a system imposed in the face of sustained popular resistance. There was privacy, but in the bleakest of surroundings, and washing, but away from home. This cleanliness reveals in a negative way how far there was to go before washing reached the extended bedroom. It also reveals how the privacy which had been transposed was only that of a separate cell, in an 'empty' structure, conceived as an arrangement of lines. It was from this geometry that other ideas had to emerge. In fact, despite the obvious differences, the cleanliness of today can already be detected in this totally bare, minimal formula: a limited space organised for individual all-over washing.

DYNAMICS

These two examples, the bourgeois bathroom and the popular shower cubicle, so close to today but yet so different, reveal two of the most important dynamics which traverse the history of cleanliness.

They reveal, firstly, the particular role of water. The cell-like cabins of the public showers were only invented after numerous experiments. Pipes, jets, and distribution seemed, for a time, to rule out individualised structures (ranks, files, etc.) such as had for long been the practice elsewhere. Water imposed its own systems; it 'resisted', and caught the imagination. The cautious elaboration of this cellular space is not the only example. There were other projects contemporary with the public shower; the first heated swimming-baths in Paris (after 1885) were primarily designed to promote cleanliness. Christmann emphasised this when promoting them. They would make it possible 'to provide baths cheaply',[40] and they were particularly effective, since the long stay in the water acted on body dirt. Swimming equalled washing. The physical activity of swimming promoted hygiene in two ways: exercise and cleansing, activating the muscles and cleaning the skin. The Paris Conseil put it succinctly

[40] P. Christmann, *La Natation et les Bains*, (Paris, 1905), p. 14.

when following up Christmann's proposals in the final years of the nineteenth century. 'If the bath in a tub is healthy, how much more so is the bath in a pool, where it is not necessary to keep still, and where the exercise of swimming serves to increase the beneficial effects.'[41] Thus the shower-bath accompanied these composite projects in which water played several roles: exercising the muscles, freeing the skin, and socialising. Within the context of this imposed cleanliness, therefore, numerous amalgams had to be untangled. The swimming-baths of the end of the century, and this multi-purpose water for the poor, remind us of all the associations from which modern cleanliness had to escape before it could come into being.

The cleanliness of the elite, at this period, revealed a second dynamic: the growth of perpetually unattainable requirements. The bourgeois bathroom does not, obviously, represent the end of a history, even if its form began to determine our daily habits. The code of distinction, both ostensible and discreet, grew ever more complex, but was never fixed. Self-imposed constraints gradually grew with the passage of time, drawing on changing models. Bourgeois cleanliness at the end of the century was not yet that of today. It was impossible to imagine a daily bath in 1880. 'One should really not take a bath every day unless it is advised by a doctor.'[42] A lingering association of water with the old images of enfeeblement, and the gradualness of the modification of the requirements of cleanliness, meant a frequency of bathing still far from our own. Practices are subject to continual modification, though the discoveries of Pasteur still retain, even for us, a distinct echo.

Nevertheless, the cleanliness of the end of the nineteenth century is crucial to the understanding of our own. It clearly applied to an invisible body, it was based on intimate sensations, and it possessed a developed scientific rationale. In this sense, it marked the last main stage preceding the cleanliness of today. With it, a history was completed, that of cleanliness finally extending to the whole of the skin, in its most visible and its most secret zones. A journey was ended when the spaces not normally seen were reached.

But it is impossible to ignore how such a journey led to a cleanliness

---

[41] Quoted by Mangenot, *Les Besoins de natation et les Ecoles primaires communales* (Paris, 1892), p. 8. Five establishments of this type were set up in Paris between 1885 and 1900. For the 'rivalry' between swimming pools and shower-baths as means for achieving popular cleanliness, cf. Cheysson, 'Piscines et bains douches', *Revue d'hygiène* (Paris, 1898).   [42] D'Alq, *Les Secrets du cabinet de toilette*, p. 40.

still different from our own. It is the psychological processes, above all, which have today gradually come to the fore. Intimate space is explored to the point of vertigo, sustained by 'keep fit' publicity, the dreams of consumerism, and attention to oneself. Care of oneself for one's own sake is ever more internalised, and ever more explicit, far removed from simple utilitarian hygiene. Narcissistic practices, in which the bathroom authorises private relaxation, are promoted. 'Pleasure' is expressed, and ever more products and objects give expression to the 'good life' and maintain a subtle blend of illusion and reality. The bath is dominated by the complex alchemy of advertising. The emphasis on personalised values, the affirmation of hedonism, often feigned, have superseded laborious hygienic justifications. The cleanliness of today, if it is to be understood, requires a close examination of contemporary individualism and the phenomena of consumption. It so far escapes, at all events, the foundations described here, that it sometimes flouts them.

Conclusion

The oldest cleanliness discussed here was a cleanliness which applied exclusively to the visible parts of the body, the hands and face. To be clean meant attending to a limited area of the skin, whatever emerged from the clothes, the only parts which could be seen. This is all that was of concern to the *Convenance* and the *Livre de courtoisie* which regulated the behaviour of noble children in the Middle Ages: keep the hands and face clean, wear decent clothing and don't scratch vermin too obviously. There was no reference to what was underneath the clothes or to how the skin felt, no allusion to intimate feelings. A bodily cleanliness existed in the Middle Ages, but it was addressed first and foremost to others, to witnesses. It applied to what was immediately visible. These archaic acts of physical cleanliness thus emerged within a tissue of sociability. Their history shows how it was the visible surfaces of the body and the regard of others which determined its code.

This ancient and long-lasting priority of the visible is understandable. Sight is probably the most intuitive and the most naturally convincing indicator, the one for which standards can most easily be formulated. They express and define the criteria of cleanliness in a few words. The rules appear crystal clear; you only need to look.

For a proper understanding of such indicators today, we need to appreciate the limited and very specific role of the bath in the Middle Ages. We need to grasp the extent to which the practices it gave rise to differed from our own. Steam-baths and baths existed in the Middle Ages, but not for the purposes of hygiene. They offered very special pleasures. Hydropathic considerations, often genuine, apart, medieval steam-baths and baths overlapped in their practices with taverns, brothels and gambling-dens. Turbulence and disorder were never far away. These steamy establishments, where beds and bedrooms prolonged the moist warmth of the bathtubs, remained places of mixed pleasures. The erotic element in bathing mattered more than washing. Water as a medium for physical activity attracted the bathers more than the act of cleansing. Play, even lust, was more involved than the state of the skin.

What a history of bodily cleanliness shows is the variety over time in the uses of, and even ideas about, water, and the distance which separates these archaic manifestations from those of today. Bathing existed in the Middle Ages but was not really aimed at cleanliness. In everyday life, the cleanliness that mattered remained that of the hands and face. Water did not really reach the intimate.

A history of cleanliness also shows the importance of the growth of a bodily privacy. A dynamic was already operating at the end of the Middle Ages – a gradual increase in the power of self-imposed constraints which took physical cleanliness beyond the visible, and a civilising process which refined and differentiated sensations, down to the least explicit. But it should be emphasised that these criteria, while changing and growing more complex, remained remote from our own. There is an obvious difference, for example, between the physical cleanliness described in the sixteenth century and that described in the Middle Ages. But this difference did not lie in a new use of water. Washing was independent of this transformation, and cleanliness was not a matter of washing. The change consisted, initially and for some considerable time, of a new use of linen. It was the treatment of clothes which, from the sixteenth century, created a new physical space for cleanliness: a sharper differentiation between inner and outer clothing, a more subtle gradation between fine and coarse cloth, and, last but not least, frequent changing of those materials which came into contact with the skin. With the manipulation of linen, the feeling of the skin seemed more explicit, the evocation of sweat more immediate. The hidden nooks and crannies of the body received a new attention. It was, paradoxically, a group of 'dry' practices which caused the perception and the sensation of cleanliness to evolve, a development all the more important in that though it, too, was a matter of sight, it completely transformed its sharpness and depth.

Linen, peeping out from men's doublets and women's dresses, brought intimations of the most secret zones onto the surface. The intimate was imperceptibly involved in the visible. This cleanliness was so dominant in classical France that it brought into play all the resources of display. Court practices multiplied the symbolism of clothing, exploiting clever layering of materials, refining deceptions, with lace lightening and extending the 'underneath' of clothes, and the texture, exploiting, according to whether it was linen, serge or canvas, variety of colour and fineness of thread to demonstrate subtle social distinctions.

This cleanliness, where the whiteness and renewal of linen took the place of cleaning the skin, is all the more striking in that it was accompanied, in the seventeenth century in particular, by a relative rejection of water. It is here, above all, that the image of the body, and of its working and functions, most clearly reveals its potential importance in a history of cleanliness. A body which had been bathed was, for the elite of classical France, a mass invaded by liquid, disturbed by surfeits and swellings, all porous coverings and impregnated flesh. The pores seemed simply so many openings, the organs so many receptacles, while examples of obscure penetrations abounded. The contagions alone provided ample illustration. Was water not similar to those elusive poisons which invaded the bodies of infected people? Bathing was no longer safe. It could even, what is more, leave the skin totally 'open'. A simplistic model of infiltration, and a rationalisation initially conceived to explain the devastating effects of plagues and epidemics, encouraged this image of a body with penetrable frontiers.

Seventeenth-century cleanliness, more extensive and more profound, was not without paradox. It concerned the concealed parts of the body, while aggrandising the role of sight. It was more secret, but had never so encouraged display. With it, the visible acquired an unparalleled sovereignty. It must be emphasised how such practices suited a court society which 'theatricalised' gestures, attitudes and clothes. The material spilling out from clothes, and symbolic renewal of linen, while giving a greater place to the intimate, allowed, as never before, the exploitation of appearance.

It should also be emphasised how it was in opposition to attaching such high value to the visible that a 'modern' cleanliness could be born. It was not that linen lost its importance, very much to the contrary. The bourgeoisie, at the end of the eighteenth and in the nineteenth century, stepped up the use of light materials and the use of white. But other values emerged, and other criteria promoted a cleanliness of what was underneath. The real transformation, which introduced the decisive change, derived from the argument of health; it was no longer a matter of appearance but of vigour. It was in seeking new strength that the bourgeoisie of the late eighteenth century adopted theories about clean skin. The pores should be freed the better to dynamise the body, and cold water employed to give firmness to the fibres. Cleanliness liberated and strengthened, so a water which tightened and hardened should be used. Changing linen was no longer enough, and external signs no longer sufficed. The skin must be touched by a liquid designed to stimulate, and the zones covered by clothes washed, but in order to strengthen them. A conception of water and a conception of the body were now exploited according to a theory of hardening. These intuitive images reveal once more how, in this slow growth of the intimate, hygiene could be the subject of rationalisations. The difference between the cleanliness of the seventeenth century, largely a question of appearance, and that of the end of the eighteenth century, with its cultivation of hidden forces, seems even symbolic, as symbolic as the difference between an aristocracy wedded to a policy of display and a bourgeoisie discovering 'vigour', a theatrical code as against a code of power.

It was an exemplary cleanliness, then, in its social significance, and in its systematic recourse to scholarly references and functional justifications. Cleanliness had a precise physical utility: it increased organic resources. These theories of the end of the eighteenth century inaugurated a mode of explanation: cleanliness was legitimised by science. The principle persisted unchanged for several decades, even though the actual mechanisms invoked altered; to be clean meant protecting and strengthening the body. Cleaning assured and maintained the efficient operation of the functions. The reasons were those of the physiologists. An energetic role for the skin, the obstruction caused by body dirt, and the danger of rotting matter became the theoretical horizons of washing and baths. The fear of microbes was the final stage; you must wash to improve your defences.

This scientific argument, dominant in the nineteenth century despite its sometimes limited and tentative application, played at least one role; it accorded a palpable utility to a cleanliness which was ever less visible, and gave a functional meaning to completely internalised requirements which were all the harder to formulate in that their target remained infinitesimal. The pursuit of the microbe neatly expressed this 'invisible' cleanliness. All the scientific reasons and all the laboriously formulated justifications bolstered a vigilance which was primarily social, and also difficult to define, so closely was it related to the imperceptible. Such science was obviously not without truth. Its role involved very real discoveries and important additions to knowledge. But the tactics of conviction in which it participated emphasised how this cleanliness, increasingly concerned with the intimate, had had to seek edifying reasons before it could become simple habit. The exhortation which the bourgeoisie employed with regard to the popular classes in the nineteenth century confirmed and extended these processes; cleanliness did not only increase resistance, it assured order. It added to the virtues. Clean skin and the discipline of washing had their psychological equivalents, a result which was physically invisible, perhaps, but morally efficacious. In any case, it was with cleanliness removing microbes that a long journey was completed, a journey from the most apparent to the most secret, and a journey which carved out the sphere of private space.

Other implications gave this journey even greater significance. These acts devoted to a cleanliness which could not be seen, were accompanied by the gradual creation of private space. Interiors grew more complex. The bedroom of the abbé de Choisy in 1680 (chapter 3) still had no special annexe where he could make his toilet. And his actions with regard to cleanliness were appropriate to this multi-purpose space: application of cosmetics and beauty-spots, change of shirt, various wipings. It was not until the eighteenth century and a distancing from the aristocratic indulgence in spectacle that there were created, in the great mansions and residences, specialised places devoted to the care of the body. Washrooms, with their bowls and pitchers, and their bidets, even though rare, corresponded to a cleanliness already more private. The rich resorted to larger and more specialised spaces precisely as this cleanliness which penetrated beyond the surface grew. Special places were created to match more elaborate cleansing.

One particular injunction became systematic at the end of the nineteenth century: the doors of washrooms and bathrooms must be firmly barred. A distance was definitively established, when the skin's every fold was explored. At the same time, a pleasure in washing which still hardly dare express itself, developed.

We should also observe how this dynamic affected quite other spaces, in towns in particular – their architecture, their communications and their water flows. Care of the body involved a total reconstruction of the world above and below cities. Water was, without doubt, one of the most important factors in urban rebuilding in the twentieth century. The water supply, like the 'breathing', of agglomerations was transformed. Thus cleanliness affected conceptions of towns, their technology, and their resistance to being criss-crossed by pipes.

The history of cleanliness consists, in the last analysis, of one dominant theme: the establishment, in western society, of a self-sufficient physical sphere, its enlargement, and the reinforcement of its frontiers, to the point of excluding the gaze of others. But such a history could not follow a linear route. It involved ideas about the body, about inhabited space, and about social groups. Thus cleanliness, tending progressively towards private attentions, is constantly rationalised. The more secretive it becomes, the more attractive is an alibi which can demonstrate its concrete utility, even functionalism. Its history is also that of these rationalisations.

Index

Past and Present Publications

General Editor: PAUL SLACK. *Exeter College, Oxford*

Family and Inheritance: Rural Society in Western Europe 1200–1800, edited by Jack Goody, Joan Thirsk and E. P. Thompson*

French Society and the Revolution, edited by Douglas Johnson

Peasants, Knights and Heretics: Studies in Medieval English Social History, edited by R. H. Hilton*

Towns in Societies: Essays in Economic History and Historical Sociology, edited by Philip Abrams and E. A. Wrigley*

Desolation of a City: Coventry and the Urban Crisis of the Late Middle Ages, Charles Phythian-Adams.

Puritanism and Theatre: Thomas Middleton and Opposition Drama under The Early Stuarts, Margot Heinemann*

Lords and Peasants in a Changing Society: The Estates of the Bishopric of Worcester 680–1540, Christopher Dyer

Life, Marriage and Death in a Medieval Parish: Economy, Society and Demography in Halesowen 1270–1400, Zvi Razi

Biology, Medicine and Society 1840–1940, edited by Charles Webster

The Invention of Tradition, edited by Eric Hobsbawm and Terence Ranger*

Industrialization before Industrialization: Rural Industry and the Genesis of Capitalism, Peter Kriedte, Hans Medick and Jürgen Schlumbohm*†

The Republic in the Village: The People of the Var from the French Revolution to the Second Republic, Maurice Agulhon†

Social Relations and Ideas: Essays in Honour of R. H. Hilton, edited by T. H. Aston, P. R. Cross, Christopher Dyer and Joan Thirsk

A Medieval Society: The West Midlands at the End of the Thirteenth Century, R. H. Hilton

Winstanley: 'The Law of Freedom' and Other Writings, edited by Christopher Hill

Crime in Seventeenth-Century England: A County Study, J. A. Sharpe†

The Crisis of Feudalism: Economy and Society in Eastern Normandy c. 1300–1500, Guy Bois†

The Development of the Family and Marriage in Europe, Jack Goody*

Disputes and Settlements: Law and Human Relations in the West, edited by John Bossy

Rebellion, Popular Protest and the Social Order in Early Modern England, edited by Paul Slack

Studies on Byzantine Literature of the Eleventh and Twelfth Centuries, Alexander Kazhdan in collaboration with Simon Franklin†

The English Rising of 1381, edited by R. H. Hilton and T. H. Aston*

* Published also as a paperback

** Published only as a paperback

† Co-published with the Maison des Sciences de l'Homme, Paris